BOOKS BY JAMES HUNEKER

Published by CHARLES SCRIBNER'S SONS

Ivory Apes and Peacocks. 12mo, . *net*, $1.50

New Cosmopolis. 12mo, . . *net*, $1.50

The Pathos of Distance. 12mo, . *net*, $2.00

Franz Liszt. Illustrated. 12mo, . *net*, $2.00

Promenades of an Impressionist. 12mo.
net, $1.50

Egoists: A Book of Supermen. 12mo, *net*, $1.50

Iconoclasts: A Book of Dramatists. 12mo,
net, $1.50

Overtones: A Book of Temperaments.
12mo, ... *. *net*, $1.50

Mezzotints in Modern Music. 12mo, *net*, $1.50

Chopin: The Man and His Music. With
Portrait. 12mo, ... *net*, $2.00

Visionaries. 12mo, . . . *net*, $1.50

Melomaniacs. 12mo, . . . *net*, $1.50

THE PATHOS OF DISTANCE

THE PATHOS OF DISTANCE

A BOOK OF
A THOUSAND AND ONE MOMENTS

BY

JAMES HUNEKER

NEW YORK
CHARLES SCRIBNER'S SONS
1916

12074

CONTENTS

CONTENTS

THE PATHOS OF DISTANCE

I

THE MAGIC LANTERN

More than a quarter of a century has passed since I first entered the Café Guerbois, on the Batignolles, where begins the avenue de Clichy. A student of music, *sans le sou*, I lived in a little street that ran off the boulevard des Batignolles, No. 5 rue Puteaux, in a sunless room, at the top of a dark, damp building. I studied finger-problems on a tuneless upright pianoforte. Like the instrument, I was out of tune myself, for I was hungry at least eighteen hours of the twenty-four. Dining, as I grandly called it, was an important event in my day; a bowl of chocolate and a dry roll had to suffice me until the evening. Then what joy! soup, succeeded by the meat of the same, followed by a salad and cheese. The wine cost eight sous a litre; it was sharp, thin, and blue: yet it warmed, and when one is not twenty, and possesses a ferocious appetite, coupled with a yearning for the ideal, the human machine needs much stoking to keep up steam and soul.

It was not every day I could afford to sit upon the terrace of the Café Guerbois; there I proudly took my coffee and smoked in flush times, after my humble dinner lower down the Batignolles.

3

The place was always crowded, specially *fête*-days and Sunday nights. I knew by sight the celebrities of the new painting crowd (a pupil of Bonnat had disdainfully named them for me): Manet, Desboutins, the engraver, giant Cladel, the novelist, Philippe Burty, Zacharie Astruc, poet-sculptor, friend of Baudelaire, and Degas, greatest of artist-psychologists. Zola came, too, though I never saw him. I had eyes for none but Manet, with his fair hair and beard, his restless gestures, so full of eloquence. He and his crowd had been sneeringly christened the Batignolles School, and the phrase stuck, much to their mingled rage and amusement.

It was one chilly March night, with occasional gusts of rain and wind, that I hugged my dreams in the Guerbois. The clicking domino games did not disturb me, nor did the high excited voices of some painters discussing divided tones distract my interior vision. I bought a *mazagran* of coffee, and I possessed a box of tobacco, and I had worked at the piano exactly ten hours that day, notwithstanding the icy temperature of my miserable attic and the intermittent objections of my neighbours, expressed in profane and at times wooden terms: bootjacks and sticks played a rataplan on my door, but without effect. I had mastered a page of Chopin; I was happy; I was at the Café Guerbois; I was in Paris; I was young. And being of a practical temperament, I read Browning every morning to prepare myself for the struggle with the world.

4

The door banged violently, and in an airy blast and amid volleys of remonstrance from a dozen disturbed groups, there entered a man, who hastily advanced to my table, embraced me, dripping wet as he was, and removing a battered silk hat, sat down, crying:

"Dear young chap, order me a drink, order yourself a drink. To-night I possess money. Yes, I!"

Our neighbours hardly glanced at him now; the painters did not cease a moment in their objurgation of burnt-umber and academic brushwork. They knew the poet. So did I; but I had never seen him with money before. It was a rare event in both our lives. His frock-coat was frayed; his shirt was carefully concealed, while about his neck there was twisted a silk handkerchief. And it was clean. If he did not show his cuffs when he folded his arms on the table, his hands were those of a poet — long, beautifully modelled, and white. Despite his poverty, an air of personal purity surrounded my friend, with his uncertain, pale-blue eyes of a dreamer. What a head he exhibited when the damp, shapeless hat was lifted. The brow was too wide for its height, but yet a brow of exceeding power and meaning; it was lined with parallel wrinkles, and there were deep depressions at the temples, which made him appear older than he was. He had led such an exhausting mental and emotional life that he seemed nearer fifty than forty. His eyeballs, swimming in mystic

light and prominent, were faded when his brain
was not excited by some ardent thought, which
was seldom. He wore a moustache and an
imperial to conceal the narrowness of his weak
chin; his jaws sloped abruptly to a point; his
whole appearance was fantastic, a little sinister,
and sometimes terrifying. But he was a gentleman. Was he not a lineal descendant of the
Grand Master of Malta? Was he not the coming glory of French literature? Tossing his long,
fair hair from his brow, and looking at me with
those faded eyes, the expression of which could
be so sparkling, so satirical, he exclaimed:

"I am a friend of Richard Wagner's." It was
as if one should proudly say, "I knew Jupiter
Tonans." Pride satanic was his foible.

We drank. I asked him: "Is Wagner agreeable in conversation?"

He shrugged his contempt for my idiotic question. "Mt. Etna, is it agreeable in conversation?"

"There are only romantics and imbeciles,"
was another of his remarks; he had forgotten
time, and did not realise that we were in the full
swing of realism of *plein-air* painting. But once
a poet, always a dreamer; except Victor Hugo,
who was both poet and business man.

He asked me if he could visit me and play
some of his compositions. He had set certain
verses of Baudelaire's. "Wagner likes it," he
said with simplicity. I had met him a few
months before, but I knew him for a man of

genius. Genius! Those were the mad days when a phrase made one ecstatic, when a word became a beckoning star. Genius was a starry word. I had talked to Walt Whitman at Camden in 1877; but Walt looked more like a Quaker farmer than a genius. Vaguely romantic, I felt that genius must be poor, unrecognised, long in hair, short as to purse. Even disrepute could not destroy my ideal. My French poet was naturally neat, charming in his manner, and the most wonderful talker in the world. Barbey d'Aurevilly could discourse with the magic tongue of a lost archangel; but Barbey, with all his coloured volubility, could not improvise for you entire stories, books, plays, during an evening in a hot, crowded, clattering café. These miracles were nightly performed by my poor dear friend. How did he do it? I do not know. He was a genius, and lived somewhere in the rue des Martyrs. That he barely managed to make ends meet we knew; we also knew that he never sold any of his stories or novels or plays. True, he seldom wrote them. He only talked them, and the prowling animals of Bohemian journalism, sniffing the feast of good things, would pay for the drinks, and later the poet had the pleasure of reading his stolen ideas, in a mediocre setting, filling some cheap journal. How he flayed the malefactors. How he reproached them in that passionate, trembling baritone of his. No matter, he always returned to the café, drank with the crew, and told other

7

tales that were as haunting. I firmly believe he had at last come to tolerate me because I did not parody his improvisations.

This night he was uneasy. He asked me the whereabouts of Manet. No, I had not seen him. Then he repeated Manet's latest *mot:* Manet, before a picture of Meissonier, the famous Charge of the Cuirassiers.

"Good, very good!" exclaimed the painter of Olympe. "All is steel except the breastplates." Meissonier was furious when a kind friend repeated this story of the painter, derided then, a king among artists to-day. The poet predicted this. "Wait," he said — "wait. Richard Wagner, Manet, the crazy Ibsen, myself — wait. Our day is to come." Remember, all this was long ago. He was a critic as well as a poet, as might be guessed of Baudelaire's cherished companion.

We drank in silence. He rattled coin in his pocket, and smiled at me imperiously. "Yes," he seemed to say, "my hour of triumph is at hand." I asked him questions with my eyes. He stretched a friendly hand across the table, fairly bursting with pride.

"*Holà*, young American! It is true; to-day I have sold a play. Here is the earnest money." He showed a palm full of gold pieces. Then he glanced furtively about him. Not a literary buzzard was in the café. Some one back of us cried the praises of a monster magic-lantern exhibition that had been given in the Clichy Quarter.

I saw that my poet was interested. He turned his head, listened for a few moments, then he scornfully said:

"They call *that* a magic lantern! I saw a magic lantern once, and on a scale that would have frightened these poor devils." I felt that something was coming; but I sat still, knowing the slightest interruption might arrest the story. He leaned back, put his pipe between his teeth, and in the tones of a noctambulist improvised his tale. His eyes at times seemed to have a delicate film over them, yet sufficiently translucent to allow a gleam of blue to penetrate the misty covering. I trembled. He spoke slowly,— and Rémy de Gourmont, philosopher and prosemaster, will bear witness to the outline of the story; once Villiers had sketched it for him:

"When I was in Africa — don't stare, I've been all over the world — I found myself, some fifteen years ago, on the border of the Red Sea. Though winter by the calendar, it was furnacehot in this gehenna of cactus and sand. I had affiliated with a small tribe of Arabs,— I was disguised *en Arabe*,— and we rode all night to escape the English, who were behind us with two battalions. El-Ferenghy, our chief, a man of profound learning and unheard-of bravery, did not act as if discouraged when the scouts he had posted at our rear reported that the red-coats were not far away. We skirted the sandy shores of the horrible sea, and reached finally a vast ravine between two gigantic heaps, rather mountains, of sand. El-Ferenghy deployed his forces into the deepest of the ravines and the most inaccessible part of this arid wilderness. It looked like the bottom of a sea the water of which had vanished after some cataclysm in a prehistoric past. We pitched no tents, but squatted under the rays of the burning sun and waited. My nerves drove me to imprudence. I ventured to ask the chief if we were not in a trap: our horses' hoofs had left clear traces for the enemy; and to give battle against such odds would be impossible. He pierced me with his magnetic eyes. '*Frank*,' he proudly said, and oh! the indescribable pride of his voice — '*Frank*, let us trust to Allah. I have magic, too. Rest.'

"The sun was still overhead; the earth a gigantic reflector; my brains wabbled in my skull as if cooking. Suddenly our captain gave orders in a harsh voice. The Arabs jumped to their feet and, in single file, raced about in circles, firing their long, archaic muskets, yelling like devils. 'We are lost,' I muttered, for my ear had distinguished the sound of answering guns from a distance. 'The English — they must be advancing.' Quivering, I awaited the onslaught. I saw El-Ferenghy in the background, on a hillock, holding a glittering dial full in the sunshine. He shifted it at every angle in the most incomprehensible manner, his devil's eyes puckered with cold malice. Was it madness? Again there was distant firing, and new pantomime on our part. A word from the chief, and

his men dropped in their tracks, crouching earthward. The rattling of shots ceased. Our men
dispersed, as the captain hid the dial in his robes,
and we sat down silently to our evening meal.

"At moonrise, after we had slept a few hours,
there was another call to arms, and once more
the mysterious manœuvres were repeated. This
time I could distinctly hear the cries of the English. They betrayed an accent of surprise —
shall I say terror? El-Ferenghy manipulated his
medal of metal, and the firing, screaming, rac-
ing, and confusion ceased only at the break of
dawn. We tethered our horses, which in this
second mock sortie had been driven full speed
around the sandy, moon-shaped enclosure. At
noon it was all begun over again. There was
half-hearted firing from the English lines. Their
men no longer cheered. We must have been
only a few hundred yards from them, for we could
note certain movements. A despairing silence
settled on their encampment. During the afternoon they neither fired nor answered our unseen
challenges. What had occurred? I asked the
chief. This time he smiled indulgently:

"'To-morrow night,' he whispered — 'to-morrow night they will no longer fight with ghosts,
but the ghosts will fight them.' I understood.
I shivered. Unhappy men, what chance had
they against devils! I am a Frenchman, I am
not a lover of the English; but, after all, they
are of our white race. I pitied them.

"The chief had spoken the truth: they were

fighting ghosts — worse still, shadows from the sky; they were warring against the impalpable, and at first, flushed by the success of their attack, by the number of seeming slain that had fallen before their volleys, they had dashed upon the Arabs only to grasp at — nothing. Even our dead had been carried away. This comedy of terror had been enacted under the moon, and the bewilderment of our foe was supplemented by something disquieting. The white soldiers refused to fight phantoms. There were devils abroad, they asserted. The troops turned sulky, and we heard the officers' agitated voices berating their cowardice, and urging them to the conflict. Then brandy must have been dealt out; during the afternoon of the third day there was a determined and vigorous sally, accompanied by a frightful fusilade. But to no avail. They felt the returning fire of the Arabs, they *saw* them tumble in heaps upon the ground, but when they attacked them with their brutal bayonets, they prodded only the sand. All this time the demon El-Ferenghy, immobile as a statue, consulted his little hellish chronometer, while his men spun around, shrieked, and shot off their pieces into the empty air. It was no longer an enigma. I gazed into the sky, knowing that there the battle was fiercest waged.

"The moon sank from sight soon after midnight. A whistle summoned us to action. This time it was no mimic war, or cruel hoax. We clambered up the sand-dunes and without warning fell upon the English. It was a too easy victory. Half of them were bloated corpses; hideous exertions under the blaze of the African sun had killed them; the others were too weak or frightened to resist. We slew them to a man. And upon their congested faces, when the sun shot its level beams in the morning, the expression was one of supreme horror. We rode away to the nearest oasis, leaving our enemy with the vultures. I refused an English sword offered me by El-Ferenghy, for I loathed the man, loathed his magic. A week later I escaped. I had been told that the motto of his band was that of the Ancient of Assassinations: 'All is permitted. Nothing is true.' Ah, my friend, in the East everything may be expected. There the old magic still prevails. There the age of miracles has not passed."

His voice came in whispers. From my corner I blinked at him with the eyes of the hypnotised. Yet I was not satisfied. What had really happened? What the magic employed? Why the tactics of the Arabs and the senseless behaviour of the brave British? I stammered:

"And — wherefore — tell me ——"

He smiled, answering:

"You spoke of magic lanterns. El-Ferenghy had a real magic lantern." I betrayed my ignorance of his meaning.

"Must one, then, explain everything in this stupid world, where electricity is performing such wonders, where my master Edison ——"

I interrupted his impending rhapsody:

"Yes, *cher maître*, I understand as far as the shining dial, but there I stop. Why should the English continue firing in the air at nothing?"

"They did not fire in the air at nothing. They fired at living Arabs; they saw them fall; and when they attempted to seize them, they had disappeared; their dead, too, had disappeared with them."

"I give it up," I sourly replied; "I never was good at riddles."

"Ha! *You* give it up, you young materialist who will not acknowledge that life is a miracle, living as we do on a ball of mud and fire balanced in space, you give up this story of a magic toy — a mere toy, I tell you, in the hands of a man who knew more than all our men of science. Yet you pretend there is no devil in our universe — you, prophet and seer not out of your teens —" He paused for want of breath. The café was quite empty. Soon the lights would be extinguished.

I grasped my chance:

"And do you, dear poet, believe in the devil?"

He crossed himself piously, for he was, even in his most blasphemous moods, a sincere Roman Catholic. Then, in a hollow voice that froze my youthful blood, he quaveringly concluded:

"El-Ferenghy was not the devil; but he understood the mechanism of the mirage. Mirages are frequent phenomena in that steaming-hot region. He knew how to control the mirage —

that's all. With his round steel mirror, his magic
lantern, he threw a mirage of his band upon the
sands, making a false picture, which the English
mistook for reality. Hence the alarums, the attacks, the firing, the ghostly pursuits, the sickening discouragement, and the cruel dénouement.
Have I made myself clear, *jeune fumiste?*"

"Oh," I cried, "there is but one master of the
mirage in Paris, and his name, his name ——"

The head waiter turned out the lights, and we
found ourselves in the avenue de Clichy. He
bade me a short, disagreeable good-night, and I
walked in a very depressed humour down the
Batignolles. It was the last time I ever enjoyed
the irony, fluted and poignant, of that rare clairvoyant soul, Villiers de l'Isle Adam.

II

THE LATER GEORGE MOORE

I

THE time has passed when a novel of Mr. George Moore is anathema to the householder in Suburbia. Indeed, some Philistines have recognised in his work a distinctly moral flavour. Such a humanitarian tale as Esther Waters, notwithstanding its condemnation by the London book stalls, has been acclaimed a victory for law and order. To-day many of Mr. Moore's admirers, possibly the author himself, find the moral stress in this book rather too obvious. But to the delight of the unregenerate who love literature quâ literature, Esther Waters was followed by Celibates, the very quintessence of Mooreishness. This volume contained one story that would have made the reputation of a half dozen "big sellers" among latter-day novelists. I refer to Mildred Lawson, of which the late Henry Harland remarked that it was worthy of Flaubert if it had been written in good English. The American novelist was more witty than truthful, for Mildred Lawson contains some of Mr. Moore's most notable achievements in prose, a fact that did not escape the eye of Mr. Harry Thurston

Peck, who had the courage to write: "George Moore is the greatest literary artist who has struck the chords of English since the death of Thackeray."

Some one has said that the English-speaking world is divided into three parts — those who read Moore and like him; those who hate his name; those who never heard of him. Certainly Moore has had the faculty — or the good luck — of bringing foam to critical lips. He is still regarded by many as a rowdy writer. The very title of Mike Fletcher evoked a shudder, and I may add that I saw Mr. Moore distinctly shudder at Bayreuth when I expressed my admiration for that virile story. But it is dangerous to indict a man for sins of coarseness as exemplified in a few of his earlier productions, when the body of his later work is of such a high order as Moore's. He has always had in him something of the gross and mystical. As a critic of painting he is one of the five or six in Europe whose opinion is worth while. He it was who first gave battle in England for the group of 1877, the Impressionists, Manet, Degas, Monet, Renoir, Pissaro, Berthe Morisot, Whistler, and the rest. He performed the same critical function for Verlaine, Rimbaud, Kahn, Jules Laforgue, to mention a few of the new men of the early eighties. An ardent Wagnerite, he has written by all odds, and in any language, the best novel of musical people, Evelyn Innes, while naturalistic tales, such as A Mummer's Wife, John Norton,

A Modern Lover — this last a study of London art life — though often unpleasant, are all very powerful.

Mr. Moore's real début in English letters caused a sensation. The Confessions of a Young Man was a book that stirred up the wrath of all patriotic Britons. It was Gallic, supercilious, modern, very iconoclastic; it was not sweet or sentimental; the youthful writer delighted in sweeping from the shelf of honest British libraries whole rows of beloved figures. Even George Meredith was not spared, and Thomas Hardy, noble master, was rudely jolted by the newly returned Parisian-Irishman. Naturally there were heard the shrieks of the wounded — not, however, Meredith's or Hardy's; but complaints emanating from soft-hearted folk who disliked this ruthless smashing of idols. "You must all disappear," cried George Moore; "you are of the past, your place is needed by new-comers." And he was one of them. Never did the younger generation come knocking so rudely at the door. Moore was called, inter alia, the Irish Swinburne, the Irish Zola, and later, the Irish Huysmans. In reality the Confessions betray a greater affinity to the early books of Maurice Barrès. Both men were individualists; both believed they had a message. And the Irish writer, when he had finished painting the artistic life of London during the last two decades of the nineteenth century, went back to his native soil, and this odyssey he soon began to relate to the world.

Sociologists say that after forty the "homing" instinct shows itself in a man. Whether this may be predicated of the man of genius I do not know. Mr. Moore was restless for several years before he fled the fogs of London, and it seemed that Paris should have been his logical stopping-place. He preferred Dublin. He was wise enough to see that despite the number of books written about Ireland there were still several unwritten. He had mocked his country and its religion in previous novels; though A Drama in Muslin (published in 1886) proved to be very stirring and a veracious picture of the hard times during the Land League. But it was not an Irishman who wrote the book; Paris and Flaubert, Paris and Zola, Paris and many other delightful things, were still fermenting in the cerebral cells of the young writer. When, however, in 1903 The Untilled Field appeared, the distinctively Celtic note was present. Abundantly so. There was superb writing in Evelyn Innes and Sister Teresa; and The Untilled Field showed no falling off in literary quality. Frankly, I am not afraid to avow that Flaubert, the Flaubert of Trois Contes, would not have been ashamed to sign some of its pages.

II

The Lake has been widely read and variously discussed in Roman Catholic circles, both at home and abroad. English reviewers praised its

delicate art and its harmonious descriptions;
but in London, as in New York, the tale of one
more recalcitrant priest matters little to those
outside the fold. The priest in fiction is becoming a drug, and his only excuse for existence between book covers is his flesh and blood qualities. Is he a viable being? That he can be
made so is proved by Mr. Moore's hero, and in
another art, that of the theatre, by Lavedan's
The Duel. But the Abbé Daniel is a different
man from Father Oliver Gogarty, parish priest,
inarticulate poet, and loving idealist. For that
easily satisfied quantity, the general public, there
would be no doubt as to the success of Lavedan's
stage puppet over Moore's religion-weary ecclesiastic. In a word, Oliver Gogarty lacks the tang
of popularity. His name and the colour of his
soul are against him.

The priest who allows himself to doubt his
mission, who rebels mentally before the dogmas
of his faith, is not so uncommon as one might
suppose. When he openly challenges the authority of Mother Church he soon finds his level.
Like rotten fruit, he drops from the branch of
the great central tree. Publicly he is not challenged for his disobedience, whatever may be
the disciplinary precautions and kind advice ten-
dered him by his bishop or friends. That the
determining, or rather, let us say, the initial
cause of his defection may have been a woman's
love is a fact too frequently observed to be
doubted. Mr. Moore in one of his early novels

said something to this effect, and he has worked out just such a problem in The Lake.

No matter what may be thought of the Irish novelist's attitude toward Catholicism, it must be admitted that in at least one trait of Father Gogarty he has sounded a true note. Rather than create an open scandal in his parish, the priest drops out of sight, letting his death be inferred. No absurd pulpit harangues, no defiance of Pope or bishop, no silly chatter about "higher criticism" and recent archæological discoveries whereby Christianity is proved a myth, the dream of some Asiatic heresiarch; in a word, no "holding the fort" with the co-operation of a sympathetic and misguided congregation and front-page interviews in the daily newspapers. Moore knew his subject too thoroughly to commit such an error. His priest was the over-ripe pear which fell on the thither side of the walled-in orchard of the faith. This fidelity to life should make his readers forgive many slippery and dangerous spots in the book.

What is it all about? your friends ask you. Nothing much happens. A priest writes letters to a woman he hardly knows, falls in love, gradually loses zeal for his sacred office, and then disappears. No thrilling adventures; no sentimental dialogues; no fun; no carnal conflagrations. Yet slowly, patiently, is evoked for the reader the portrait of a real man, a genuine woman. You may not care for the calling of the one or the temperament of the other. You may ask, as do most of us American grown-up children, why something does not happen. But when you have finished you have peeped into the souls of a man and a woman and witnessed their struggles. What occurs to us in the street is not of the same importance as the ideas that float at the base of our consciousness. And to tell a simple story of simple lives is thrice as difficult a task as to relate in huge and resounding prose the astonishing happenings in the careers of kings and queens, dukes and titled dullards.

Briefly, this is the slender anecdote from which has sprung Mr. Moore's story. Oliver Gogarty was born in a little village somewhere on the west coast of Ireland. He had two sisters. The family was poor, but it had always boasted a priest. The boy was of a mystic mind. He fed upon old chronicles, misty legends. He loved the lake, the woods, the clouds, the mountains. Particularly did the early centuries before the advent of the hated Sassenach make a potent appeal. He wished that he had been born in those times when a hermit could spend his days praising God and loving the tender flowers and the little creatures of the air. A ruined hermitage on a deserted lake island touched his imagination. Slowly his sister Eliza instilled into his thoughts the idea of priesthood. She was determined to be a nun and, as he did not relish the notion of marrying Annie McGrath and becoming a manufacturer, he ended by being ordained. His parish consisted of simple peasant souls. He had one assistant, Father Moran, a priest who battled against the liquor madness. One day Father Gogarty heard whispers of a scandal about Rose Leicester, a young, good-looking woman who played the organ in his church. She was a girl of unusual mental attainments and the priest occasionally rehearsed with her.

His indignation, then, may be imagined when the evil story was brought to him by a gossiping female parishioner. Rose had a lover. Worse still, she could not remain long in the parish without palpable exposure. Burning with rage at the sinner, forgetful of all mercy, the priest preached a wrathful sermon one Sunday morning, levelling lances at the unfortunate girl, though not openly mentioning her name. But it sufficed. Next day Rose Leicester disappeared, and for months the rumour persisted that she had sought the lake to drown therein her shame. Father Gogarty allowed this idea to become a fixed one within the walls of his brain. Day and night the image of a desperate soul drowning herself ravaged his conscience. He was of a poetic nature. His imagination played him queer pranks, and his life soon became a torture. Great was the relief some time afterward to hear from an Irish priest in London that Rose had quietly gone away, with her child, and was supporting both by her work in London.

Grateful because of the load lifted from his conscience, Gogarty wrote a letter of apology to Rose. It was answered. And then began a long correspondence, in which we see the growth of familiar affection, artistically manipulated by the author; the social advancement of Rose, her intellectual development, and her artful communication of these facts to the curious and interested priest. He is fearful for her soul's salvation. He is also jealous because of her surroundings, because of the man — a free-thinker — who is giving her so many opportunities for culture and travel; because — and this motive appears at the close of the book — the priest falls hopelessly in love with the fair letter-writer. Not once do we meet her in the story. She reveals herself only in her letters. She writes from Holland, from Belgium, from Germany, from Italy. She talks of Wagner's music and Rembrandt and Hals, of the River Rhine, of wine, of women, of song. Over in Ireland, where the upright rain falls, remorselessly, from week's end to week's end, the priest, his soul aflame for beautiful paintings, music, marbles, cathedrals, and palaces, hungrily reads of these lovely and desirable things, reads of skies as blue, as hard as turquoise. He has an old woman in his cottage who looks after his humble wants. Occasionally Father Moran visits him — once to beg for whiskey, for he is overtaken by the thirst craze at intervals. There are the usual kind-hearted peasants, but set before us by a master hand. And there is the lake — the symbol of the play.

Bereft even of the letters, for the woman revenges herself when she has led the priest to an avowal by dropping the correspondence, Father Gogarty plans an escape. His soul is empty. God has withdrawn from him. Worse, far worse than the thirst for strong drink which devours his fellow-priest is the thirst that makes his present life dry and stale. He resolves to escape. But how? He has a sister, now an abbess. He will not make her life wretched. He will not precipitate a scandal in his flock, perhaps send some weak souls to perdition. So he leaves his old clothes on the banks of the lake, swims it, and with another garb makes his way to Cork and to America, where he purposes to become a journalist.

Unhappy man, and in New York! Far better the dreary parish by the lakeside.

"There is," he reflects on the deck of the steamer, "a lake in every man's heart. And every man must ungird his loins for the crossing." Thus the book ends, symbol-wise.

The Moore people are neither fantastic nor anarchs; they are, whether vulgar or visionary, fashioned from the common clay of humanity. Their author may now say with his own hero: "Surely the possession of one's soul is a great reality." For those with Irish blood in their veins this book is full of that magic we call Celtic. It is enchanting, wistful, melancholy, and poetic, and across its pages sound the sad undertones of a worsted race. It fills one with a veritable home-sickness.

III

MEMOIRS OF MY DEAD LIFE

An astoundingly frank book is Moore's Memoirs of My Dead Life; frank and brutal and fascinating. The title is not altogether happy, lacking the straightforward ring of his early Confessions of a Young Man and the excellent simplicity of that occasional series of literary papers he has chosen to call Avowals. But if we cavil at the name of the new book there is no mistaking its quality. Memoirs these pages are, a veritable baring of the writer's bosom. In his Confessions of a Young Man there are few episodes of such intimate human revelation. George Moore was too youthful then for profound experiences; instead he told us what he thought of some modern books and pictures and people. In 1877 he had achieved no foregrounds and, as Nietzsche might have said, there is pathos in perspective whether linear or emotional.

Not so are the contents of these later Memoirs. There is talk about art and literature; but the bulk of the volume is given over to the narration of various events in the life of Mr. Moore, events as a rule published after a man has joined his forefathers across the rim of the unconscious — that is, if some indignant and conscientious relative does not burn the manuscript. This must not be construed that George Moore is a second Casanova with his indiscreet outpourings; nor is he as coarse as a comedy of the Restoration. Yet, no book has appeared in England since Sterne that so plainly deals with matters usually left unwritten, if not unsaid. It is one of the glories of this Irish author that he is always leagues away from hypocrisy. He never calls a leg a limb. He is not afraid to remind us that the facts of sex, of birth, of death, are gross. Nor is he mealy-mouthed and mincing. Prurient he is not, though very often coarse, with a tang of the eighteenth century.

It was all very shocking to our American fiction-fed public, this outspoken declaration of a man who is not afraid to declare that the love passion is a blessing, good wine a boon, art alone enduring. We heard the moral cackling of the hen-minded — forever be praised for that phrase, Mr. Howells! — and the wincing of that "refined" New England school in whose veins slowly courses ink and ice-water. To be brief, in the English edition and unexpurgated form, Memoirs of My Dead Life is a shocking book, and its present reviewer delights in the statement.

Consummate art is displayed in the handling of the narrative, a mingling of artificial simplicity and the most subtle interbalancing of phrase and idea. Some one complained recently that in the review of current English and American fiction little or nothing is said of the style or scholarship displayed by authors. The reason is quite simple. The majority of such books are badly written. As for style, it may go hang. It is considered insincere to polish one's periods. The quality that makes Edith Wharton's short stories loom above many of her contemporaries is a despised quality for those manly practitioners of the art to whom cow-boys and motor-car collisions, embalmed politicians and youthful female idiots who play tennis and speak English through their nasal ducts, are the choicest pabulum of fiction. Therefore to write moving English about the human soul has been pronounced morbid by prominent critics.

With Mr. Moore's book little fault may be found on the score of individual style and charm. He is always charming even in those days of the Nouvelle Athènes, when he was so superciliously chilly, so arrogant in his assumption of æsthetic superiority. It may then be said that the Memoirs is written in distinguished English, often in the key of confidential babblings, often rising in pitch to the loftier tones of passion and melancholy. There is passion, the Celtic passion which exhales from the memories of a man who has loved many women, yet who is not cursed with the sentimental temperament. It is a burden for readers of discrimination when the sentimental stop is pulled out in the organ piece of confession. George Moore is still pagan enough not to regret having lived his life — as the odious phrase goes; rather does he seem to regret missed opportunities — something that men dare not often avow though they may believe it. It is still the same

George Moore, artist, poet, egoist, lover; somewhat softened to be sure — has he not fought the fights of Verlaine, Manet, Monet, Degas — and George Moore! But across that rather cruel, if always poetic, temperament — one may not be morally tumefied, yet remain a poet — there has descended a rich mist that blurs egotistical angles, that robs of their harshness several episodes which, otherwise, would wear the air of vain boastings. Nor has Mr. Moore's unconscious humour deserted him. He writes magnificently humorous passages without a spark of consciousness as to their destination. If, like Théophile Gautier's, his periods fall, as do cats, on their feet, so do his meanings. But he skirts many narrow corners. Precipices yawn at the bottom of certain pages. And we often wipe our brow in relief as we are helped over some spiny fence of dialogue or some terrifying admission. He even peeps and botanises on his mother's grave. And by the way, he got his title in a novel by Goncourt, Charles Demailly by name.

IV

THE RECRUDESCENCE OF EVELYN

Mr. Moore once asked regarding a certain writer, What was he the author of? When we say Shakespeare, Balzac, Goethe, Wagner, we do not think of the titles of their works. But Flaubert we know as the author of Madame Bovary,

Bizet as the composer of Carmen, or Moreau
as the artist who gave the world a marvellous
Salome. Of what is George Moore the author?
Several critics whose opinions have the ring of
finality believe that in painting the portrait of
the mean-souled Mildred Lawson he created
a new figure in fiction. What then of Esther
Waters? It may be suggested that after all
Esther is the type, a poor, colourless type at that,
of thousands of unhappy English servant-girls.
Nevertheless, it was a feat to set her before us so
vividly, in a manner that at moments recalls both
Dickens and Zola. Moore spent his formative
years in Paris and could not escape the turbid
surf of the new naturalism. He shows its colour
and mass in that real story, A Mummer's Wife,
which contains descriptions of the pottery country that Thomas Hardy might have signed, and
for a heroine — if Kate Ede can be allotted such
a high-sounding title — a woman who has a little
of Emma Bovary and something of Zola's Ger-
vaise in her make-up; the pretty vanity of the
one and the terrible thirst of the other. A human tale, and in spirit not French at all. Dick
Lenox, "sensual as a mutton-chop," is a character
absolutely vital and familiar. We have learned
to hate the phrase "a human document," so
uncritically abused has it been, yet it suits A
Mummer's Wife.

It is said by those who know him that Moore
is far from pleased when any one talks of his
early novels. Mike Fletcher he considers a

youthful error, though plenty of his admirers see it as a big, bold, gross, and unequal book. Mike is also a living person, not a pale adumbration of polite fiction. That he was both a blackguard and poet need not concern us. The amalgam is not infrequently encountered. As for Mildred Lawson, she is the most selfish girl we ever encountered between book covers; not wicked, but temperamentally chilly, and egotist to the bone. Even Balzac, Turgenief, and Tolstoy did not anticipate her. She is as modern as to-morrow, as modern as Hedda Gabler. What then shall we say is George Moore to be considered the author of? If we follow his lead it will be an easy answer: Evelyn Innes and Sister Teresa (they are both one story and have been revised and rewritten several times). Evidently the work is its author's favourite, and his devotion in thus remoulding what he considered his early faulty efforts, while not without a precedent, must have been a labour of love. And what a labour.

The preface to the first edition of Sister Teresa (1901) tells of the publisher's dismay when in 1898 he was shown three hundred thousand words, being the adventures of the Wagner singer Evelyn Innes. She had made her bow to the English reading world that year and was well received. But a novel of three hundred thousand words was an impossibility in our hurried days. The story was chopped in the middle, and we left Evelyn riding home to London from the nuns of the Wimbledon convent. Her mind was made up — she would become a nun. Three years later appeared Sister Teresa. As Evelyn Innes was overburdened with musical analysis, the sequel — rather, the last half — was saturated with a conventual atmosphere. We all wondered how Moore could have caught the note so accurately, despite several shocking incidents, only fit for the literature that delights in decrying the purity of a nun's life. The streak of sensuality in the Irish writer may be recognised in all of his novels.

Those who are faithful Moorians thought that they had read the end of Evelyn, of Sir Owen Asher, of Ulick Dean. It was not to be. The artistic conscience of Moore began to ring him up at Bayreuth, at Versailles, at Dublin, and London. A third edition of Evelyn Innes came out in 1901, a sixpenny edition, but its perusal soon proved that it contained many new episodes, though ninety pages shorter than the original. The mystifying love-making between Evelyn and Ulick in her dressing-room at Covent Garden during the third act of Tristan is missing. Possibly it was suggested to Moore that Isolde's great aria would have been indeed a *Liebestod* if she had attempted to sing on that occasion. And Ulick Dean, more Rosicrucian than ever, tells of Grania, and Diarmid, Bran, and Cuchulain in Ireland, at Chapelizod, the spot where Isolde walked and talked in actual life with Tristan. However, this edition kept fairly close to the original scheme.

Again Moore was haunted by the simulacrum
of Evelyn. Reproachfully she asked him if he
had really spilled her soul. For seven years he
laboured at a complete recasting of her story.
In 1908 a new Evelyn greeted us, shorn of much
of her waywardness, a less cold but not a more
charming woman. Too many overpaintings had
effaced some original features. We hope she is
the last incarnation, for though she is not such
a theologian in petticoats as in her former guises,
she is not as a character large and generous
enough to stand another reorchestration. In a
word, revising does not always mean re-vision.
Mr. Moore quotes Shakespeare, Balzac, Goethe,
Wagner, Fitzgerald, George Meredith, and W. B.
Yeats as precedents in this matter of rewriting an
early book. But it is hard on the average reader;
besides, there are some who prefer the confused
composition and multifarious details of the early
Evelyn to the clearer-cut profile and swifter-told
tale of the later version. Why not rake up the
history of Beethoven's four overtures to his opera
Fidelio? the Fidelio overture and the three Leo-
nora overtures? Mr. Moore is still one behind
in the running with the German composer.

We are inclined to grumble at the attenuated
new version of Evelyn's first meeting after her
elopement with her father. It was a thrilling
bit of art in the 1898 edition, and the psychology of the singing actress was masterfully exposed as she sank to her knees asking her simple-
minded parent for forgiveness. Like Magda's

homecoming in Sudermann's play, the comedian came to the surface. Evelyn could not forbear humming "War es so schmählich?" the phrase Wagner puts in Brunhilde's mouth as she bends before Wotan. In the first version Evelyn's father, who knows Palestrina better than Wagner, does not note the mixture of acting and genuine emotion. In the new edition he is more sophisticated and begs her to stop her foolery — which may be natural, but not as effective as when he had the innocence of the ear. And those who remember Ulick Dean as an Irish mystic and music critic may be displeased to find another young man who fiddles a little and is yet a "smart" business man. Vanished the perfumed atmosphere of mysticism and poetry and the long rumbling, delightful conversations about music, art, and literature. The original Ulick was possibly a too-well-known portrait of Yeats, hence the suppressions.

But if the new Evelyn Innes may not please, there is little doubt that Sister Teresa will not fail to win admiration. It is a better-planned book and more logical than the first edition, because Teresa after four years at the convent leaves it knowing that she has not a true vocation. She pays the debts of the convent, and into the world she returns. She devotes herself to charity and singing-lessons. The original Teresa was pictured as a nun who had lost her voice and was quite resigned to her life, but this psychology was weak, at no time did Evelyn

34

Innes suggest the possession of a religious nature. She had a vein of cold sensuality that was incompatible with a genuine conversion. She always thought of men. Too long before the foot-lights she had been to change in a few years. Sir Owen, who is the most static character in the novel, knew this, and thus the fictive Evelyn has asserted her fictive rights and worried her creator into changing her destiny. Sister Teresa now abounds in brilliant descriptions of desert life; Sir Owen goes to the Sahara to see Arabian falconry. The painter that is in George Moore exercises his art in the most delectable style. At the final meeting recorded of Evelyn and Owen, they recognise that they are too mature for romance; they become good friends. The book ends in a suspended cadence, one that leaves something for the imagination. You are conscious that the last page overflows into real life and does not end abruptly with the covers. Evelyn Innes was formerly a novel of musical and religious life; it is now a connected love story, one that Mr. Moore does not hesitate to proclaim as "the first written in English for three hundred years." Mr. Moore has never valued modesty as one of the fine arts, and he gives chapter and verse for his assertion. They may not convince readers of Richard Feverel, but what cares George Moore — the survivor of the Three Georges in English fiction (the other two being Meredith and Gissing), the "last of the Realists and the first of the Symbolists."

V

MORE MEMORIES

The memory of George Moore borders on the abnormal. Sights, sounds, and scents of childhood are recalled after the lapse of years by the majority of persons, but not so easily the events of one's middle years. Mr. Moore confesses to having been born in 1857; he is therefore over the ridge-pole of life. His new book, the first of the trilogy Hail and Farewell, which is entitled Ave, is a still sharper test of his retentive memory than the Memoirs of his dead life or the Confessions of his youth, for it deals with occurrences in his life that happened not more than fifteen or twenty years ago. Only on the supposition that the author kept a diary can we understand his mental drag-net, and Mr. Moore does not, we have been told, indulge in the habit. That the book has shocked his Irish contemporaries we can readily realise, but it was inevitable; like Dante he has placed friend and foe alike in his pleasant inferno, and doubtless has told many truths. Our chief amazement is caused by the army of details, the thousands of facts which are the bone and sinew of Ave.

The book is not precisely an autobiography, for there is a fictional air about the performance which testifies to the most exquisite art; nevertheless the story deals with the careers of George Moore and of his friends, Edward Martyn, author of The Heather Field and other plays; the poet W. B. Yeats; Lady Gregory, indeed the entire Abbey Theatre group. It begins with Moore's introduction to the new movement in Dublin to restore the study of Erse, and ends with his departure from London at the outbreak of the Boer war. He was a Little Englander, and it may be remembered that he issued a manifesto in which he gave his reason for abandoning England to her fate, a proclamation that moved Max Beerbohm to a mocking discourse.

On the first page we find Mr. Moore living in a garret — the year 1894, his poverty temporary — in King's Bench Walk, and Edward Martyn in another at Pump Court. From him he learned of the new literature in Irish and was duly incredulous. "I began to think of the soul which Edward Martyn had told me I lost in Paris and in London; and if it were true that whoever cast off tradition is like a tree planted in uncongenial soil. Turgenief was of that opinion: 'Russia can do without any of us, but none of us can do without Russia.' True, perhaps, of Russia, but not true of Ireland. Far more true would it be to say that an Irishman must fly from Ireland if he would be himself. Englishmen, Scotchmen, Jews, do well in Ireland — Irishmen never; even the patriot must leave Ireland to get a hearing." And later he declares with true Moravian logic that "a Protestant can never know Ireland intimately." This, coming from this Celtic St. George, stirred Ulster to its centre.

The interest and value of the book do not consist in its fable, but in its art. Mr. Moore goes to Dublin, raises ructions, falls out with his friends, falls in again; goes to Bayreuth, makes remarks about the absence of decent plumbing, returns to London, and again raises a row. He is a living embodiment, or rather the literary equivalent, of "tread on the tail of me coat." But if any one repeats the hoary falsehood that George Moore lacks the sense of humour his Ave will be the best answer. It is full of implicit humour, naïve, subtle, never exuberant.

He met Cosima Wagner at Bayreuth in 1897. "Liszt lives again in her, the same inveigling manner; she casts her spells like her father. But how is all this to end? Am I going to run away with her?" We submit that as a truly humorous outbreak. And his portrait of Siegfried Wagner: "The son is the father in everything except his genius; the same large head, the same brow, the same chin and jaw. 'A sort of deserted shrine,' I cried to myself, and gasped for words." The late Anton Seidl is as happily described. He conducted Parsifal in Bayreuth that year. The search for chambers in the stuffy little town is the real Moore. There is much criticism of Wagner and Wagner singers scattered through this section of the book, some of which may make the reader stare.

The Dublin experiences ought to prove fascinating to the leaders of the Celtic renaissance.

Lady Gregory is sketched at full length and with surprising amiability considering the tart tongue of the writer, who did not spare his mother in his earlier memoirs. Speaking of her literary interest in Yeats he says: "As the moon is more interested in the earth than in any other thing, there is always some woman more interested in a man's mind than in anything else, and is willing to follow it sentence by sentence. A great deal of Yeats's work must come to her in fragments — a line and a half, two lines — and these she faithfully copies on her type-writer, and even those that his ultimate taste has rejected are treasured up and perhaps one day will appear in a stately variorum edition." Mr. Moore describes her as he first saw her some twenty-five years ago: "She was then a young woman, very earnest, who divided her hair in the middle and wore it smooth on either side of a broad and handsome brow. . . . In her drawing-room were to be met men of assured reputation and politics, and there was always the best reading of the time upon her tables. There was nothing, however, in her conversation to suggest literary faculty. Some years after she edited her husband's memoirs, and did the work well, . . . and thinking how happy their [Yeats's and Lady Gregory's] life must be at Coole, my heart went out to her in sudden sympathy. I said she knew him to be her need at once, and she never hesitated . . . yet she knew me before she knew him." Perhaps this may account for the slightly curdled milk in the cocoa-nut. Otherwise Lady Gregory is a charming lady and the very pattern of a doting grandmother.

Again, the value of the portraiture in Ave depends less on its fidelity to the unconscious and presumably unwilling sitters and more upon the wonderful art displayed. Occasionally the firm, nervously incisive line of the writer flattens and falters into caricature, but not often. That dinner at which Moore met certain Dublin celebrities is one of the best chapters in his memoirs. There were Gill with his beard, Tom the Trimmer, and Rolleston, with too little back to his head; John O'Leary, the ancient beard; Standish O'Grady, whose talent reminded one of the shaft of a beautiful column rising from amid rubble heaps. "O'Grady tells me that he found Rolleston a West Briton, but after a few lessons in Irish history Rolleston donned a long black cloak and a slouch hat and attended meetings, speaking in favour of secret societies," and altogether scaring O'Grady by his impetuousness. Moore murmured to himself: "What a good tutor he would make if I had children." And the professor! What a joy he must experience as he gazes upon his portrait as here limned by Moore. Is it Dowden or Mahaffy? Impossible! Certainly a literary somebody. He abhors their wine, but likes Marsala. His appetite is fair. He says to the waiter: "Nothing much to-day, John. Just a dozen of oysters and a few cutlets and a quart of that excellent ale." And says the professor: "After that I had nothing at all until something brought me to the cupboard, and there, behold! I found a bottle of lager. I said 'Smith has been remiss. He has mixed the Bass and the lager.' But no. They were all full, twelve bottles of Bass and only one of lager. So I took it, as it seemed a stray and lonely thing." George Moore not charitable not humorous? Eh?

Yeats, who sat with "his head drooping on his shirt-front like a crane," was there, and there was a letter read from W. E. H. Lecky. Horace Plunket was alluded to; but when Moore was called on for a speech he answered: "No, no! I will not. My one claim to originality among Irishmen is that I never made a speech." Then Hyde was called upon, Douglas Hyde. "A shape strangely opposite to Rolleston, who has very little back to his head. All Hyde's head seemed at the back, like a walrus, and the drooping black moustache seemed to bear out the likeness. . . . Without doubt an aboriginal." But he grew to admire Hyde. Of "A. E.," the poet-painter (George Russell), Moore said: "Here is the mind of Corot in verse and prose." John Eglington reminded him of both Emerson and Thoreau, — a Thoreau of the suburbs. "The hard north is better than the soft, peaty Catholic stuff which comes from Connaught," adds the author. Moore never fails to strike out sweet sounds for his one-time co-religionists. His name in Ireland nowadays is responsible for much mild objurgation, for he is in a manner the playboy of the "far-down" world.

There are no sentimental episodes in Ave, but too many long-drawn-out discussions about the making of plays. Edward Martyn seems to Mr. Moore singularly obstinate, for he refuses to alter his play and is well abused for his stubbornness. Mr. Yeats comes in for his share of criticism. There are so many felicitous pages of musical English, English that expands before the eye into sudden little sceneries: Ireland the land of beauty, Ireland misty and melancholy, that we forgive the gall for the honey. Like most Irishmen George Moore is lyric only in the presence of nature; for his fellow-countrymen he reserves his irony.

The fact is that Moore is an æsthetic firebrand. He is always applying his torch to some reverent institution, to some hay-mow of prejudice. He has reviled British painting and novel-writing. He has called by hard names persons in popular favour. When he announced that he would shake the dust of London from his shoes there were thanksgivings offered up in some English newspapers.

And yet a milder-mannered man never scuttled the ship of conventionality than this same George Moore. I last saw him on the esplanade in front of the Wagner Theatre at Bayreuth. We talked during the long entr'actes about music, literature, the Erse language, and America. Every attempt I made to trip him into a dis-

cussion of his own novels met with a gentle but
unmistakable rebuff. He shivered when I spoke
of his earlier stories of A Modern Lover, Spring
Days, and Mike Fletcher, that very remarkable trilogy of London life (and to-day they are
reprinted in a new edition). But he said many
things on other themes.

"You Americans are always on the right side
in a struggling cause. You freed Cuba, and even
if you do gain a material profit the end justifies
the means. You did right."

"I don't believe in books," apropos of Flaubert. "We all read too much. It is better to
sit on a fence in the sunshine and look at things
than to bury one's head in a book. If you read
a half-dozen books in a lifetime, read and re-read
them, you have conquered all bookish wisdom."

Shakespeare's, Balzac's, Turgenief's, Tolstoy's,
and Flaubert's names were mentioned as a comprehensive list. "No one can hope to equal such
writing as Flaubert's. Why attempt it? We are
all imitators." Naturally, as Mr. Moore has
read all the books and written a lot, he has his
doubting moods.

"The theatre is the only field for the twentieth-
century artist. By placing before the eyes and
ears of the people your story you gain an im-
measurable advantage over the written word.
The spoken word — always. Consider the power
of Wagner! His is the real art of the new century — speech reinforced by tone, and such
tone!"

43

After hearing Sir Edward Elgar's Dream of Gerontius in London he was asked his opinion of the music. "Holy water in a German beer barrel," was his wicked if not altogether convincing reply.

Mr. Moore read in a newspaper this sentence: "We often speak of the trouble that servants give us, but do we ever think of the trouble that we give servants?" This was illuminating. "Of course we give servants a great deal of trouble." And then he began to consider the vicissitudes in the life, say of a cook-maid. The poor wretch earns from fourteen to sixteen pounds a year. She may get into trouble. There is another life to be looked after. How can she support herself and a child on such a meagre sum? All the horrors of baby-farming were set forth in Esther Waters with such clearness that the English nation was revolted. George Moore came in for his share of opprobrium, but he stood to his thesis. He was right, and the public realised that he spoke the truth.

From an equally slight beginning grew the novel of Evelyn Innes. A French actress weary of her life went into a convent to escape the men who trailed after her. She found the nuns too childish — which was natural in a sophisticated creature of the stage. Evelyn Innes stays and becomes a nun in earnest. She loses her voice, but not her faith.

To show you how popular Mr. Moore must be let me quote a few of his ideas on various subjects. He declared that "morals are like the veering wind, but beauty is a fixed star." "We should beware of whatever we write in a book, for what we write will happen to us." (Not a consoling thought for penmen.) His opinion of women in art has endeared him to the sex wherever English is spoken. This opinion accounts possibly for the expressions of velvety wrath his books arouse from women in this land of "lady novelists."

"They [women] are very unlike men. . . . The male animal seems to us more beautiful than the female in every kind but our own. We have doubted the beauty of women very little. De Musset said that most of woman's beauty existed in man's love for her. . . . Our concern is with the mental rather than the physical woman, but mentality is dependent on physical structure. Woman is beautiful in detail and she excels in detail, but she never attains synthesis, for she herself is not synthesis. Every generation pours thousands of women into the art schools, and after a few years they marry and art is forgotten. . . . Women like art until the more serious concerns of life begin for them, and George Eliot, who had no children, continued to stir a sticky porridge all her life long, a substance compounded of rationalism and morality without God. . . . Women have succeeded as actresses and courtesans — yes, and as saints; best of all as saints; they have worshipped worthily the gods that men have created."

He pays his respects to Jane Austen, with her "wool-work style."

He agrees with Dvorak, that since "the Indian is gone America must look to the negro, for only a primitive people can produce language." I wonder if the Irish writer ever heard Dvorak's so-called American symphony, which sounds so Slavic and is so full of quotations from Schubert and Wagner. Mr. Moore makes sport of English painting, and one of his most fantastic ideas was that a writer's name may have determined his talent.

"Dickens — a mean name, a name without atmosphere, a black out-of-elbows, backstairs name, a name good enough for loud comedy and louder pathos. John Milton — a splendid name for a Puritan poet. Algernon Charles Swinburne — only a name for a reed through which every wind blows music." Shelley and Byron's poetry is like their beautiful names. "Now, it is a fact," he continues, "that we find no fine names among novelists. We find only colourless names, dry-as-dust names, or vulgar names, round names like pot-hats, those names like mackintoshes, names that are squashy as goloshes. We have charged Scott with a lack of personal passion, but could personal passion dwell in such a jog-trot name — a round-faced name, a snub-nosed, spectacled, pot-bellied name, a placid, beneficent, worthy old bachelor name, a name that evokes all conventional ideas and formulas, a Grub Street name, a nerveless name, an armchair name, an old oak and Abbotsford name? And Thackeray's name is a poor one — the syllables clatter like plates. 'We shall want the carriage at half-past two, Thackeray.' Dickens is surely a name for a page boy. George Eliot's real name, Marian Evans, is a chaw-bacon, thick-loined name."

Moore speaks of Tolstoy as "a sort of Jules Verne in morals." Kipling is a cinematograph (his soul was like a music hall to Arthur Symons). "Real, solid English novels are composed to prescription — so much curate, so much Bible, so much religious doubt, so much settling down, so much money. We hate those novels as we hate an English lunch. Indeed, they are very like an English lunch — the father and the mother at the ends of the table, the children and their governess at the sides, and the governess telling a child she must not take the rhubarb pie in her lap."

A man whose eye was educated by Corot — didn't Corot paint a Lake in the Louvre? — whose brain has fed on Turgenief and Flaubert, cannot be expected to admire the painted anecdotes of modern British schools or the clumsy, formless novels of dear old England. So Mr. Moore has sown a goodly crop of enemies by his outspoken criticism. If he doesn't like a thing he sounds his dislike to the four quarters of heaven. And the wind thus bred of his fierce discourse often returns in the guise of a critical typhoon.

He has been misrepresented — nay libelled — by his pictures. William Orpen has painted him as he looked when I saw him at Bayreuth — tall, slender, with sloping shoulders, a lemon blond, with gray about the temples. His eyes are pale blue, the shape of his head oval. He dresses with rare taste. His gaze is vague unless he is interested, and the easiest way to interest him is to contradict any one of his pet theories. Disillusioned, incurious, a quiet-spoken, charming gentleman, he has at a moment's notice a large amount of nervous energy. Théodore Duret declares that he once looked like the famous Manet portrait, a pastel, with the anarchistic beard. Rothenstein's sketch is not too flattering. The three pictures presented above may enable you to form a fair average of the Irish iconoclast, the man who is ever on the side of humanity, right or wrong; the writer of exquisitely modulated prose, the pantheist, who has said "that life is an end in itself, and the object of art is to help us to live."

In Salve, the second volume of his projected Trilogy, he paints a complete portrait of George Russell, poet and painter, though the work lacks the variety of its predecessor. I suppose when the final book appears it means that George Moore has put up the shutters of his soul, not to say his shop. But I have my serious doubts.

III

A HALF–FORGOTTEN ROMANCE

I

ABOUT thirty years ago there was a small family hotel at the northeast corner of Irving Place and Seventeenth Street; kept by an elderly German married couple, the place was noted for its excellent cooking, its home-like atmosphere. Many well-known Americans and Germans in literary and artistic life made a rendezvous at Werle's, and at the table d'hôte dinner you could always count on meeting entertaining companions. It was one of those houses where at any time before midnight the sounds of pianofortes, violins, violoncellos, even the elegiac flute, might be heard and, invariably, played by skilled professional hands. There was, I recall, a small vine-covered entrance, on the steps of which we sat listening to some passionately played Chopin Ballade, or to string music made by Victor Herbert and his friends across the street.

For several weeks I had been a frequenter of the place, when the mistress of the establishment told me that the Red Countess would be at one of the dinner-tables. Later I saw sitting near the centre of the dining-room, which was in the basement, a large, rather heavy woman, with red hair of the rich hue called Titian by æsthetic hair-dressers and ardent reporters. Her face was too fleshy for beauty, but the brows and the intense expression of the eyes made up for any lineal deficiency. She must have been in the forties, and the contours of her finely moulded head, her aristocratic bearing and the air of one accustomed to command attracted my attention. This lady spoke four or five languages and was the very hub of the company. Finally, after watching her and listening to her very musical voice, often disturbed by ironic intonations, I asked a friend her name.

"The Red Countess, otherwise the Golden Serpent, otherwise Countess Shevitch, otherwise the Princess Racowitza, otherwise Helena von——"

"Stop!" I exclaimed. "Is this the heroine of Meredith's novel, The Tragic Comedians?"

"The same," was the answer; my companion read English, even the English of Meredith, an unusual feat for a German three decades ago. The moment was hardly historic for me, but it sent me back to Meredith and to his exasperatingly clever story. After the tragic death of Ferdinand Lassalle, Helena von Doenniges married Prince Yanko Racowitza, and some time after his death the widow married a Russian of birth, Count Shevitch, a political agitator, and with him came to New York. The Russian Government had expropriated the estate of her husband, and as they were active nihilists, or anarchists, or any one of the names invented for the public so as to discredit the war for liberty, the Shevitches had to make their living, the Count in journalism, for the propaganda, the Countess as a writer. I barely recall a volume of short stories signed with her name, the theme of which was devoted to proletarian life on the East Side, a theme that is thrice familiar now, but in those days had the merits of novelty. (Gorky has since taught us how the submerged tenth lives and rots and dies.) Soon after I encountered her, the Countess Shevitch with her husband returned to Europe, and the pair settled in Munich, where their home was a magnet for the literary, musical, and artistic elements of that delightful city on the green river Isar.

If you have read Meredith's vivid but one-sided book you will not need to be told that its Tragic Comedians, Clotilde von Rüdiger and Sigismund Alvan, are masks for the high-born Helena von Doenniges, daughter of General von Doenniges, Bavarian ambassador to Switzerland — it was before the consolidation of the German Empire — and the celebrated agitator, brilliant writer, so-called father of German socialism, Ferdinand Lassalle. Meredith told the story in his own crackling, incendiary style, after the appearance of Helena's book — veritable confessions of her relations with Lassalle. She was a Christian, educated in a Hebrew-hating house (though it was whispered that on her

maternal side a trace of Oriental blood was not
to be denied), and Lassalle was the fine flower
of the Jewish-German; a thinker, a born leader,
and one of the handsomest men of his day in the
Oriental style, the style of which Meredith writes:
"The noble Jew is grave in age, but in his youth
he is the arrow to the bow of his fiery eastern
blood, and in his manhood he is . . . a figure of
easy and superb preponderance, whose fire has
mounted to inspirit and be tempered by the intellect." It was the love romance, now a half-
forgotten one, that set all Europe gossiping, wondering and, finally, sent it into semi-hysterics,
as the affair turned into a tragedy, for which the
woman was universally condemned.

The main events in this lamentable case are
not so simple as they appeared in the published
reports of the time, 1864; nor as distorted as
they stand in Meredith's account. It must be
kept in view that the chief cause of the Von
Doenniges' contempt for Lassalle was not alone
because of his Jewish ancestry — he was known
to be a free-thinker; nor was his connection with
the German-Democratic party an absolute bar
to his hopes of an alliance with Helena — was
not Lassalle on intimate terms with Bismarck?
Had not Bismarck jokingly remarked that if
Lassalle seriously entered the political arena, he,
Bismarck, would put up the shutters of his shop?
(There was a grim *nuance* to this joke, as some
remember Bismarck's curious behaviour at the
news of Lassalle's sudden death.) Did not Las-

salle persuade Bismarck not to impose a property qualification for the electoral franchise in the Reichstag? No, Lassalle was far from being a negligible suitor; his father was rich, he had been given a liberal education, he was considered one of the most learned jurists and brilliant pleaders at the contemporary bar, the one hope of the social democracy — why should the Von Doenniges have objected to such a union? They occupied the best of social positions in Munich, though they were not very wealthy. Helena had in her own right seventy thousand thalers. But her parents were narrow, prejudiced, with old-fashioned notions about manners and morals. They were strict Protestants. And it is here the shoe pinched. Ferdinand Lassalle was considered one of the most dissolute men in Germany. That he found time to gamble, drink, and pursue the never-too-elusive siren and also work fifteen hours a day, like the intellectual giant he was, must be set down to the prevalence of the legendary in the lives of public men. If Liszt had led the existence with which he was accredited he would not have composed all the music he did; not to speak of his pianoforte performances. It may be said without further discussion that Lassalle was neither a great saint nor a prodigious sinner. And being fluent of tongue, always on view, and the participator in a half-dozen scandals, he was credited by his enemies — and he had, luckily for him, a legion — with leading a loose life. Which was manifestly impossible. Yet the Von Doenniges were only too glad to believe the talk, and as there was one ugly spot in Lassalle's career, they invariably pointed it out to the exclusion of his indisputable record for accomplishing remarkable things. A reckless man in speech and bearing, Lassalle was named by some of his co-religionists. *Chutzpe*, i. e., a daring, impertinent fellow.

He was born at Breslau, April 11, 1825. After a stormy youth he entered the legal profession and astonished every one by his knowledge of Roman law and Hegelian philosophy. Heraclitus the Dark was the thesis of one of his books; Franz von Sickingen the name of his only drama. He became a fighting socialist, absorbing, it is asserted, most of his socialistic learning from Karl Marx and Ricardo. He was called "The Social Luther," and though opposed to duelling — he refused many challenges — he was a dead shot and a dangerous swordsman. Lassalle was the first president of the General Workingman's Club. His fighting motto was: "State support for co-operative production." He was not in sympathy with "passive resistance" as a weapon against the government. A fallacy, he cried: "Passive resistance is the resistance which does not resist." It might be easy to maintain that Lassalle, if he had lived and not married into the philistine Munich family, might have drifted into the ranks of the militant anarchists. That he would have broken with Marx is almost a certainty. The blood ran too hotly in his veins to long endure the opportunism of his cooler-headed colleague. Possibly Bakounine — Richard Wagner's associate in the Dresden insurrection of 1849 — would have charmed the younger man; there were seventy thousand Bakounistes in Spain alone in 1873. And would Lassalle have espoused Marx's side in the polemical duel at Geneva between Bakounine and Marx, Marx, who had contemptuously called Proudhon's philosophy of want, "a want of philosophy"? Germany has never been the home of anarchy; socialism has always outnumbered its adherents. Marx, with his international-social democracy, was pinching Lassalle's national ideal, and though Bismarck was flattering the youthful agitator by adopting some of his ideas, Lassalle was in reality dissatisfied. Either Bakounine or Prince Krapotkin might have won him over. But his ambition was insatiable. He did not believe in a divided throne. He was romantic, and romanticism is one parent of philosophic anarchism, though Flaubert wittily called the god of the Romanticists "an upholsterer." But Russian revolutionists had not made their appearance on the map of European unrest before Lassalle died.

He was a powerfully built man, five feet six inches in height, with a broad, deep chest. Brown-haired and blue-eyed, he was vain of his appearance, dressing in dandy fashion and always carrying the gold-headed cane of Robespierre, which was presented to him by the novelist Förster; temperamentally, Lassalle recalled

Mirabeau. In 1841 Heinrich Heine met him in Paris and admired him exceedingly. He said of him: "Ferdinand Lassalle is a young man of the most distinguished gifts of mind; with the profoundest learning, the widest knowledge, the greatest acuteness — uniting the ardent gifts of exposition and energy of will to a decisiveness in action which is astounding." He furthermore addressed him as "the son of the new Time." To the gaze of the sick poet, Lassalle was the one man destined to lead his beloved people forth from the wilderness to the promised land; — "people" in Heine's sense, being all the poor and oppressed of this world, not merely his tribal forebears. Unhappily, Lassalle failed to realise the golden dreams of the German prophet. A few years later he became immersed in the legal affairs of Countess Hatzfeldt, who, desiring to sever her marriage with a gay husband, employed the young lawyer with the eloquent tongue. If Helena von Doenniges was his fate, so was this Hatzfeldt woman, who stood by him in all his troubles, always playing the friend — some deny she was anything else — and giving him an annuity of seven thousand thalers for winning the case against her husband, that gave her a share in large landed estates. But there was a disagreeable occurrence during the progress of the trial. Count Hatzfeldt presented a certain feminine acquaintance of his with an annuity bond of one thousand pounds value. Lassalle, they say, instigated the pursuit of both bond and lady and secured the former for the Countess. His companions in the undertaking were arrested, indicted, condemned to prison. Ferdinand escaped only after a trial in Cologne, in 1848, and because of his irresistible address in the court-room. Nevertheless the story of the stolen *casette* stuck to him, and coupled with the fact that he had been imprisoned six months for participation in the socialist riots at Düsseldorf in 1846, his reputation was too much for the Von Doenniges. Wagner disliked him; some say he was jealous of his personal success. Von Bülow, the pianoforte virtuoso, admired him, though Lassalle offended him when he declared that Cosima von Bülow was a blue-stocking. "Citizen of the world," as he delighted to call himself, Lassalle was at the height of his powers, intellectual and physical, when he was introduced to Helena von Doenniges.

This must have been some time in January, 1862. They had heard of each other from mutual friends: he of her beauty, she of his brilliancy and witty insolence. She was very beautiful; a gold-crested serpent and golden fox, Lassalle had christened her. A glance at her portrait painted by Von Lenbach shows us a girl of the Mrs. Scott-Siddons type; poetic, emotional, impulsive, weak — very weak — as to will, altogether a young woman spoiled by a doting grandmother, a *schwärmer*, and of a rebellious, warm-blooded temperament. Just because Lassalle was abused at home for a Jew, a demagogue, and a man who

was said to live on the bounty of a titled woman
— the latter was a false assertion — just because of these wellnigh inscrutable barriers, the
capricious young person fell in love with him;
while he, desirous of settling in life and not
blandly indifferent to the social flesh-pots of the
proud Munich family, assumed the attitude of
the accepted conqueror. Meredith gives an
electric presentment of the first meeting; but
for a more sober, more truthful rendering of the
same incident, it is better to go to Helena von
Doenniges-Shevitch herself. She published in
Breslau, 1879, a little volume entitled Meine
Beziehungen zu Ferdinand Lassalle (My Relations with Ferdinand Lassalle). It is said that
when a woman writes her confession she is never
further from the truth. Heine once made a
wicked jest about women who write with one
eye on the paper, the other on a man; adding
that the Countess Hahn-Hahn must alone be excepted because she was one-eyed. There are
many *lacunæ* in this confession of an unhappy
woman, yet the impression of sincerity is unmistakable; too much so for Meredith, who was
in search of a human document over which he
could play his staccato wit and the sheet-
lightnings of his irony.

We learn from Helena that she was no novice
at flirtation and that, like many girls of high
spirit, she refused to be auctioned off to the highest bidder by her worldly parents. She resolved
to marry Lassalle. There were cries of indigna-

tion. She was sent to Switzerland, but at the Righi she contrived to meet Lassalle. Contemporaneous with her passion for him, she permitted the amiable attentions of a young Wallachian prince, Von Racowitza, a Danube osier with Indian-idol eyes, as Meredith calls him. This prince, affectionate, good-hearted, rich, was the choice of Helena's parents. She told him that she loved Lassalle and that she intended to marry him. The prince concurred in her plans. He was a nice youth and as pliant as a reed. Finally, at Geneva, in the summer of 1864, seeing that she would be sequestrated by her father, she left his roof and went to Lassalle's hotel, accompanied by her faithful servant, Marie-Thérèse — a venal wretch, as she found out later.

Then Lassalle assumed his most operatic attitude. Elopement? Never! Either you come to me, a gift from your father's hands — ! You may guess the pose of the fiery orator. Bewildered, the girl could not understand that the man feared the loss of political prestige if he carried off the daughter of a prominent government official. So he procrastinated — those whom the gods hate they make put off the things of to-day until to-morrow. Proudly—Lassalle's pride was veritably satanic — he returned Helena to a family friend — she refused to go home — and her parents were summoned. There was a painful interview between the mother and Lassalle — Helena in the background — one that would make a magnificent fourth act for an ambitious dramatist. Meredith puts epigrams in the mouths of these disturbed people that are so much sawdust — do not all his people talk as brilliantly and as inhumanly, from Father Feverel to the comedians of the Amazing Marriage? This page is a darker one in the Confessions. The angry mother used outrageous language; Lassalle kept his temper and went away decidedly the hero of the occasion. Alas! he also left Helena to the tender mercies of two enraged parents. The General entered cursing and actually dragged his daughter by the hair through the dark avenues to her home. Locked up, without the slightest hope of reaching Lassalle — she was told that he had immediately left the city — threatened with severer personal abuse, for General von Doenniges was an old-style Teutonic father, the wretched girl lost all hope. Daily was she upbraided by her parents, by her sister and brother. The sister's engagement had been just announced to a member of some old family; so old that it was dusty. The brother played on her feelings with his tears. He would lose caste if his sister married a Hebrew. (He didn't say "Hebrew," but something opprobrious, patterning after his father.) In a word, the entire family battery was trained on her, and as she despaired of Lassalle — she was assured by forged proofs that he was glad to get rid of her — and was sick in body as well as soul, she capitulated. She promised not to see him. What she didn't know

was that Lassalle was raising heaven and earth
to get at her; that he had appealed to Church,
State, to the Court itself; that he had recruited
a regiment of friends, and, finally, that he had
bribed the unspeakable Thérèse, Helena's maid,
with one hundred and eighty francs to carry a
letter, planning an escape, to her mistress.
Thérèse took the letter to the General and was
given twenty francs more, thus selling the poor
Helena for forty dollars. Police guarded the
house. Negotiations were forced on Von Doenniges by the now aroused Lassalle, who realised
what a mistake he made when he had juggled
with fortune, no matter what his exalted motives.

But the blind bow-god had shot his last arrow, a spent one, and Mars entered as Cupid
fled. Lassalle, at bay and furious after Helena
had been forced to declare in the presence of his
two friends — false ones she declares — that she
would not see him, sent a challenge, accompanied
by an insulting message, to the General. One
day Von Racowitza entered and bade her good-
bye. He was going to fight Lassalle instead of
her father, who was too old and feeble. She was
incredulous. Lassalle in a duel! Impossible! And
he a dead shot—unhappy boy! The next day the
prince returned, pale, fearful. She was aghast.
Lassalle wounded! A falsehood! Yet so he
was, and fatally. Three days later, August 31,
1864, the hope of Heinrich Heine, the hope of
young Germany, died in agony of peritonitis, an

agony that opium could not mitigate. At his death-bed was Countess Hatzfeldt. It is said he died repenting his crazy action. His funeral was followed by thousands. Torch-light processions moved through Germany. He was a dead god, a hero translated to the clouds. Many believed that he had been crucified because of his love for the people. A bullet, fired from the pistol of a novice, had snuffed out the life of a man who was the most commanding figure in Germany at the time. He had been denounced as a brilliant charlatan. He was much more, though perhaps partially deserving that appellation. However, a man whom Bismarck feared and respected was something more than a brilliant firebrand.

And now our credulity must be strained. Six months after Lassalle's interment, Helena von Doenniges, hating her parents, at war with the world and herself, turned to the only friend she had in all Germany — Yanko von Racowitza. He was half dying. The shock of events had been too much for his frail, sensitive nature. In pity and as a terrible penance Helena outraged the world by marrying the slayer of her lover. Five months later she buried him. What hell this woman traversed during her earthly pilgrimage not even her book reveals. She admits her weak will; she was between the devil and the deep sea — her parents and Lassalle. She was young, trusting, without an adviser. Her father was brutal, the flesh weak. She asks us to remember "que tout comprendre, c'est tout pardonner." But no one has pardoned her, least of all George Meredith, who in his most merciless manner has served readers with much psychology for "those acrobats of the affections," as Helena and Ferdinand have been called. Meredith depicts Clotilde as the "imperishable type of that feminine cowardice" to which he says all women are trained. This may be true of the characters in the book, not of Helena. Young women who are imprisoned and stuffed with lies about their lover are not cowardly if they weaken, especially after the shocking experience Helena had undergone with Lassalle. She had, brave as she was, put all to the test and had lost. Is it any wonder that her nerves played her false when the man — as she thought — had deserted her? At least she cannot be compared with the lady in Browning's Statue and the Bust. Helena greatly dared.

As to her marriage, it was both an expiation, a charitable act to Racowitza, a defiance to the world, and also a cruel self-laceration. And there was possibly another, a more subtle reason than any of these. Flaubert at the close of Madame Bovary shows us Charles Bovary almost happy to talk about his Emma with her former lover, Rodolphe. Racowitza was the one person on earth to whom Helena could talk of Lassalle. Possibly her reminiscences hastened the poor lad's death. And young women don't kill themselves for love; that notion is the invention of conceited males or romantic feminine novelists. To live and to suffer was more difficult for the woman than to evade the consequences of her weakness by sliding out of existence. She was a martyr, no longer a weakling, after her marriage. She has been banned by all the sentimentalists; whereas, if she had run away, as did Cosima Liszt-von Bülow, with a great composer (poor Von Bülow, who sacrificed himself to his wife and to his friend, Richard Wagner, is always left in the cold by these same sentimental folk), then Helena von Doenniges might have been called a heroine. Nothing succeeds like bathos. She should be pitied, not censured. And behind all this really tragic romance (not a tragic comedy) was something the English novelist forgot — the mating of a young man with a young woman; which is, whether we subscribe to Schopenhauer's view or not, the most significant fact in the life of our planet. The world was well lost for love by Lassalle; for Helena von Doenniges nothing remained but the mastication of dead sea fruit.

II

A TRAGIC COMEDIAN

A few years ago still another book by Mme. Racowitza, as she chooses to call herself, though two other husbands have given her their names, appeared in Germany entitled Von Anderen und Mir. From the summit of nearly sixty-eight years the heroine of one of the most romantic stories that filled all Europe with astonishment, pity, and indignation now surveys her past to the tune of over three hundred pages, and again has unstopped the tongue of scandal and has brushed away the dust from several forgotten tombs. Mme. von Racowitza has been more than frank. Her skill as a writer, her vast worldly experience, her brilliancy, vivacity, and anything but grandmotherly regard for the conventions have resulted in a fascinating autobiography that is sure to shock many and in which we find significant light thrown on the memorable intrigue and death of Lassalle.

The author's object in this second rehashing of the thrice-told tale is something besides Lassalle. With a self-confidence that borders on the naïveté of Marie Bashkirtseff she begins with her love affairs when she was in pinafores. Her precocity, like that of Lassalle, suggested genius. Because of her family she met all of the shining lights and big bow-wows of art, literature, fashion, and politics. Upon her intellect there is little need to dwell; she assures her readers of its existence on every page. Of her beauty much could be said. Painted as a girl by Wilhelm von Kaulbach, with the famous Justus von Liebig an admiring third; portrayed by Lenbach in the first lovely flush of womanhood, we might, nevertheless, set down to legend the miraculous reports of her beauty if there were not those alive who still remember her. She could write excellent English and was a fluent conversation-alist on many themes. In her last book there are three photographs, one after the Lenbach portrait, one taken in 1895, the third in 1905. The last betrays no relaxation of the pose nick-named "grande dame." She is the aristocrat who became a social outlaw, the Cleopatra, slightly matured, who outlived her Antony. The russet coronal has been replaced by venerable white hair; yet Mme. von Racowitza, to judge from her book, is anything but venerable.

She was born in 1843; this she does not tell us. Her father, General von Doenniges, came of northern stock. He was proud of his Viking (?) blood. Handsome and accomplished, he was taken up by the Prince Royal of Bavaria, after-ward Maximilian II. The young Pomeranian Protestant developed such a predilection for public life (he was at first protected by Humboldt at the Berlin University) that he followed his royal friend to Munich and from the household service was promoted to Minister and Bavarian Ambassador. As a girl Helena von Doenniges romped with Ludwig II, later the patron of Wagner. She relates that once she was caught by some of the servants engaged in pulling his curly black hair. Her mother, she admits, was the daughter of a rich and cultivated Hebrew family of Berlin, a member of the most cultured circle, to which the Von Mendelssohns, bankers; Rahel, Heine, Varnhagen von Ense, and other well-known people belonged. We say "admitted," for it may be remembered that one of the reasons given for excluding Lassalle from the company of Helena was his Jewish birth. When Rustow, the Swiss officer, friend of Lassalle, sought to calm the enraged General von Doenniges at Geneva he asked him: "Your wife, Mme. von Doenniges, was she not born a Hebrew?" "Yes," was the grudging reply, "but that was many years ago." As there always has been doubt expressed on this subject it is refreshing to find that Mme. von Racowitza is so plain in her statement. Lassalle asked her if she had had many love affairs before their meeting. She put him off with a poetic allusion, but in her last volume she opens widely the closet of her heart and displays without mock modesty the skeletons that hang in it. There is quite a neat little row of them. At ten she analysed love like a Stendhal in petticoats. At twelve she was betrothed to a soldier of fifty, "ugly as an old monkey"; later she lost her heart to a young officer. It was a Romeo and Juliet episode, moonlit gardens, sighs and vows, and the odour of wild roses; but Lassalle drove away these idle flirtings with Cupid (serious enough, she is fain to admit) and made hot love to the beautiful, capricious creature. She was nineteen, he thirty-eight.

After Lassalle's death Marx, when asked by Sophie Hatzfeldt, the elderly lady who was Lassalle's benefactor, to write a brochure attacking Helena von Doenniges, refused. Liebknecht and

Bebel intervened and the pamphlet became a veiled attack against the partisans of Lassalle, Hasselmann and Hasenclever. We mention these things, as Mme. von Racowitza has apparently forgotten some of them. In the Reichstag, September 17, 1873, nine years after Lassalle's death, Bismarck in the course of his historical controversy with Bebel said: "The most intelligent and charming man I ever knew was Ferdinand Lassalle."

After the death of Racowitza his widow went on the stage. Her hatred of her family was the chief reason; and she was penniless. She married Siegwart Friedmann, a German actor and a handsome man. In five years they separated; tired of each other, she hints. Her marriage with Serge von Schevitsch proved happier.

Her pages teem with portraits of men and women whose names to-day are memories. Bulwer, Dickens, Liszt, Napoleon III, Eugénie, Makart, Paul Lindau, Paul Heyse, Wagner, Cosima Wagner — the list is long. Her flight to America in 1877 with Graf von Schevitsch and her life here until 1890 gives her readers some interesting reading. She was friendly with the late Joseph Keppler of Puck, with the littérateur Udo von Brachvogel, and Fred Douglass. Of the last and his treatment in certain social circles she has something to say; a thorough-going democrat, she cannot forgive America for its handling of the colour problem. She writes sharp and not always just or sensible words of us. We do not believe that Lassalle actually uttered all of the sentiments which she quotes. The most amazing confession of this woman is one she omitted to make in her book of 1879 (My Relations to Ferdinand Lassalle). It is this. She admits that hearing he was at Righi-Kaltbad for his health she slipped away from Geneva and sought out the man she loved. There had been a separation and Lassalle believed the affair was at an end. Mme. Racowitza glosses over this meeting in the first revelation, but is very explicit in the second. This meeting in the mountains, cunningly planned by the girl, was the first link in the fatal chain of circumstances that ended in the catastrophe. The book is well worth translating. Perhaps if George Meredith had read it we should not have had The Tragic Comedians, for one survivor of the twain has told the tale in different fashion. Perhaps on the other hand the great analyst might have exclaimed: "See! She is my Clotilde Rüdiger after all." She certainly remains more the tragic comedian than ever in Von Anderen und Mir.

The sequel to her adventurous life was in the proper romantic key. She committed suicide in October, 1911, at Munich.

IV

THE REAL ISOLDE — WAGNER'S
AUTOBIOGRAPHY

I

"That I should have written Tristan I owe to you and I thank you for all eternity from the bottom of my heart."—Richard Wagner to Mathilde Wesendonck.

It was Nietzsche, was it not, who warned us against setting too much store by the auto-biographies of great men? Now the autobiography of Richard Wagner still reposes inviolate in the care of his widow at Bayreuth. Yet all his life was a self-confession, whether in deed, letter, or music. Music is the most subjective of the arts, and Wagner was the most subjective composer who ever put pen to paper. Every important act of his life — one is almost tempted to add unimportant, too — was speedily recorded in tone; and his music if it could be translated into speech would tell tales compared to which other modern tragedies might pale their romantic fires.

To write a music drama like Tristan and Isolde, to paint in tones its swirling undertow of passion and guilt, demands a poet-composer who must feel first, subjectively at least, a tithe of the sensations he attempts to depict. The greatest love story in the world — for it is more complete and vaster in its consequences than the unhappy loves of Paolo and Francesca — set to the thrilling musical-dramatic score, is what Richard Wagner accomplished in Tristan and Isolde; and to achieve the gigantic task he underwent the tortures of an unhappy love second only in intensity to his music. What the man put into his music he had experienced. His drama throbs at times like an open wound, as did the souls of the enraptured pair in real life. This proceeding of poets and composers — perhaps of mathematicians and philosophers if we could but interpret their work — is as old as mankind. Goethe embalmed his loves in deathless verse and thus eased the aching pain of his heart — better say hearts! Heine made of the formula a tiny exquisite lyric, and at last the higher criticism is beginning to suspect that Shakespeare, who conceived Hamlet and Iago, Lear and Macbeth, Ophelia and Juliet, was himself made up of the elements of all these and a myriad other characters. Browning averred that it was the lesser Shakespeare who wrote the sonnets; all the worse for Browning's judgment. It may have been the lesser Wagner who almost disrupted the Wesendonck household; but why should we complain! We are the gainers. Have we not a precious possession in Tristan and Isolde? This is the pagan view of the situation, not the ethical one.

Nearly all the Wagner biographers have slurred the details of the musician's life at Zürich from 1853 to 1858. The reason is a simple one: those who knew the facts were not allowed to or would not divulge them, and those who did not know perforce left an unexplained gap. Occasional rumours were blown by the wind of surmise about the globe. Every one has since been corroborated in the published letters of Wagner and Madame Wesendonck and the Bélart study. These letters are volcanic on Wagner's side, though he does speak much of the weather, and his pains; the few included in the volume of Mathilde are by no means passionate. One more love affair in the career of a musical Ishmael like Wagner need not particularly interest the world. But this one, the Zürich episode, is of prime æsthetic importance. It gave birth to a magnificent music drama and its outcome made of Wagner again a wanderer, without a home. For a time he had been an anchored parasite in the household of the amiable Otto Wesendonck, and it is safe to assert that if the love and its subsequent catastrophe had not occurred we should have been the poorer of a masterpiece, perhaps several; for Die Walküre was written at Zürich, as were parts of Die Meistersinger, Siegfried, even Parsifal — that bizarre compound of rickety Buddhism and *bric-à-brac* Christianity — was planned, so rich and ripening were the influences of this love upon the fecund brain of Wagner. He began the music of Rheingold in

1853, finished it in 1854; and the June of that year began Die Walküre, finished in 1856; worked over Siegfried and finished several acts by 1857; from 1857 to 1858 was busy with Tristan, wrote the five songs — words by Mathilde Wesendonck — and in 1859 finished Tristan. It is no exaggeration then to say that these five years were the most significant in Wagner's life, the very flowering of his genius.

So much for statistics. These tiresome figures are given to prove that Wagner himself, and following him, the majority of his biographers, created the impression that his second spouse, Cosima Liszt, the divorced wife of Hans von Bülow, was the one passion of his lifetime, the mainspring of his music, the Eternal Feminine at whose loving command the little wizard wrought his miracles in tone. So were we all educated to believe this. Did not Richard Wagner swear to the fact many times? Did he not lay his hand on his heart and solemnly assure the world that to Cosima, his well-beloved, he owed all? And in doing so he was only as human as the rest of his sex — the last woman usually counts the most in the life of a man; this natural fact possibly gave birth to the proverb about straws on the back of camels. Some day the demi-god nonsense about this composer will be entirely dissipated and then behold — a man will emerge, with all a man's failings and virtues. Ernest Newman has knocked Wagner's philosophical pretensions to smithereens, as did

Dmitri Merejkowsky the hollow sham of Tolstoy's prophetic and religious vapourings. So the official autobiography of Wagner given to the world does not after all paint for us the composer's true portrait.

'Therefore, it was not Cosima Wagner, but Mathilde Wesendonck who started Wagner's imaginative machinery whirring. And the most singular part about the mutual letters of Richard and Mathilde is that they were issued with the official stamp of Bayreuth. That Madame Wagner permitted this at once makes us suspicious. How many letters are not in the collection, for there are many unaccountable omissions in this apparently frank volume! Let us relate the main facts. Wagner had been in love with Mathilde Wesendonck, the wife of a wealthy Zürich merchant, for six years. This is stated in a letter to the lady dated August 21, 1858. He met her in 1852, and a year later they were both immersed in a sea of passion and trouble. Yet we have been told by Glasenapp and Chamberlain that Wagner only fell in love with her in 1857, when he lived in a small cottage, "on the green hillock," close by Wesendonck's stately villa. Hans Bélart, in his Richard Wagner in Zürich, published some years ago, was very frank in his disclosures of the affair, treating Wagner as if he were the veriest ingrate and home-wrecker; whereas, if Otto Wesendonck had cared to put his foot down, the intrigue, probably platonic, would have been soon stopped.

But he did not choose to do so, and why is not discoverable in the letters that Wagner wrote Madame Wesendonck, or Otto Wesendonck — that is, in the published letters. What Wagner thought of this husband we may see in the figure of King Marke in Tristan and Isolde, who sings: "O Tristan!" so sonorously and so sorrowfully when he discovers the pair.

The sad side of the story was not Wesendonck, but Wagner's wife, Minna Planer-Wagner, who, sick, old, and neglected, ate her bread in sorrow at his table, a table provided by the bounty of others. She knew that Mathilde's influence had become paramount, and the letters and diaries of Wagner are full of naïve complaints of her selfishness! "Destiny dooms me; having been constantly too good, and having submitted always, I have spoiled my wife so that her demands on me are becoming impossible." The principal demand was only for his love — impossible, indeed. He dedicated the Walküre prelude to Mathilde in 1854. In the original poem of Gottfried of Strasburg, the potion it is which arouses Tristan and Isolde to their fatal undoing.

Mathilde, with a keener precision than Wagner of the psychologic possibilities of the situation, caused him to change this rather mechanical operation of fate to the mutual glances of the lovers. "His eyes on mine were fastened."

Minna did not like this spiritual friendship. She was a simple soul, and the complexity of her husband's genius, its many voracious tentacles groping in the void for sympathy — is not genius always selfishly cruel! — made her miserable. And then, worst of all, she did not comprehend his music. Rienzi was her favourite. Its theatric pomp and post-Meyerbeerian brassbands were to her, educated as an actress, the acme of greatness. Rienzi, too, made money. It was popular. She loathed Walküre; she declared that "It is an erotic and an immoral stupidity." Of the latter drama she wrote from Dresden, where she went for a cure: "They — Tristan and Isolde — remain nevertheless a couple too amorous." Fancy Robert Browning misunderstood by his poet wife. What tragedy is all this. Minna did not suspect the greatness of her little lord, who shook off his early operas with disgust. The future was to be his — and who was to pay the rent? quoth Minna. Ah, these practical wives of men of genius — why will they persist in feeding and lodging their husbands! Poor women — no Daudet has ever espoused their cause, has sung their praises!

In the letter alluded to there occur the most damaging charges. (This letter, or for that matter many of the following details, are naturally not in the letters of Wagner and Madame Wesendonck.) Minna writes:

"The fatal Tristan, which decidedly I do not care for (though not because of the reasons of its origins) is, I think, coming laboriously into the world, with long periods of intermission and great efforts! It seems to me that the travail under such conditions cannot be a happy one. The news of the death of the little Guido, youngest son of the Wesendoncks, has depressed me terribly. I believe it is but the dispensation of Providence that God visits affliction on this heartless woman, spoiled by a happy life. How many times have I hoped that the Lord would bring about a change in her through sickness of one of her children; but see! I still tremble with the terror of the thought."

"Reasons of its origins!" "Heartless woman!" These are strong phrases. In the meantime Wagner up at the villa — Minna at the cottage — was revelling in the bliss of a sympathetic soul. A beautiful creature, young, intellectual, poetic, Mathilde was a prolific author. Not only did she write five poems which were set by Wagner for soprano voice and piano, but dramas, Märchen, poems, epic and lyric, puppet-plays. Her muse was inspired by such themes as Frederick the Great, Edith, Gudrun — three dramas of hers — and also by the rhythms of music. Her work reads rather commonplace nowadays, though fluent in the romantic imagery of her time. To Wagner it must have appealed, for two of the five songs, In the Hothouse and Dreams, he called Studies for Tristan and Isolde. Dreams was utilised in the duo of the second act of Tristan, while in the prelude to the third we recognise the profile of In the Hothouse.

Of rare culture then, Mathilde Wesendonck

caught the many-coloured soul of Richard Wagner up into a fiery cloud, and only did he return to earth when Minna complained or his purse grew light. How the Wagners lived at this period was never exactly known until the recollections of the composer Roberd Freihern von Hornstein were published. Wagner was comfortably housed. For form's sake he paid a nominal rental. Every year from his friend Alexander von Ritter's mother he received eight hundred thalers. His Zürich admirer, Jacob Sulzer, looked after the table; a sportsman, he weekly sent him fish and game. The wine came from Wesendonck's cellar. Brockhaus, the publisher, gave him royalties on his books. And there were *tantièmes* from early operas. Von Hornstein relates that somehow or other money always flowed in — was there not Franz Liszt, golden-hearted Liszt! Elegance, plenty, refined surroundings, company — Ah, the Wagner legend pales day by day, that charming legend of his continual poverty! He had friends rich and eager to assist him. The only mortifying thing there is to note is that so many of these friends have since told the world how they helped the struggling genius. Always let the world, as well as your right and left hand, know how much you lend, seems to have been the motto of this band. Liszt was the exception. He gave like a prince of the Renaissance and never took heed of his bounty. I, for one, am glad that Wagner accepted assistance. If ever the world owed a man a living, he was that man.

We should be grateful to those who helped him to the leisure which gave us masterpieces — only wondering at the bad taste displayed by some in publishing their generosity.

Gossip began to breed. Minna's attitude toward Mathilde was that of the implacably jealous wife. Von Bülow wrote Richter in 1858 that Wagner was financially embarrassed, "something occurred between him and Wesendonck." And Wagner hints to a friend: "I have good reasons for not asking him" — Wesendonck — "to aid me." Liszt's Princess Sayn-Wittgenstein was called by the friends of both the enamoured ones, and replied, as might have been expected: "I do not believe the worst. But even should this be, one can say honestly that in this world everything is relative, even justice and fidelity. . . . We truly say that genius belongs to all the world, and that every one claims his portion." Spoken like a merciful woman — and also as one rowing in the same boat with Mathilde Wesendonck.

The crash occurred in 1858. It was not unexpected. Otto Wesendonck's patience had been sorely tried. He loved Wagner, the man, and adored the genius of the musician. But there were limits. His wife gave a concert at the villa in 1858 and Wagner conducted. It was an event; musicians came from Germany to hear the new music of the exiled revolutionist. He was presented with a gold baton. It was the gift of Mathilde and supposedly from Paris. Herr

Siber, a Zürich goldsmith, made it and told the story to Bélart of the pious deception practised by the donor. Evidently Mathilde knew her Richard! Liszt was expected to visit Zürich August 20. When he arrived, great was his amazement to find that Wagner had left three days before, left precipitately, better say fled the city. Why? Silence again, even in these new letters. In 1859 Mathilde wrote that Wagner had left "voluntarily." She continues: "But what is the use of questioning birds? We have commemorated that event in Tristan and Isolde. The rest is silence."

But it was not silence. The facts are these — never printed until Bélart, through his dogged industry, unearthed them. The day of August 11, 1858, Minna Wagner went to Otto Wesendonck's villa, and after telling the mistress of the establishment what she thought of her, she informed the husband of the state of affairs as she believed them to be. Wesendonck sent for Wagner. What happened then only two men could tell and they never did, though Wesendonck curtly informed Wagner's curious friends that he had advised the composer to leave the town. Broken-hearted Wagner asked Mathilde: "Where Tristan is going wilt thou Isolde follow?" But there were children and a comfortable home and a reputation to be considered — Isolde did not wave the burning signal torch, and the miserable man left after borrowing from Sulzer money enough to get to Geneva. There old Jakob Susstrunk, the barber, gave him the necessary means for a further flight to Venice. In Venice he arrived, sick, almost penniless, alone, all that he loved in Zürich, the future a wall of despair.

He has related his experiences. While confined to his bed, the plaintive cry of a gondolier on a lonely canal gave him the piping of the shepherd in Tristan — at death's door, the instinct of the artist was not subdued. He noted down the melody, as he also registered for future use the heart-throbs of his passion and Isolde's.

Wagner fell to keeping a diary. This he sent from time to time to Zürich. Mathilde answered discreetly. Otto was evidently in the secret, and his jealousy appeased. Doubtless he said to himself after the manner of fatuous musical amateurs: "It is a great thing that my wife has inspired the harmless passion of an extraordinary composer." At any rate, the correspondence which languished ceased, was renewed, and lasted until 1871. In the interim, Wagner had met Ludwig of Bavaria, and become famous, had seen Cosima von Bülow and stolen her from her husband; had, after the death of Minna in 1866 — poor sacrificed Minna! — married Cosima, and the old romance went up in smoke. Wagner had plotted suicide in Venice; luckily he changed his mood. A perfect final cadence this self-murder would have been for the greatest romance of his life. That it ended in chilly proprieties; that he wrote Mathilde, adding a postscript, regards from Cosima; that Siegfried, his son, was years later petted in the household of Mathilde (Wagner died in 1883, Mathilde in 1902, a widow since 1896; she was born 1828) —Subtle are the ways Life, the comedian, has of ending our little frenzies. "Auf Wiedersehen! Auf Wiedersehen! Soul of my soul, farewell! Auf Wiedersehen!" wrote Wagner before he left Zürich. He did not believe it was a genuine farewell; but the Comic Spirit, which, according to George Meredith, enjoys the merry hamstringing of our destinies, took Wagner at his word, and though he saw Mathilde once more, the two were doomed to remain apart, and tragic comedians that they were, to end their lives in the odour of respectable married folk; Tristan and Isolde settled down in bourgeois comfort — but not together! Destiny shook the dice and made of these two rebels conventional tax-payers and not citizens of eternity. Perhaps Paolo and Francesca, those contemporaries of the stars, were braver.

II

WAGNER'S AUTOBIOGRAPHY

If the long-expected autobiography of Richard Wagner, My Life, had appeared after the death of Cosima Wagner a cynic would have been justified in saying that the composer's widow was indulging in a posthumous revenge. Certainly nothing he ever wrote in his voluminous literary works has produced in the minds of his readers so definite an impression of meanness and mightiness as do these memoirs. The marked impression is that Wagner was more Mime and Alberich, even Fafner, than Siegfried or Tristan or Wotan. His contemporaries have described Will Shakespeare as a lovable man, both merry and melancholy in his moods. We like to think of him as a Hamlet or a Prospero. But Wagner kept all that was great, noble, poetic for his scores; in his private life he often behaved like a malicious, a malignant monkey. He lied. He whimpered when he begged, and he was always begging. He invariably deceived women attracted by his genius and a magnetic personality. And he abused every friend he ever had, abused them when living and after death in this book. A singularly repulsive, fascinating man and a brave one. What was his reason for giving to the world so unflattering a portrait of himself?

In his lifetime he made enemies daily because of his venomous tongue. Some evil fairy bestowed upon him the gift of saying aloud what was in his mind, and not infrequently he hit the nail on the head, told the truth in high places where concealment would have been a virtue. He was a moral or immoral typhoon that swept away the evil and good alike in its elemental fury.

I

We are informed that between the years 1868 and 1873 Wagner compiled these memoirs from diaries and other memoranda which he had preserved for thirty-five years. He dictated from these notes to Cosima and, it is said, to Ludwig II of Bavaria. The book was set up by French compositors who did not understand German; twelve copies were printed and the type then distributed. Of these twelve copies eight were held by his wife and four were entrusted among some other friends. It is a significant fact that Friedrich Nietzsche read the proofs of the work, and while he never broke the seal of secrecy his knowledge of the peculiar Wagner psychology enabled him to write his later attacks on the master from superior vantage-ground. Strictly speaking, there is less novelty in My Life than we had expected. The earlier biographies by Glasenapp and Henry T. Finck, the last-named being the best in English and ranking with the best in German, not to mention Wagner's own writings, contain much that is here retold by the composer. The funeral ceremonies of Weber, the story of Spontini, the first performances of Liebesverbot and Beethoven's Ninth Symphony, and a score of other anecdotes have long since been in print. What is fresh is the details of Wagner's childhood, his courting of and marriage with Minna Planer, and the account of his first meetings with Cosima Liszt, then the wife of his dearest friend and worshipper Hans von Bülow. What he has omitted — or is it the fault of Bayreuth? — would fill two more volumes of the same size as these. He slurs over the Wesendonck affair, which is all the more curious because only a few years ago Bayreuth permitted, nay edited, the publication of the Wagner-Wesendonck correspondence, chiefly his letters. Furthermore Wagner, the friend of kings when he died, seems to have forgotten completely his share in the Dresden uprising of 1849. That he was a red-hot revolutionist is proved by his Art and Revolution. An intimate friend of that sombre, enigmatic nihilist Bakunin (Bakounine is the better spelling), Wagner it was who inducted the harmless Roeckel into the movement, and not, as he vaguely insinuates, he who was led away by Roeckel. Ferdinand Praeger's Wagner as I Knew Him is a document of profound value, one that was not invalidated by Ashton Ellis's pamphlet entitled, 1849; a Vindication. But after all Wagner was only an amateur socialist.

All the composers of his day, the big as well as the little, Schumann, Mendelssohn, Meyerbeer, Spohr, Marschner, Spontini, Hiller, Berlioz, were attacked by Wagner, who saw with the clairvoyant's eye of hatred and with a touch of his baneful pen transformed them into mean, grotesque, even vile personalities. Heine didn't escape, nor Hebbel and Auerbach. But all this is the obverse side of the medal, as we shall pres-

ently see. This little, selfish monster of genius,
sickly, puny in size, his mask of appalling ugliness, bowlegged (he wore a long cloak to hide
this defect, for, as he said, he didn't wish to be
taken for a Jew), with large, protuberant blue
eyes, from which at times gleamed the most extraordinary fire; this stunted man, hated and
despised, nevertheless could make himself very
attractive. He was full of fun and boyish antics
to old age. Praeger relates that when in London
conducting the stodgy Philharmonic Orchestra
Wagner's exuberance took the form of standing
on his head. Wagner never grew up; his was a
case of arrested moral development. He retained the naïve spites and vanities and sav-
ageries of his boyhood, while his intellect and
emotional development had become those of a
superman. He neither forgot nor forgave. He
was Dantesque in his memory of personal af-
fronts, and if he couldn't put all his adversaries
in hell, as did the Italian poet, he remembered
them in his autobiography, and in at least one
instance he transferred the personality of a hostile critic into the scene of Die Meistersinger —
Beckmesser is a supposed portrait of Eduard
Hanslick, the Vienna music critic. Hanslick was
present when the poem was read, and Wagner
relates that he left deeply offended. Is it anything to wonder over? Nor is it surprising that
Hanslick too never forgot. A trait of Wagner's
is his constant amazement when a man or a woman he has insulted or betrayed dares to man-

ifest feelings of retaliation. In these matters he is genuinely childish. To the very end, despite his imperial success, he never succeeded in bringing his inner nature into harmony with the external world. A man of genius, he was a stranger in his own land to the end.

We have said that the significant portions of these memoirs are set forth not in those sections that deal with the artist's psychology but in his purely human relations. Of him it might be said that nothing inhuman was foreign to him. And we propose to deal with this side of him. Mr. Finck has painted a very sympathetic portrait, while Glasenapp is too much of Bayreuth to offer the entire truth. It is a pity that the monumental life begun by the late Hon. Mrs. Burrell was not finished. It is not printed but engraved throughout and illustrated in facsimiles of every document quoted. A copy is in the British Museum, and the original is in the possession of her husband. As a critic has said, "many as have been the biographies of the composer, and loud as has been the chorus of praise bestowed upon each, it was reserved for Mrs. Burrell to establish the accurate form of his mother's maiden name." My Life, notwithstanding its revelation of a mean, tricky, lofty soul, one that wavered along the scale from Caliban to Prospero, will rank among the great autobiographies of literature. Its place on the shelf will be between Benvenuto Cellini and Goethe. (Wahrheit und Dichtung aus Mei-

nem Leben.) The irresponsible sculptor and
the wise poet — surely Wagner had in him something of the stuff of both. Unmoral, reckless,
consumed by the loftiest of ideals, shoving aside
all that opposed him, breaking faith with man
and woman alike, turning his sorrows into passionate song, vainglorious and cowardly, lust-
ful and outrageous for his ideal, always keeping
his star in view, he was kin to Cellini and he was
kin to Goethe. The world will not willingly let
die such a book as this.

II

Nietzsche wrote some time about 1887–88,
"Was Wagner German at all? We have some
reason for asking this. It is difficult to discern
in him any German trait whatever. Being a
great learner, he has learned to imitate much
that is German; that is all. His character itself is in opposition to what has hitherto been
regarded as German, not to speak of the German
musician! His father was a stage-player named
Geyer. A Geyer is almost an Adler (Jewish
names both). What has hitherto been put into
circulation as the Life of Wagner is *fable con-
venue*, if not worse. I confess my distrust of
every point which rests solely on the testimony
of Wagner himself. He had not pride enough for
any truth whatever about himself; nobody was
less proud; he remained just like Victor Hugo,
true to himself even in biographical matters —

he remained a stage-player." Elsewhere Nietzsche warns us against the autobiographies of great men.

"His father was a stage-player named Geyer." Coming from Nietzsche this statement is not surprising, for he had read these memoirs while at Villa Triebschen. Why then, it will be asked, does this fact not appear in the first page of the autobiography? Despite asseverations to the contrary we suspect that Bayreuth edited not wisely but too well. Others besides Nietzsche had seen the opening line of the work: "I am the son of Ludwig Geyer." The late Felix Mottl in the presence of several well-known music critics of New York city declared in 1904 that he had read the above statement. He also told the same story to German journalists. Mr. Finck as long ago as 1896 informed the present writer that at Wahnfried one could see the portrait of Ludwig Geyer, Wagner's "step-father," and of Wagner's mother, but not a sign of the real (or putative) father. This statement we personally corroborated. Now this doesn't prove that Richard Wagner was of Jewish descent, though there is a strong reason for believing that the versatile Geyer, painter, poet, musician, and actor, may have had Jewish blood in his veins. To tell the truth, Wagner's mother displayed more marked Hebraic lineaments; her name was Bertz, as Mrs. Burrell discovered. Stranger still is the fact that Richard Geyer, as he was known at school, looks more like the Wagners than Geyer; he resembles his elder brother, a veritable Wagner, much more than he does his half (or whole) sister, Cecilia Geyer. So the physiognomists must make of this anomaly what they will. Of course the chief point of interest is Wagner's chronic hatred of the Jews, and his attack on the Jewish element in music.

If the Geyer story be the truth, then the music of Wagner, sensuous, Oriental, brilliant, pompous, richly coloured, is Jewish, more Jewish than the music of Meyerbeer, Mendelssohn, or Goldmark. But let us see what the original of this contention has to say himself on the subject.

Of Wagner's own opinion concerning his paternity he leaves no doubt in the mind of the reader. Before such frankness the most seasoned will quail. Sir William Davenant is said to have blackened the memory of his mother in his not very laudable endeavour to prove that he was the natural son of William Shakespeare. Possibly that is why he is known to posterity as "Rare Sir William Davenant." Perhaps Wagner, in his anxiety to demonstrate that his father was a man of lively talents, hinted that his supposed father, Friedrich Wagner, was too much away from home of nights and that "even when the police official, his father, was spending his evenings at the theatre, the worthy actor, Ludwig Geyer, generally filled his place in the family circle, and it seems had frequently to appease my mother, who, rightly or wrongly, complained of her husband." This is simply breath-catching.

"Seems, good mother." Was there ever such a Hamlet-son to such a queen-mother? Geyer married her and her big brood after the elder Wagner had gone to another world. Richard was not called Richard Wagner till the age of fourteen. He was born May 22, 1813, in Leipsic. The house was once a Judengasse, and is now the quarter of the fur merchants.

Geyer did not live long. He took the liveliest interest in Richard, especially when he suspected that the boy had musical ability. The mother of Wagner came from Weissenfels, and she told her son that her parents had been bakers there; later authorities say mill-owners. There was an air of mystery surrounding her antecedents, perhaps because of some personal caprice. She would never give the correct spelling of her name, Perthes, not Bertz, being then the accepted form. A "Weimar prince" had seen to her education at a high-class Leipsic boarding-school. More romantics! That she was a clever, witty, well-educated woman there is no doubt. Harassed by poverty and a large family, she contrived through all of it to keep her head above water. Wagner writes that "her chief characteristics seem to have been a keen sense of humour and an amiable temper, so we need not suppose that it was merely a sense of duty toward the family of a departed comrade that afterward induced the admirable Ludwig Geyer to enter into matrimony with her when she was no longer youthful, but rather that he was impelled to that step by a sincere and warm regard for the widow of his friend." Wagner always spoke better of Geyer than of his father or mother.

The first volume is in two parts. Part I, 1813 to 1842, is devoted to his childhood and school-days, musical studies, travels in Germany, first marriage, and Paris, 1839 to 1842. Part II is devoted to the years in Dresden, 1842 to 1850, and comprises descriptions of Rienzi, The Flying Dutchman, Liszt, Spontini, Marschner, Tann-häuser, Franck, Schumann, Semper, the archi-tect; Gutzkow, Auerbach, Lohengrin, Spohr, Gluck, Heller, Devrient, his mother's death, Bakunin and the May insurrection, his flight to Weimar, Zürich, Paris, Bordeaux, Geneva, and again to Zürich. The prose style of the orig-inal, not of the English translation, is free from Wagner's accustomed obscurities and clogged sentences, which we meet in his pretentious and turgid studies of music and the drama. Doubt-less Cosima, aided by Nietzsche, made these memoirs presentable, for Wagner, while a copious writer, is absolutely devoid of ear for the finer harmonies of prose; indeed, his prose is only one degree worse than the doggerel he too often calls poetry.

His childhood was spent in dreams. He was very sensitive to things that terrified, such as ghosts, shadows, and the whole battery of Ger-man fairy tales. He read Hoffman's stories and they did him no good. He composed tragedies in the style of Hamlet and Lear; he adored Weber and Freischütz; but the major impression of his life was Beethoven's Fidelio. Later came the symphonies and the string quartets; yet the opera was, musically speaking, Wagner's starting-point. What will be matter of surprise to many is the fact that Wagner was no middle-aged student of music, as has been generally understood. He was always studying, only he began earlier than musical histories have told us. He was not a prodigy; he never half mastered the technique of the pianoforte, an instrument which he cursed, yet could never satisfactorily compose unless at the key-board, and sang like a crow. He began with Müller and ended with Weinlig in theory. He had composed a pianoforte sonata by nineteen. He wrote songs. He longed to be a composer of opera. He was omnivorous in his reading, but passed his school examinations with difficulty if at all. In a word, a lad of genius who was determined to seek such spiritual nourishment as he craved and none other. No wonder his schoolmasters shook their heads. At the university he indulged in all the student vices. His particular adventures as a gambler, while dramatic, even thrilling, sound a trifle too much like French fiction to be credible. Petted by his sisters, alternately spoiled and neglected by a capricious though well-meaning mother, Wagner's home-life made up in affection what it lacked in discipline. His life long he was to feel the loss of a father, who would have shaped his conduct as well as his genius.

His mother could not endure the notion of a theatrical career for her son — her dislike of the theatre was well grounded — so she allowed him to become a musician. He literally began conducting before he could read a score. However, the operas he waved his wand over were by Auber and Donizetti, and no doubt the youthful leader used a piano partition. At Lauchstadt he met Minna Planer, a pretty, vivacious actress. Wagner was the musical director of the Magdeburg Theatre Company, of which Minna was also a member. They were both young; they loved, and oddly enough it was Richard who urged a legitimate union. The lady had been imprudent so often that it did not occur to her that any one would be foolish enough to marry her. She had a past, a daughter, Nathalie, being one of its witnesses. Wagner knew this. He tells, not without a certain gusto, the sordid story of her life, her early seduction. Why in the name of all that is decent he should dwell upon such details we may only wonder. If it is to blacken the memory of an unhappy woman who was his best, his only friend through the most awful trials, well and good; base as is the motive, it is at least understandable. But while this aspersion puts Cosima on a pedestal it lowers Wagner, for he confesses he took the woman for better or worse; that after she ran away from him with a certain Dietrich he received her back;

he accepted the illegitimate child; he accepted
her doubtful temper, her ignorance, finally her
tippling and drug-eating habits. At times he
behaved like an angel of light. He forgave so
much that you wonder that he didn't forgive all.
Minna was not a companion for a man of sensitive nerves, as was Richard. What other
woman would have been? And those critics who,
inspired by Bayreuth, attack the unfortunate
actress should remember that she it was who
washed his linen in Paris during the three dark
years from 1839 to 1842; who cooked, slaved,
and saved for him; who stood with rock-bottom
fortitude his terrific outbursts, his peevishness,
his fickleness.

It is a risky business, this judging the respec-
tive rights and wrongs of a husband and wife;
nevertheless justice should be done Minna. He
did not love her long; yet such a dance of death
did this self-absorbed musician fiddle for his
weary spouse that one reads with relief of her
death, not described in these memoirs. Goethe,
the superb and icy egoist, as is commonly supposed, broke down entirely at the death of his
wife, Christiane Vulpius, an uneducated woman
of intemperate habits, pretty but of common
clay. Kneeling at her bedside and seizing her
hands cold in death, this so-called impassive poet
and voluptuary cried: "Thou wilt not forsake
me! No, no; thou must not forsake me!" And
Goethe was a greater poet than Wagner and a
greater man. But Wagner was only too glad to

be relieved of his matrimonial burden. He was already the lover of his friend's wife.

III

Perhaps Cosima may enlighten the world some day as to the methods she employed in managing her hitherto untamable spouse. Past fifty, past the storm and stress of a life rich in miseries and economical in its distribution of favours, Wagner knew that he was in safe harbour after he became the friend of the King. Cosima knew it too. Von Bülow was an exacting husband. Ferdinand Lassalle has described Cosima as a pedant in petticoats, though a true daughter of Liszt in her brilliancy and personal charm. She saw that Von Bülow would always remain a pianist, a very dry, though intellectual artist; that the future was Wagner's. She did not hesitate to sacrifice all, her husband, her father, and she went off with Wagner. Nietzsche, who later was intimate in this circle, must there have formed his conception of supermen and superwomen. Nothing counted but personal inclination; Siegmund and Sieglinde, Siegfried and Brünnhilde, Tristan and Isolde — each a law to himself, to herself. Poor Liszt was shocked not alone because of the moral aspect of the case, but because of the unhappiness brought upon his favourite pupil, Von Bülow; last and principally, Cosima to remarry had to become a Protestant.

Wagner describes his growing love for Cosima. Once it took the freakishly sentimental desire to lift her into a wheel-barrow and wheel her home. Hardly Teutonic this, as Nietzsche would have said. (Nietzsche did not come off without scars in his friendship for Cosima. He, so it was asserted by competent authorities, loved her more than he did the music of Richard.) Minna was cognisant of the growing intrigue between her man and the other woman. She must have been quite broken by this time, for she had gone through the Wesendonck affair and it must be confessed had come off with flying colours in that stormy encounter. After the Dresden revolution Wagner, who had only manipulated the church-bells and had risked his friend Roeckel's life by sending him across the line for a water-ice, the day being hot, fled to Weimar, where he enjoyed for a few days the hospitality of Franz Liszt and his Princess Sayn-Wittgenstein at their house on the hill overlooking the river Ilm, called the Altenburg. Naturally he says little of how he repaid his hosts at a banquet given in his honour. He abused all the guests, got drunk, and was only brought to his senses when Liszt threatened him with expulsion if he didn't apologise to Von Bülow, Tausig, Cornelius, and the others. He knew Liszt too well to hesitate, and did as he was told; therefore Liszt, Liszt who gave Lohengrin its first production, who sent Wagner thousands of dollars, who furnished him musical ideas, also a devoted spouse, Cosima, Liszt is shown in anything but flattering colours in this book. Verily Wagner was obsessed by the evil angel of truth-telling. Like the little child in Hans Andersen's story, he always saw the king naked. And this, whether we like his ingratitude or not, may constitute in the future the weightiest value to his utterances.

But, honest to the point of shocking, he exhibits a clamlike reticence in a quarter where he might have been more expansive. Not that his comparative silence regarding his relations at Zürich with the Wesendoncks was actuated by any awakened sense of chivalry. No, his letters reveal the reverse. The truth is he cut a poor figure in that ugly episode. He tells his story as obliquely as he dare, but the facts are against him. There were too many witnesses for him to prevaricate, and we wonder that Frau Cosima printed this present story when the Wagner-Wesendonck letters (and Wagner's words) do so contradict the autobiography.

If readers of My Life when disgusted by the pettiness of the author would only recollect that this pigmy with the giant brain gave us the sublime last act of Götterdämmerung — as sublime as a page from Æschylus or an act from King Lear; gave us the Shakespearian humour, fantasy, and rich humanity of Die Meistersinger, and, finally, the glowing love poem of Tristan and Isolde, then Wagner the sorely beset and erring mortal would be forgotten in Wagner the

Titan. We smile at John Ruskin's attempt to prove that only a moral man can produce great art. Alas! What would he have said of Richard Wagner? Therefore, why should we sit in judgment on the man? His temperament was abnormal, his health wretched. He was all intellect and emotion, and if in his last years he became unduly sentimental over the sufferings of dogs and guinea-pigs, also became a vague socialist, and indulged in some decidedly queer pranks during the Ludwig affair, we had better set it down to the strain of his early years, to his age, as was the Tolstoy case, and to his protracted conflict for his ideals. And what a glorious fighter he was! In the deepest despair he would rouse himself and begin anew, and this lasted over thirty years. You forgive his childlike enjoyment of luxury when it did come, after his fiftieth year. He was a "wicked" man like Tolstoy in his youth; both ended in a vapour of sentimental humanitarianism, though Wagner remained "harder" — in the Nietzschian sense.

We confess to finding the second volume — a trifle less interesting than the first. It ranges from 1850 to 1861; the entire work is over nine hundred pages, and deals with the Nibelungen Ring, Zürich, Liszt, Schopenhauer, London, Venice, the various stadia in the progress of Tristan and Isolde, Weimar, Paris, and the fiasco of Tannhäuser, Vienna, and again Zürich, Stuttgart, and finally Munich. He had to flee Vienna because of debts, although he insulted a wealthy Jewish banker by borrowing one thousand gulden from him, giving a banquet to singers and musicians, and when the banker visited him, calling down the stairs: "No dirty Jews are admitted." This phrase "dirty Jew" was often on Wagner's tongue. He insulted the great conductor Herman Levi thus. He mocked Tichhatschek, the tenor, who "created" his Rienzi, and retailed scandal about his early idol, Wilhelmine Schroeder-Devrient, who was said to be fond of handsome young officers. Wagner spared no one. Karl Ritter, whose mother did so much for him, giving him an annual pension; Van Hornstein, who refused him at the last a huge sum; Princess Metternich, Duc de Morny, Louis Napoleon, all lent him large sums, as did Otto Wesendonck, yet he mentions them coldly. His brothers-in-law, Brockhaus and Avenarius, he slights for the same reason — they refused him money. To discover the real Wagner read the Liszt-Wagner correspondence. The two men stand revealed, Liszt, the antipodes of Wagner, noble, patient, always giving, always praising or encouraging, seldom criticising. And it may be confessed that at this period Wagner's feelings toward Liszt, as shown in the letters, are edifying. He was not altogether spoiled, else so many people wouldn't have loved, have worshipped him. Adversities, if they strengthened the keystone of his art, made his temper unbearable. But no idiosyncrasy can be summoned as an apology for his behaviour in the Jessie Laussot affair at Bordeaux. And he tells it all so disinterestedly.

By temperament pessimistic, nevertheless in his artistic theories Wagner was an optimist. He had begun as a disciple in philosophy of Feuerbach, but a copy of The World as Will and Representation, by Arthur Schopenhauer, topsy-turvied the composer, whose later poems became tinged with the world-woe (Weltschmerz) of the cynical sage of Frankfort. This pessimism was personal in Wagner's case; it was not so much Weltschmerz as Selbstschmerz (self-pity). He sent the poem of The Ring to Schopenhauer, who abused it heartily to his disciples. Yet Wagner writes with smirking self-satisfaction that Schopenhauer had been much impressed. How much impressed he was we all know now. He pencilled at the end of the first act of Die Walküre, where the stage direction is "quick curtain!" — "high time" (höchste Zeit). Schopenhauer, who admired the music of Rossini and blew plaintive melodies on the flute, disliked the incest theme in Die Walküre, and even denied the composer any musical ability whatever. Possibly this same Schopenhauer, whose chief work also opened the eyes of Nietzsche, was at the close one of the causes of the break between Wagner and his ardent apostle, the author of that brilliant, enthusiastic book, Richard Wagner in Bayreuth.

Nietzsche had outgrown Schopenhauer when the music festival of 1876 inaugurated the opening of the Bayreuth music drama. His Wagner-worship had begun to wane; he saw his god in the full glare of worldly glory and he noted the feet of clay, noted that the ex-revolutionist of 1849 bowed very low to royalty, and also realised that Wagner did not propose to share his throne, not even the lowest step, with any one. He left Bayreuth thoroughly disillusionised, though he joined the Wagner family at Sorrento the following November. He published his Thoughts Out of Season, and there were those who detected the tiny rift in the lute of friendship. Wagner too felt the coolness, but he wrote Nietzsche a brief, cordial letter. In 1878 appeared Human, All Too Human, and henceforth Bayreuth was silent as the tomb on the name of Nietzsche. The friends never met again, and when Parsifal was produced in 1882 at Bayreuth Nietzsche threw overboard his Wagnerian baggage and forswore the ideals of his former master. The master had long since thrown Nietzsche to the winds. When a disciple ceased to be useful he was dropped, as were Von Bülow, Von Hornstein, Ritter, and Liszt. In Meyerbeer Wagner encountered metal of his own kind; he could never catch this wily Berlin-born composer off his guard. Hence his eloquent abuse.

V

CERTAIN AMERICAN PAINTERS

I

WHISTLER

THE exhibition of Whistler's paintings and
pastels at the Metropolitan Museum (1910)
ought to dislodge the last cobweb of prejudice
clinging to the Whistler legend. Time, which
disentangles all critical snarls, has allowed us to
place in its true perspective the work of this
American genius. He is no longer a barbarous
solitary, a ferocious eccentric, nor is his originality indisputable. Genius never drops from
the skies. Wagner we know was a complex product, stemming from Beethoven, Weber, Liszt;
Chopin, the unique Chopin, was firmly founded
on Bach and Hummel. Swinburne, who amazed
our fathers with his fiery metres, had in him
much of Sappho and Baudelaire. And Whistler,
a stumbling-block to criticism for so many years,
was caught at various periods in the eddies of
Courbet and Fantin-Latour, the Japanese, and
Rossetti; even such an antipodal talent as Alma-
Tadema's he did not disdain to profit from.
The loan exhibition, arranged with such tact,
tells us these things, and Whistler emerges

more Whistler than ever. A stylist like Poe
and Pater, not devoid of preciosity and at times
of mysticism, he selected — his art is the very
efflorescence of selection — a narrow path, realising that his salvation lay in finesse, not virility; in languor, not ecstasy. Within his restricted compass he contrived to beat out a
highly individual style. He is Whistler as Chopin is Chopin and Poe Poe. The names of this
musician and of this poet are not dragged in
haphazard. With both the painter had singular affinities. And like Renan, he soon outgrew
the "mania of certitude."

It is a commonplace in the history of criticism that a great man is unappreciated during
his epoch; yes, too often unappreciated, but not
always unperceived. Sensible strictures were
passed on the music-dramas of Wagner, strictures that to-day are as valid as when they were
first published. Manet was badly treated by his
contemporaries, yet what was said of his de-
ficiencies still holds good. Whistler, personally
a cloud by day and a pillar of fire at night, made
confusion worse confounded by his antics, his
butterfly affectations and waspish vanity. (Oh,
if Wagner hadn't written those terrifying books
of his to prove that he was Wagner, when the
first bar of the introduction to Tristan and
Isolde stamped him as a god among composers!)
Whistler, like Baudelaire, and doubtless patterning after the poet of spleen and ideal, fashioned his own legend. He was not only a genius

but he acted like one; thus would the world better understand him. If he had retreated to his ivory tower as did De Vigny, we might not have found him out until after his death. This was the case with Rembrandt. "I'll show you!" said James, and he did show them. Knowing that in London he would shine by sheer comparison, he left Paris, where he was but Whistler, in such company as Fantin, Manet, Degas, Courbet. He had his admirers in England, and they fought as the Irish at Fontenoy in his behalf. He had his enemies, and they put their fingers on his sore spots and he winced. But they, too, advertised him. The mystery is not that Ruskin failed to understand Whistler but that Whistler was so lacking in humour as to fight Ruskin with such a weapon as The Falling Rocket; Ruskin, who had missed Velasquez and how many masters, what could he say before such a picture? Let us not mince words. Time is not treating the Whistler canvases with a gentle touch; the " tone of time " is not for his surfaces. More disquieting still is the fact that he does not seem so wonderful as he did two decades ago. Some of his works are hopelessly outmoded. Nor is this because better acquaintance has bred a certain sense of satiety. On the contrary, what is beautiful in Whistler will remain beautiful until the last patch of paint has peeled off the canvas. In a word, we mean that all Whistler is not great. He was ever experimenting and he was often uneven.

The collection lacked the three master-works: the portraits of his mother, of Carlyle, of Miss Alexander. Yet it was very satisfying, as it gave us a glimpse at the various stages of his development. How normal that development was! A romantic at the start, he played with the formula of realism. His Blue Wave is decorative if compared with Courbet's. The Japanese motive was then sounded. Paris at one time was Japanese mad, thanks to De Goncourt. Whistler saw the possibilities of this new art and he absorbed it as Wagner absorbed Liszt and Berlioz. It added another note in the gamut of the painter's palette. Symmetry was not altogether supplanted by asymmetry, but the slight perpetual surprise and deviation from the normal line introduced a strange and delicious dissonance in the harmonies of a man for whom music was the arch type of the arts. He saw the rhythmic irregularities of the Japanese, saw their "going to nature in a frank, gipsylike manner," above all realised their harmonic sense, and grafted all upon Western art, making it richer, bolder, more novel. Withal he remained Whistler.

How Whistlerian we may see in his portraits and nocturnes. As through a palimpsest there struggle to light several texts, so in the Whistler pictures we can say: Here he went to Japan. There he knew Rossetti (the White Girl). Here and there he saw through the eyes of Velasquez. But he was invincibly Whistler in spirit. And this is the key-note of him. He is psychic. He paints the spiritual emanations of a personality. He would have jested if any one had said that to him, for like all great artists he was hugely concerned with the mastery of his material. Yet who ever plunged deeper (among modern masters, Carrière perhaps excepted) into the enigmatic well-pit, into the core of personality? Those transcripts of souls, of Lady Archibald Campbell, of Sarasate, of Rosa Corder, of the Lady Sophie of Soho, of Francis Leyland (for that portrait of Florence Leyland is an apparition), of Miss Alexander, finally of his mother (we believe that the Carlyle just misses fire as a psychological document despite the magnificent painting), are something more than harmonies, arrangements, and symphonies; as the scherzos and ballades, impromptus and études of Chopin are more than decorative titles. The decorative side of Whistler's gifts has in the end been over-emphasised. He feared the literary pitfall as Chopin feared the sentimental. Their escape was but a sign that both men were more preoccupied with subject matter than they would acknowledge. Both were capable of pyrotechnical flights into the azure, where they trilled in company with the morning stars; Whistler like Chopin could toss aloft a tone and spin from it variations that dazzled. But then he was not the greater Whistler any more than the Pole was the greater Chopin when he wrote his variations on the themes of other composers.

Whistler is not "literary"; he is a poet, and a

poet as mysterious and intangible as Poe. The psychology of his sitters he sought, and then having seized the salient trait, he placed the portrait in a penumbra at once mystic and evocative. It was as if he wished to hide their secret. We know as we never knew before the virtuoso of Pampeluna, Pablo de Sarasate, as he fingers his fiddle-strings and with his transverse bow makes an unforgettable decorative fulcrum for the composition. Accepting Whistler's word literally, we are looking at the Spaniard as he comes down stage, his eyes, his white shirt, his swarthy face so many notes in the colour scheme; nevertheless, spiritual overtones are sounded, and in the silver silences the soul of the violinist is singing. There is muted music in many of the canvases; not without reason did Whistler search for analogies to music. He was a profound harmonist, one who at the last cared little for the pattern; when younger the pattern curiously intrigued him. The Music Room — which looks old-fashioned and mid-Victorian in its sharp definitions — the Golden Screen, Lange Leizen, these are excursions into the rare country of porcelain and linear falsifications. Virtuosity rules, humanity is all but excluded. The rather opaque paint of The White Girl is not very seductive (white against white is no longer a miracle; besides, some of his admirers had never seen Velasquez). To call the picture a symphony was pretty. Whistler did not borrow the word from the critic Mantz but from a poem by his friend

Théophile Gautier, Symphonie en Blanc-Major, which appeared in Emaux et Camées (1852). The three girls in white are too suggestive of Albert Moore, are thin and unreal. The sentiment in the Little White Girl is not only Rossettian, but the pose, hair, and forms of the head are also his. A picture of exceeding charm.

There is more character divination in the Rosa Corder, which is as aristocratic as the art of the aristocratic Whistler. She is not the dear Lady Disdain who looks over her shoulder in the portrait of Lady Archibald Campbell; yet what a proud profile, what superb placing of the figure! How Whistler sets echoing the browns and blacks! A masterpiece, which ought to be rechristened Noli me Tangere. Obviously the Little Lady of Soho was the result of a visit to the Monna Lisa. The sweetly folded hands, the pose of one who listens to an invisible presence, and with the nuance of a smile exquisitely expressed — all this and a nameless aura of memories tell us that Whistler, consciously or unconsciously, was affected by the great Italian at the Louvre. We cannot admire much his male portraits. Whistler's was not a masculine genius. The salt of sex is missing. His Blacksmith is a *poseur*. There is nothing but papier mâché in those muscles, and the countenance is operatically fierce. We never hear the fundamental basses of Velasquez, Holbein, Rembrandt. Nor need we miss them. There are crepuscular compensations. And for his lack of substance (not overlooked by his early critics) have we not the subtlest play of harmonies since Velasquez? His lyric, vaporous creatures are of the same stuff as the Lenore, Ligeia, and Annabel of Poe; wraith-like, they belong to a No-Man's Land. But Whistler does not sound the morbid note of Poe. He is sane, and his strangeness is never bizarre. He is primarily concerned with essences. In the true sense he is the delineator of the moral nature. With a veiled intensity that is absolutely magnetic in its power he adumbrates the moral temperament of his model. Doubt this and you doubt the truth that irradiates from the portrait of Comte Robert Montesquiou de Fézenzac.

Those Tanagra-like female figures in the pastels are for many the chief attraction. Colour notes, they proclaim the master of values. Here is the transfiguration of the real, the transposition of earth and sky and the eternal feminine into the most evanescent terms of art. What simplifications! What fluidity! No hint of the effort to conceal the effort of an effortless art — occasionally felt in the larger compositions, despite Whistler's famous boast. Here he is impressionist, not, like Monet, juxtaposing tones, but playing diaphanous variations on a single tone in artful loops — Velasquez is not subtler in his modulations. George Moore's theory, that if the American artist had been physically a bigger man he might have painted masterpieces like the Spaniard, gives us a shock. Then we should have lost the mystic chord, and that absent the less Whistler he. And at the risk of being disloyal to his paintings, let us confess to our belief that the real Whistler is the magician of the etchings and lithographs. With Rembrandt and Méryon he makes one of the glorious trinity of visionaries.

II

ARTHUR B. DAVIES

A PAINTER-VISIONARY

As painter Arthur B. Davies is a realist, though a mystic in temperament. The conjunction is not rare even in this derided land of dollars. Now your true mystic abhors the vague; with crystalline clearness his vision embraces the minute and magnificent things of the world about him. And equally real is the life of the spirit. A very wrong notion it is that the mystical man, let him be artist, priest, statesman, or poet, possesses a rambling intellect or stammers enigmas or deals in the minor black arts. The mystic is eminently practical. Clairvoyant in spiritual matters, the very intensity of his inward vision when applied to mundane affairs enables him to solve problems which puzzle practical persons. All men of action are dreamers. Little need to offer examples. Saint Teresa, a mystic of fiery imagination, was an astounding organiser. Many other names come to the memory.

Davies is a man for whom the invisible world exists — a world which flows harshly or rages serenely about us, soundless, pervasive, puissant as magnetic waves that beat upon the shores of an electric ocean. But endowed with acute organs of observation and a master of technique he is enabled to record upon canvas his dream of the visible and invisible. That is why we call him both realist and mystic. He is no purveyor of fuliginous incantations, of shadowy nightmares and esoteric hysteria. A primitive, he sides neither with Blake nor Botticelli, admiring both. He has remote affinities with some of the English Pre-Raphaelites, but at the very point where their system breaks down, where their vision becomes schematic and not vital, Davies has passed on. He is often elliptical in his themes, but never obscure. His ideas may be philosophical, but they are emotionally set forth. A Romantic, he never loses view of the significant. The commonplace is charged with miracles for him. You return to his pictures not alone for any lurking messages but for their magic beauty; they are at once a gracious pattern and a noble symbol.

The mental processes of an artist at work, no matter if tracked down by himself, always contain an incommensurable quality. With an idea an artist begins to weave his arabesques; it is the validity or the strength of that idea which conditions the ultimate fate of the pictorial composition. Davies starts with a well-defined idea.

He never improvises on canvas. The aspect of a scene, say in California, appeals to him, not only for its suggestion of space composition — in which element of his art he is a master — but for some idea which we may call mystic. From his functional line — and what a virile white line it is! — to the last spot of colour, he develops his subject like a musician building up a symphony. Yet there is in all remarkable art some spot where the creative process seems to focus more fiercely. It may be in the rhythmic flow of the sky-line with cloudshine overhead; it may be in the values of movement as expressed by the indolent gait of a woman, or a conflict or an out-cry of tones. Subject doesn't much matter: the painter's genius is not always spilt in illustration. Three passionate scratches of a Rodin sketch or the flight of exotic birds in a Japanese print sometimes tell us more of the artist's soul than would an entire museum. So we discover in the Davies pictures those dissonances of form, feeling, colour, which leap like flame to the eyes. His romanticism is less the choice of an obvious situation or landscape than it is his ingrained manner of considering the bright appearances of life as a symbol; but this symbolism must be interpreted in terms of paint. His world is all out of doors, clear, smiling, sinister, prophetic, but nature ever. Sheer fantasy, and perhaps a touch of the perverse, forces him at times to twist his patterns, and he loves to introduce into his landscapes gentle unicorns and other fabulous beasts, as did

Arnold Boecklin, or, earlier, Pier di Cosimo (Piero di Lorenzo), the gay inventor of Florentine masques and the master of Andrea del Sarto. Davies admires Piero for his animated humour and for his slight deflection from the normal.

To set the American painter speaking of Botticelli is to discover in his sincere utterances what would be considered heresy. For instance, he is entirely with Bernhard Berenson when that writer declared that Botticelli is the greatest artist of lineal design that Europe has ever had. Educated here in the technical requirements of his art, Davies visited Europe only for spiritual nourishment. He is not the product of the schools, and while the academic artists may question his power he is suspiciously regarded by the younger men, who are now all for realisation. Nevertheless, you may note that Davies has not neglected manual dexterity. His studies of the nude display a mastery of tactile values and of the values of movement that are astonishing. Seldom does he carry a figure as far in oils as in black and white. Is it his subject matter that puzzles and offends? Hardly. There are Boecklin the Swiss, Franz Von Stuck of Munich, Max Klinger in his etchings, Gustave Moreau — these artists dead and alive painted and etched more fantastic scenes with satyrs and mermaids, centaurs and Daughters of the Devil, than Davies could accomplish in a lifetime. No one disputes their technical facility. But

Davies is different. His abundant gifts of drawing, colouring, designing, while they stamp him as the artist born as well as trained, are at the service of a potent imagination, an individual imagination. One does not hesitate to adjudge him the most original of American painters and the peer of those living European artists who are dominated by ideas and not by the brush. Imagination, then, is the master trait of Arthur B. Davies. Let us see to what use he puts it.

First as to his artistic ancestry. We have called him a Primitive for want of a more suitable phrase. He has retained much of the naiveté of the Primitives, something wellnigh impossible in this age of inartistic conventionalism. That childlike delight in the presence of nature and of children which we are pleased to credit to the early Italian painters only is another trait of his. He has the "innocence of the eye," though his formulas often resemble those of the Florentines. But to slight one's age is impossible. Davies belongs to his century; furthermore he is an American. The escape which art offers he presents in individual symbols. Arcady with sleepy damosels as seen in the dark glass of Burne-Jones's wizardry is not shown by Davies; it is with the vital impulses of nature that he is concerned. His Californian landscapes proclaim the artist of the New World, not the dreamer of the Old born out of his day. His handling recalls certain traditions of Florence. He may be entitled archaic. What precisely is an archaic painter? Mr. Berenson answers the question: "For no art can hope to become classic that has not been archaic first. The distinction between archaistic imitation and archaic reconstruction, simple as it is, must be clearly borne in mind. An art that is merely adopting the ready-made models handed down from an earlier time is archaistic, while an art that is going through the process of learning to reconstruct the figures and discover the attitudes required for the presentation of tactile values and movement is archaic. On the other hand, an art that has completed the process is classic. . . . A painter still among us, Degas, may boast of being archaic."

Davies is archaic. His art is a "becoming" and not frozen into a rigid symbolism. He is an admirer of Degas, and he places Cézanne above Monet for the significance of his landscapes, just as he recognises the power of his nudes. And after all the nude is the touchstone. With Botticelli the passion for presenting movement-values closed his eyes to many other fascinating possibilities. Blake's swirling lines are an abstract of the idea of form; and that ceaseless experimenter Edgar Degas has arrived almost to the disintegration of movement that we see in the Rodin sketches. Davies severely practises elimination of non-essentials. He completes but never finishes a picture, using the word in its ordinary connotation. His themes overflow their frames, and like some poetry the memory is full of their spiritual repercussions and overtones. Technically speaking, he paints with great directness. Those who believe his work to be the outcome of laborious "cookery" and a *pasticcio* of many styles would be surprised to know with what clarity he plots in advance his pictures, with what boldness and fire he attacks them, in what a fury of execution he terminates them. Yes, those majestic, sweeping landscapes with luminous washes of sun and cloud, trees that loom up grave and giantlike to the sky, those long-limbed nudes with mystical gaze and strange gestures, are all planned largely, are the result of much pondering. Davies creates beauty. Sometimes he nods — all imaginative souls do — though he nods less often than one would think if his fecund invention and versatility be considered; that he has not yet fully realised himself, he knows. The dreamer and painter wage daily a conflict. But he is slowly achieving a unity of matter and manner.

His landscapes are not mineral or metallic like the airless backgrounds of Gustave Moreau; they exist in the West. California is Davies's favourite region. He gives us the living panorama of glorious California. He has discovered the soul of California. Men have been painting there for a lifetime and they have seen her beauties through the eyes of the Barbizon tradition. Not so Davies. He shows some valleys from a pinnacle, valleys upon which the hosts of heaven and hell could war, a carpeted plain for Armageddon. His interpretation of what he sees springs spontaneously. A woman's figure points earthward or crooks a beckoning finger as if the sons and daughters of men were invited to enjoy the fulness and plenty of the earth. No hint here of the scene-painter's California. And on the borders of what exquisite and mysterious seas does Davies conduct us. The limpidity of his lakes, the hieratic awe he infuses in the enlacing attitudes and gestures of the anonymous groups in his foregrounds! It is not paradise, for his earth is real; these women whose eyes are as subtle as Da Vinci's, whose limbs are as fluent and lean as Botticelli's, whose hair is blown upon by strange airs — these women may claim Davies as their artistic progenitor. And how strong is the salt and savour of sex in all his compositions! No mere arabesques are his creatures. The virility of Davies is unmistakable, but it never takes the questionable grimace of a conventional voluptuousness, nor has it the suggestion of decadent paganism. It is clear and sweet, this conception of sex. When he clothes his people in modern garb they are quite as vital — that is, if anything draped is ever as thrilling as the nude.

And that Harlem Bridge picture. It is not a set landscape, but an interpretation of a mood, the fusing of Davies's nocturnal vision and the actual forms and facts of the vicinity. How those children interest. The Davies children are real, but seen through the prism of a mystic.

Look at his Sea Wind and Sea. Or his mighty
Forest with its mænads. He is filled with the
earth spirit. Hemmed in by thousands of questions, dumb yet eloquent, this poet-mystic has
no need to summon spirits from the vasty deep.
His very existence, the earth beneath his feet,
the azure above him, are miracles. We walk
with the "tender and growing night" in the
symbol-land of Davies. Nature possesses him
not so much for her lovely and enticing curves —
and those he has not failed to praise — as for
her deathless interrogations. He portrays the
salient characteristics of the landscape, but in its
general composition he searches for its universal
import. It is the key-note, the releasing answer
of the Davies art; in tune with the universal is
only phrasing a very old truth. To achieve this
harmony, to compass the larger rhythms, our
painter has thrown overboard much ballast.
He has avoided the genre picture, the obviously
dramatic anecdote, the pretty, shallow landscape and decoration for the sake of decoration
and the banal rhetoric of the flesh. For motive
he has gone to myth. But what myth? What
countries have furnished the myths of Davies?
We believe that his myths are his own, though he
reads the poets, and in Horne's Orion — to give
one example — he found inspiration for a hunt-
ing-scene, one is tempted to say *the* hunting-
scene, so universal is its application. The hunts-
men are indeed up in this novel America. As a
space composer Davies produces in us the sensa-

tion of a "happy liberation." There is hugeness without emptiness on his mountain tops and under his monster trees. Unless we are greatly mistaken he has all the qualifications for a mural decorator on an epical scale.

But he prefers his myths, his panels covered with radiant creatures, unclothed and in their right mind, moving in processional rhythms to some unknown goal. Nor do we wish to know this goal. Great art is an instant arrested in eternity. These men and women are enigmatic, their secret in the skies. One woman of noble contour walks as in a dream through a delicious landscape. (A Measure of Dreams, now hanging in the Metropolitan Museum.) She has come from a dream and is crossing the bridge of transition; soon she shall be enveloped in the splendours and terrors of a new dream. She is ever in motion. Is she the ideal that haunts the artist soul? We have the sense of something vanishing, like music overheard in sleep, or of a beautiful mournful face that melts into the chambers of your brain, elusive yet more real than the noises of the naked day. Such pictures as these translate into paint Mallarmé's "silent thunder afloat in the leaves." The uneven silhouette of a mountain top, the incandescent glow of light, a light in which human forms are decomposed, yet endure and weave the measures of some antique dance, a country out of time but not of space — these luscious and sonorous landscapes fill us with wonder at their beauty.

Davies by reason of his imaginative temperament can sound the notes of the profound, of the sublime. Indeed, he is too much given to the apocalyptic. Like Maeterlinck he can evoke a nameless fear oppressing vast multitudes. Nor is Davies so breath-taking, as if in a cell without windows or doors, as was the early Maeterlinck. He knows the secret of "life-enhancing" values. There is a panel which was covered with humans expecting some mighty visitation, some spiritual or cosmic upheaval. The trees bend helplessly before the invisible wrath and iron wind of destiny. Horror is exhaled from the canvas, a mystic fear that crisps the nerves. Yet unintelligible symbols are not employed. A key is seldom needed for these pictures; on the contrary, their titles too often confuse. We saw the designs for his exhibited but unfinished work, The Girdle of Ares (which is literally Greek), and were stirred by the writhing Titans, with their Angelesque vigour of line and movement.

One of the rivals to A Measure of Dreams is the large, symbolic picture Maya, Mirror of Illusions. The ten elect virgins with mauve dappling their nude backs and thighs gaze wistfully into the mirror of Maya; Maya, the great mother of illusions. The landscape might serve for D'Annunzio's novel, Virgin of the Rocks; we are content to suggest it stenographically. The colouring is rather pallid, the mood chilly, but as ice burns, so is there spiritual heat in this enraptured parable. The only masters we may compare it to are Botticelli — the women make a sweet Botticellian loop — or to Edward Burne-Jones's Mirror of Venus. Yet it does not proceed from the Primavera, nor has it the rich, smoky enchantment of the Burne-Jones. What does it signify? Isn't the title expressive enough? Maya — Illusion! Of all earthly illusions, is there any other comparable to woman — even when she boasts mauve reflects? The mirror may be the mirror of matrimony! But hush! These are fables for the disillusionised middle-aged. Crescendo shows seven girls (seven, the mystic number; seven, the number of tones in the scale), and the crescendo is unmistakable.

The best way to approach the art of Davies is with an open mind. Like what you like, dislike what you dislike. One man's paint may be another's poison. If a figure seems backed like a whale, weasel, or camel, then it is — for you; but don't expect your neighbour to follow your suit. He may see shrewder into the clear-obscure of the painter-poet's mirror and discern fairer visions. If we could only realise how simple in expression are the best of his canvases, notwithstanding the supposed complexity of his ideas, we might let his thrice subtle magic work its will upon us.

Mr. James remarks that "there are two kinds of taste in the appreciation of imaginative literature — the taste for emotions of surprise and the taste for emotions of recognition." It is the same with pictorial art. In the case of the other men our emotions of recognition are gratified. But with Davies it is always the emotion of surprise. His imagination plays him pranks; it leads him into dangerous spots. This seer of visions, this poet who would penetrate the earthly envelope and surprise the secret fevers of the soul, disengage the solemn emotions of subliminal personality, evoke magical scenes in a no-man's-land with Botticellian figures, primitive seas and hills, a sort of pre-Raphaelitic mood disquietingly interfused by a delicate modern feeling; a neurotic strain of ascetic music, with the hills of a celestial Florence for a frame and the antique nymphs of the brake moving or reclining melodiously — into what category may we compress Davies? He is obstinately mediæval, until he carelessly brushes in the grandeur of a California forest. His women, nympholepts, affect the imagination as do the bacchantes of Maurice de Guérin. And yet he catches with exquisite tact the virginal lines of a young girl who surely lives not far from Central Park. He has the apocalyptic strain in him and many of his canvases are darkened by symbols. But beauty is always present, else its fragrance hinted at. Those fragile, mysterious women, haunted by visions of the great god Dionysos, or perhaps Pan, where do they come from, where are they going? One can ask of Davies as did the Centaur of another: "The jealous gods have buried somewhere proofs of the origins of all things, but upon the shores of what ocean have they rolled the stone that hides them, O Macareus?" Upon the crust of what planet have you seen your picture visions, O Arthur Davies?

VI

MATISSE, PICASSO, AND OTHERS

I

AFTER a performance of Tristan und Isolde, March, 1876, at Berlin, the well-known music-critic Louis Ehlert registers the remarks of two friends who sat on either side of him. The younger man exclaimed: "The world holds no pleasure after this"; the elder whispered: "A few more evenings like this and my strength will sink into the grave." These widely diverging views of two opposed temperaments, not to consider as a factor the different ages, might serve as a classic example of the attitudes invariably struck in the presence of a new work of art. Not that old age always faces the past — we know that the reverse is often the case — but the lack of apprehension or sympathy is usually the result of a certain way of seeing or hearing things, and it is quite useless to attempt to convert such people into your manner of thinking. Why upset the picture of the world you have so laboriously built up simply because an impudent nobody comes along and shows you his version, the outcome of disordered vision or a desire for self-advertisement! Such a thing were impossible. The young man of the Ehlert story was a Wagnerian lover and later in his life would have been the first to hiss the music of Richard Strauss. The men to-day who fought so valiantly for the impressionistic movement are hurling contemptuous epithets at the neo-impressionists and the post-impressionists. The younger generation bangs at the door, the older fires its critical blunderbuss at the intruders from the first floor, and no one is wounded, neither is any one convinced against his will. The strange part of it all is that about every quarter of a century the operation is repeated, yet no one learns the lesson of the past. Perhaps it is better so, else no real progress would be made. After the fat the lean, after the feast the famine, after Manet, Matisse; after Wagner, Richard Strauss; after Flaubert, Zola; after Zola — the deluge. And so will it continue; otherwise artistic stagnation. Change and criticism are inevitable if a living organism is to be conserved; we do not discuss the dead. Therefore let us talk of the post-impressionists, a vital issue now in the world of art.

Every law has its holidays, said the worthy Professor Ehlert, and in each new manifestation of the artistic spirit the laws that governed the arts we first learned seem to be cast aside as useless; we say seem because it is only self-deception evoked by the strangeness of the method, the inclusion of new material, and the personality of the new man. After a time the novelty wears away and intrinsic qualities remain to be judged. Ibsen was called an immoralist and a revolutionary dramatist; to-day we know that his work and character are all of a piece, sound in art and spirit and in the direct line of his great dramatic forebears. What hasn't Wagner been called, Wagner a melodist of Mozartian fecundity if you compare him with his successors? And Charles Baudelaire, prosecuted for a few poems that no one reads nowadays except as a duty or a matter of curiosity, what of this rare poet, who actually brought fresh subject matter into the formal and faded garden of French verse! We do not speak here of the sonorous Victor Hugo, for man cannot live by rhetoric alone. Baudelaire treated evil as a theme without the sugary sentiment of a Coppée or the impassive perfection of the Parnassians. Naturally he was misunderstood. Manet fought a lifelong battle with people who could not see his artistic descent from Velasquez and Goya. Claude Monet, the first and, we are tempted to add, the only impressionist, now a classic, was a few years ago regarded as a dauber; his exquisite tonalities were smears made by one who possessed no craftsmanship. The slanting sun of a decrepit civilization feebly shone on French art, so averred the enemies of impressionism, though by 1880 the group had won the battle, and this same year also proved a marking date for the victories of Wagner, and of the realistic school in fiction, French and Russian. In a phrase, the tumescence of the classicists, of the romantics, had set in; antique stale formulas were discarded, and new facets of art, the eternal Proteus, were discovered. Paul Gauguin has said that in art one is either a plagiarist or a revolutionary. He might have added that the secret of success in art is excess.

But does this new art, do these inhuman, nay esoteric arabesques represent a veracious mood? What becomes of the rainbows and flutes, the ivory, apes, and peacocks, the pomegranates and persimmons of the past? They can't endure forever. After Monet? Not Matisse, because a strong man intervened, Paul Cézanne; and the new movement dates from Cézanne; as surely as evolution from Charles Darwin. In literature the firm prose and lucid lubricity of Huysmans revealed to the clairvoyant Zola that this descendant of Flemish painters was the true realist of the naturalistic school, and not Maupassant, who, as George Moore so happily put it, absorbed as much of the genius of Flaubert as he could and then proceeded to "cut it into numberless walking sticks." And when Cézanne was understood he and not Monet became chief of the school. Why Cézanne? We know that naturalism is dead for the present, that symbolism has gone the way of all things born flawed, yet the younger men are obsessed by a mixture of realism and symbolism that almost defies analysis. Through the gates of ivory or the gates of horn will you steer your bark? Degas and Manet are called "old hat" in Paris; there are no younger men of such vigorous personality and gift of painting as Monet, Renoir, Pissarro. Is this the reason that Paul Cézanne, who, much as we admire him, is inferior as a sheer manipulator of paint if compared to the five men just named, was shoved into the place of honour? Or was there some fundamental reason why he of all others was selected as a starting-point by Gauguin and Van Gogh? You may recall his acid criticism of this pair and his violent disclaimer that they were pupils of his or that they continued his tradition. And just here we come across the name of Emile Bernard, for it was that painter who recorded the utterances of Cézanne after he had visited him at Aix in Provence.

Now Bernard, who is an excellent artist, has shocked many by what he calls a refutation of impressionising, and if it had been written by the late Albert Wolff of the *Figaro* it couldn't have been more destructive, in sentiment at least, although as it came from the pen of a painter the technical side is dealt with more drastically than if it had been composed by the shallow, prejudiced, but clever Wolff. Bernard seeks to demolish the theory that impressionism is nature traversed by or viewed through a temperament, on the score that nature, not the individual, should count; which is very modest, but rather weak in metaphysics. He finds fault with the colour theories of Chevreul and Rood, not as theories, but in their applica-

129

tion by such artists as Seurat, Signac, Anquetin. The science of chromatics has naught to do with the practice of art, he contends. He reproaches the impressionists for their meagre palette— black being banned, consequently chiaro-oscuro; dark shadows do not exist for the pleinairistes. And their much vaunted subject matter, modern life, what has that led them to? To the exclusion of the imaginative, the spiritual; to baseness, to vulgarity, even as Zola and others caricatured Flaubert and brought their readers to the dunghill of romanticism, which is naturalism. These impressionistic painters are uglicists! You seem to hear the voice of Kenyon Cox preaching in the wilderness of our Academy when too many impressionistic canvases are hung. No more savoury impasto, no modulation of tones, no rich *couche* of underpainting; instead, all glaring, direct painting, themes so literal as to be meaningless, above all, no emotional quality. Impressionism then is a feeble rill losing itself in the arid sands of the obvious.

We quote Emile Bernard, not only because he is a backslider but as an instance of a critic like a certain man down South who didn't know the Civil War was over. There is no necessity of a propaganda for Richard Wagner. He is a classic. It is the doings in tone of the other Richard that puzzle the critics. Manet, Monet, Renoir are all ranged. Cézanne is still a bone of contention, for he attempted not only to improve upon the technical methods of his contemporaries, the impressionists, but also to give to painting the content that it lacked. Mr. Cox and Cézanne could have shaken hands on that side of the question, but when it comes to Henri Matisse the American critic would look another way. What though Matisse endeavours to return to the subject in art, above all dower the theme with the note of intensity! Mr. Cox would probably quote Hamlet at him, saying, "Thou com'st in such a questionable shape." Yes, it is the shape that affrights the conservative, a shape that seeks to be more plastic than music and as emotional.

The waves raised by the first exhibition of the post-impressionists at the Grafton Gallery in London have not yet subsided, are still reverberating on distant shores where the local critical Canutes stand, measuring tape in hand, crying: "Thus far and no further." One of the fruits of the discussion is a book entitled The Post-Impressionists, by the art writer, Mr. C. Lewis Hind, another is the news that Mr. Roger Fry, also an expert, who knows a Mantegna from a Matisse, or a hawk from a handsaw, has succumbed to the malady and exhibited in London, so it is said, a roomful of horrors, staring doll-like nudes, queer landscapes in which the perspective falls away as if the earth were sinking, the colours of which are poisonous greens or jaundiced yellows. We quote from various amiable English sources. Mr. Fry was formerly a painter of delicate water-colours. Why this defection from the revered standards of beauty?

In his interesting monograph Mr. Hind tells us in his agreeable style why—not specifically of Mr. Fry, but of the ideals of the movement generally. Let us examine more closely this latest bubble on the turbulent stream of early twentieth-century art.

There is no absolute in beauty; expression, not beauty, is the aim of art. All the rest is mere illustration. Beauty is relative. It is topographical, nay parochial. The beauty of Chinese art is not the same beauty that informs Occidental art. When the Wagnerian music was first heard it gave much pain to people whose aural organs had been soothed by the charming music of Mendelssohn. But Wagner didn't care, for he couldn't use the saccharine Mendelssohn palette to paint the full-length portraits of the brutal Hunding, the acrid Alberich, or of the incomparable Brünnhilde. Nietzsche has pointed out that our present system of morality may dangerously approach immorality if practised at the antipodes. Cézanne felt that the mellifluous, shimmering tones of the poetic pantheist Claude Monet would not serve to express his sober, solid picture of a section of the universe (and how modest he was, for his universe, his Motive, was a slice of a hill near his home). Paul Gauguin, sickening of the ninety times nine thousand times represented life of Paris and the provinces, fled to the South Sea Islands and there lived the existence of a glorified beachcomber. But he formed for himself a fresh synthesis, painted extraordinary sights, painted massive decorations in which ecstasy lives. Van Gogh, the genius of this ill-assorted new trinity of paint-gods, went the way of those who live too intensely. To understand him fully one must study Ricciotto Canudo's Les Libères, in which the madman is revealed, not as a sick being, but as one overflowing with so much health that the brain and body crumble in the fierce conflagration — a refreshing variation of Nordau's degeneration theme. Vincent Van Gogh hovered on the borderland of madness and genius. But he was the best-equipped of the three in the gifts of painter and visionary. From these men stem Matisse and the new crowd. Away with all the old stock attitudes and gestures; a new synthesis, an immobility Asiatic in its hieratic immobility, a different mosaic of tones, are their watchwords.

Mr. Hind prefers expressionism as a term to define the ideal of the movement rather than the clumsy compound post-impressionism. To express an idea emotionally in a medium of only two dimensions is not easy. Is it possible? The Sistine Chapel arouses the sensation of awe in the mind of the spectator. Raphael fills us with a calm joy. Dürer puzzles as well as stirs, and Da Vinci is wholly beautiful, with the threefold beauties of colour, form, and suggestion. What, then, are these crazy new chaps after? Isn't the vision of their grandfathers good enough? Evidently they think not; yet wrestle as they

do to extort novel ideas, their art recalls some
art that has pre-existed, and lying dormant
for centuries has gained a new dynamic force.
Behold Assyria and Egypt in Pablo Picasso's
work. The cubists or geometricians, or what
not — how they love new names for old things
— are not precisely novel. Despite Edwin
Björkman to the contrary, there is no new thing
under the sun, not even his assertion. Let us
not pale before the ugly manifestations of young
France. They may be gods, after all, as Baudelaire said when somebody in his presence attacked strange idols. But with so many other
practitioners of this school the cleavage between
idea and image is appalling.

It has been said that you may not have seen a
man or woman or landscape such as Cézanne
shows in his canvases, but after seeing them you
can never forget them, for you will see them
again in life. Who before Corot showed us a
landscape like this? You need not go to Ville
d'Avray to see such. It is the individual vision
of the artist that teaches anew the innocence of
our eye. Consider the school of English face
painters — can they stand the test of criticism,
the sort of criticism you apply to Rembrandt,
Hals, Velasquez, Titian, Raphael (the portrait-
ist), or Manet? For more than one modern
critic the colour of Reynolds, Hoppner, Lawrence, Romney — not Raeburn — is a mere
shining poultice, as glistening and insincere as
what a German writer calls "snail slime with

raspberry sauce" ("Schneckenschleim mit Him-beer sauce"). As to form, how weak the line and what conventional simplifications, above all what insipid prettifications. This iconoclastic criticism is not rare. And can our painters go on for ever imitating the Barbizon school, so called, or for that matter the impressionists of 1880? But the new wine is very heady for young folk, a sort of epileptic cider; isn't all cham-pagne epileptic cider? Yet after the giddiness, the intoxication, the morning headaches have vanished there may be a residue of art remaining. Matisse has been much abused. We confess a weakness for his drawings, as we do for the drawings of Rodin, of Augustus John, of Davies. Frank J. Mather, Jr., than whom we recognise no more competent critic to deal with this thrill-ing theme, asserted that the line of Matisse re-minded him of the line of Antonio Pollaiuolo, which statement is rather a startling one com-ing from the distinguished Marquand professor of Princeton, who cannot be accused of an un-due liking for latter-day movements in art. Un-fortunately sterile eccentricities mar the painted work of Matisse.

What is post-impressionism? What is this cruel alchemy that deforms the supple curves of the human figure into images both hideous and ter-rifying? Into what backward abysm are we being led? Mr. Hind does not altogether succeed in answering the somewhat illusive question. We only know that, weary of the externalism of the

impressionists, a new group began experimenting and broke the old linear mould, altered the
old colour schemes. To each man his own vision,
and except a certain sincerity there is not much
sameness in the technical procedures of Cézanne or Gauguin or Van Gogh or Matisse. The
imitators need not be discussed; epigones always
exaggerate. What do we care, for example, for
a Kees Van Dongen and his paradoxes in paint?
But if post-impressionism means the work of
Davies or Augustus John or the line of Matisse,
then we are believers in post-impressionism. No
matter the strangeness of image, the eternal emotion of the cosmos must sing, else it is no art. Let
us be catholic, let us be open-minded. Depend
upon it, if these artists paint as they do they
do so for sufficient reasons. Hanslick once wrote
"not the opera, but the public was a failure."
For many years it was the public that failed,
not Tristan und Isolde; for a long time Manet
was accused of deforming the ideal of beauty
(meaning of course the academic Lefebvre,
Bouguereau & Co.). Eyes there were too few
to appreciate his genius. Rhythmic intensity is
the key to the new school; line, not colour, is
king. Not beauty, but, as Rodin said, character,
character is the aim of the new art.

II

THE MATISSE DRAWINGS

The second batch of Matisse drawings were fascinating; where his followers plod panting miles behind, he leaps the stiffest barriers by reason of his sheer virtuosity. His real friends (not the sort who moan in ecstasy over his new monkeyshines) and critics have noted, not without regret, that the Master (he has attained the dignity of capitalisation) is given to the bootless task of shocking the bourgeois. Poor old bourgeois; how they have been shocked from the Hernani days of Théophile Gautier to the macabre merry-making of Huysmans and the *fumisterie* of Paul Gauguin! And the young fellows are still at it. Who hasn't contributed his share, if his boyhood were worthy the name? The small boy snow-balling the fat teacher is as much a symbol of the revolt of youth against sleek authority as is an Emma Goldman lecture on Ibsen for the instruction of our police. But why Matisse? Here is a chap whose talent is distinguished. He can make his pencil or brush sing at the bidding of his brain; better still, that brain is fed by eyes which refuse to see humanity or landscape in the conventional terms of the school. He wishes not only to astonish worthy folk but also to charm their cheque books. Paris is always the prey of the *dernier cri*, and Matisse, unless he has been ousted during the last month,

is not only the latest cry but, we hope, the
ultimate scream. At his worst he shocks; at his
best his art is as attractive as an art can be that
reveals while it dazzles, makes captive when it
consoles.

The two dozen and more sketches on the walls
of Mr. Stieglitz's gallery were of a range and intensity that set tingling the pulse of any honest
craftsman. It is not alone the elliptical route
pursued by Matisse in his desire to escape the
obvious and suppress the inutile, but the creative force of his sinuous emotional line. It is a
richly fed line, bounding, but not wiry, as is
Blake's. Its power of evoking tactile sensations
is as vigorous, rhythmic, and subtle as the orchestration of Richard Strauss. Little wonder
collectors in Paris are buying Matisse just because of his emotional suggestiveness. There is
a sketch in the middle of the east wall before
which William Blake would have paused and
wondered. It is worthy of Blake, or it might
have been signed, despite its casual air, by one
of the early Italian masters. Orphic or Bacchic,
we can't say which, these tiny figures hold their
own in a composition simple to bareness, each
endowed with an ecstatic individual life. In the
right foreground, as seen by the spectator, a
woman lies on the ground, a man sits hunched
up near by. The pair, without the remotest hint
of the conventional erotic, tell more in a few
lines than could a volume. Only Rodin has
compassed such, though his is the stenographic

method of the sculptor, not of the painter, especially of a painter whose colour is so bewilderingly opulent as that of Matisse.

After all, nature is a dictionary; the artist goes to her for words, not to copy; he must phrase in his own personal way if he expects to achieve originality. With the exceptions of Whistler and Cézanne no one has studied the patterns of the East as Matisse. He always sees the decoration and makes you see it, unless you are blinded by the memory of some other man's line. There is no monopoly in the conventional, and because thousands of painters have envisaged the nude in a certain — and usually the same — monotonous fashion, that should not attenuate our agreement with the vision of Matisse. His knowledge is great, his simplicity greater. Such problems as are set forth and mastered in that woman — we only see her back — who has thrown herself forward in sheer weariness must extort a tribute of admiration from any fair-minded lover of art. Another woman places one arm over the other close at the wrists. A series of delicate muscular acts are involved. Immobility is the result, but even when the body is at rest the muscles are never quite still. The rich interplay of flexor and extensor in the muscles of the Matisse models delights and appals. Who has ever dared before to push so far, dared to annex territory that is supposed to belong to the anatomist proper? Yet no suspicion of the anatomy lesson is conveyed in these singularly alive nudes. Matisse is dominated by an idea, but it is not a didactic idea. His colour sense is profound. Fancy black and white still-life that brings to you the jewelled sensation of fruit and flowers! Patterns, whether Persian or Japanese, are to be detected in his landscape bits and still-life. And what mastery in spacing. Far back his art is rooted in Manet and Cézanne; the abridgments of the one and the sense of structural bulk and weight of the other, with much of his harmonic sense, are suggested in both the portraits and the flower pieces; yet you feel the subtle pull of the East throughout all. Some of his creatures are not presentable in academic studios, but you forget their pose and pessimism and the hollow pits that serve for their ferocious eyes in the truth and magic of their contours. One woman with balloon hips is almost a caricature until you discover the repetitions of curves in sky, bodily structure, and earth. In a word, an amazing artist, original in observation and a scorner of the facile line, the line called graceful, sweet, genteel; worse yet, moral. Men like Matisse and Richard Strauss do good in stirring the stale swamp of respectability, notwithstanding the violence of their methods. Otherwise art would become, does become, a frozen symbol. These barbarous natures bring with them fresh rhythms — and then they too succumb to the love of the sensational; they too, more's the pity, cultivate their hysteria, following the evil advice of Charles Baudelaire, and finally become locked in the relentless grip of their own limitations. All things pass and perish and in a dozen years children may be taken to special matinées of Elektra, there to be amused, as they are amused to-day, by the antics of the animals and monsters in Wagner's Ring, and the Matisse drawings may be used for the instruction of maidenly beginners. Who knows! This exhibition was more instructive and moving than a century of academy shows.

III

PABLO PICASSO

A dozen years or more ago Pablo Picasso arrived in Paris, having an excellent equipment with which to conquer the world artistic. He was a superior draughtsman, a born colourist, a passionate harmonist; he incarnated in his production the temperament of his Iberian race. Mr. Stieglitz has shown us at the galleries of the Photo-Secession a few drawings of that period; they are supple, alert, savant, above all charged with vitality. Then the spirit of Henri Matisse moved across the waters of his imagination, as did that of Debussy in the misty wild regions of Ravel and Dukas. To-day Picasso has surpassed his master in hardihood, as Matisse left lagging both Gauguin and Cézanne, St. Paul the Minor and St. Paul the Major, in the rear. When exhibiting in the Galerie Volard, Paris, critical commentary made one gasp; he is either a satyr or a Hyperion; there is no middle point in the chorus of execration and exaltation. We believe this is wrong and makes for critical confusion.

In an illuminating address Mr. W. C. Brownell remarked that "every important piece of literature, as every important work of plastic art, is the expression of a personality, and it is not the material of it but the mind behind it that invites critical interpretation." Precisely so, though we do not believe that either to the reason or to the imagination of this distinguished critic the pioneer Picasso would make much of an appeal. And even this opinion we put forth diffidently, remembering that when the name of Rodin was still anathema Mr. Brownell had written almost a book about the sculptor. Picasso is miles away from Rodin, yet he is striving for a new method of expression, one that will show us his new vision of the powers and principalities of the earth. (At present Satan is chanting the chief rôle in his composition.) It's anarchic, certainly; that's why we tolerate it despite its appalling ugliness; anything is better than the parrot-like repetitions of the academic.

What is meant by the new "vision"? Why shouldn't the vision that pleased our great-grandfather content his great-grandchildren? You must go to Stendhal for an answer. Because each generation, whether for better or worse, sees the world anew, or thinks it does; at least it is "different" in the Stendhalian sense. For a keener definition let us quote D. S. MacColl: "This new vision that has been growing up among the landscape painters simplifies as well as complicates the old. For purposes of analysis it sees the world as a mosaic of patches of colour, such and such a hue of such and such a tone of such and such a shape. The old vision had beaten out three separate acts, the determination of the edges and limits of things, the shading and modelling of the spaces in between with black and white, and the tinting of those spaces with their local colour. The new analysis looked first for colour and for a different colour in each patch of shade or light. The old painting followed the old vision by its three processes of drawing the contours, modelling the chiaro-oscuro in dead colour, and finally colouring this white and black preparation. The new analysis left the contours to be determined by the junction, more or less fused, of the colour patches, instead of rigidly defining them as they are known to be defined when seen near at hand or felt. Its precepts were to recover the innocence of the eye, to forget the thing as an object with its shapes and colours as they are known to exist under other aspects, to follow the fact of vision, however surprising, recognise that contours are lost and found, that local colour in light and shade becomes different not only in tone but also in hue. And painting tended to follow this new vision by substituting one process for three; the painter matched the hue and tone at once of each patch, and shaped a patch on the canvas of the corresponding shape, ceasing to think in lines except as the boundaries by which these patches limit one another." Elsewhere Mr. MacColl asserts that the true history of man would be the history of his imagination. It would prove, we think, a more stupendous undertaking than Lord Acton's projected history of ideas.

For over a quarter of a century the impressionists did cease to think in lines and modelled in patches, but curiously enough the return to the academic, so called, was led by the least academic of painters, Paul Cézanne. Strictly speaking, he was not a genius, though a far better painter than his misguided follower (Cézanne's own words) Gauguin, who, despite his strong decorative talent, never learned how to handle paint as a master. Cézanne was for returning to the much neglected form. "Don't make Chinese images like Gauguin," he cried; "all nature must be modelled after the sphere, cone, and cylinder. As for the colours, the more the colours harmonise the more the design becomes precise." Cézanne is the father of the post-impressionists, and it is a mistake to suppose that they are impressionists with the "new vision" so clearly described above by MacColl. They have gone on and consider the division-of-tones men, Monet included, as old-fashioned as Gérôme and Bouguereau. And as extremes meet, the contemporary crowd are primitives, who have a word of

praise for Ingres but a hatred of Delacroix.
They also loathe Courbet and call the first impressionism mere materialism. To spiritualise
or make more emotional the line, to be personal
and not the follower of formulas — ah, mirage
of each succeeding artistic generation! — are the
main ideas of this school, which abhors the classic, romantic, impressionistic schools. It has one
painter of great distinction, Henri Matisse; from
him a mob of disciples have emanated. Among
the Americans are Weber, Maurer, Marsden
Hartley, John Marin, and others.

Picasso is also one, but a disciple who has
thrown off the influence of the master. He goes
his own way, which is the geometrical. He sees
the world and mankind in cubes or pyramids.
His ideal form is pyramidal. There is the
back of a giantess corseted. Her torso is powerfully modelled; no dim hint of indecision here.
The lines are pyramidal. Power is in them.
Obsessed by the Egyptians, Picasso has deserted his earlier linear suavity for a hieratic
rigidity, which nevertheless does not altogether
cut off emotional expressiveness. There are attitudes and gestures that register profound feeling, grotesque as may be the outer envelope.
He gives us his emotion in studying a figure.
And remember this is a trained artist who has
dropped the entire baggage of a lifetime's study
to follow his beckoning star. To set it all down
to a desire to stir up philistia would be to classify
Picasso as a madman, for there are easier routes

to the blazing land of réclame than the particularly thorny and ugly one he has chosen. There is method in his wildest performances, method and at times achievement even to the uninitiated eye. His is not the cult of the ugly for the sake of ugliness, but the search after the expressive in the heart of ugliness. A new æsthetic? No, a very old one revivified, and perhaps because of its modern rebirth all the uglier, and as yet a mere diabolic, not divine, stammering.

The best, or worst, of Picasso was not at this little exposition. Our objection to it and to others of its kind (though we are grateful to Mr. Stieglitz for his unselfish impresarioship in these affairs) is that such drawing and painting are only for a few artists. It is all very well to say that the public will learn later to appreciate; we doubt it. It either gasps or mocks; sympathy it seldom develops. To a vision like Picasso's the external of the human form is only a rind to be peeled away. At times he is an anatomist, not an analyst; the ugly asymmetry of the human body is pitilessly revealed, but as a rule he abstracts the shell and seeks to give shape and expression to his vision. Alas, nearly always do we shudder or else smile! Those inanimate blocks, kindergarten idols of wood and bronze, what do they mean? You dream of immemorial Asiatic monsters and also of the verses of Emile Verhaeren: "The desert of my soul is peopled with black gods, huge blocks of wood"; or of Baudelaire's spleen and ideal beauty: "Je hais le mouvement qui déplace les lignes; et jamais je ne pleure et jamais je ne ris." Benjamin De Casseres in his brilliant summary of the poetry of Leconte de Lisle shows us the genius of immobility, and his description would fit Gustave Moreau's picture as well: "When he walked he left abysses behind him. Where his eye fell objects relapsed into rigidity. There is no motion in his images. The universe is static, all things are turned marble. Motion is spent. . . . Silence, impassivity, sterility, trance, in a few magical strokes the universe of living things, is caught in the sin of motion — vibration is seized flagrante delicto — and stiffened in its multicoloured shrouds. The organic and inorganic worlds have stopped at high tide, turned to adamant as at the sudden vision of some stupendous revelation."

Will Pablo Picasso restore form to its sovereignty in modern art? His art is not significant, yet with all its deformations, its simplifications, the breath of life does traverse the design; as for his colour we must imagine what it was formerly, as Mark Twain's German musical public loyally recalled the long-time dead voice of their favourite tenor. One Parisian critic accused Picasso of painting the portraits of anthropoid apes that had been inoculated by M. Metchnikoff. Gracious Apollo! Is this irony? To paint a counterfeit of a monkey, sick or otherwise, is sound art, isn't it?

IV

TEN YEARS LATER

I

Ten years ago I was present at the first varnishing day of the Autumn Salon in the Grand Palais des Champs-Elysées, and last fall (1912) I attended the tenth exhibition of all these young and mature Independents, Cubists, Futurists, Post-Impressionists, and other wild animals from the remotest jungles of Darkest Art, and I was able to estimate the progress made since the first function. Great has been the change. Whereas a decade ago the god of that time was Paul Cézanne, to-day there are a dozen rival claimants for the job, vying with one another in every form of extravagance, so as to catch the eye. Manet, Monet, Degas, Pissarro, Sisley were in the eyes of his admirers dethroned ten years ago by Cézanne, Paul Gauguin, Vincent Van Gogh; now it's Matisse, Picasso, Picabia, Van Dongen, to mention a few, who look upon the trio of Post-Impressionists as "old masters," and, to tell the truth, seem masters in comparison with the new crowd who have contemptuously pitched overboard everything that we oldsters consider as essentials in pictorial or plastic art.

Will they, too, be voted "played out" ten years hence? Is there a still profounder level of ugliness and repulsiveness and idiotic trickery, or has the lowest been reached?

To answer these questions one must not resort to the old argument as does a writer in the catalogue of the Autumn Salon, pointing out that Manet, Wagner, Ibsen, Maeterlinck, Rodin were voted incomprehensible. That is too easy. Even in the depths of uncritical ignorance there were gleams of sympathy for the above-mentioned men. And in all the ruck and welter of the new movements there are a few men whose work will stand the test of time, and to-day shows mastery, originality, obscured as it may be by wilful eccentricities and occasional posturing to the gallery — a gallery, be it understood, composed of the gay young dogs who yawp in paint and screech themselves hoarse whenever a colleague cuts up infernal didoes. One of the "new" men I think will come to something is Henri Matisse.

I am not a prophet, though I listen to prophets. I met one ten years ago who had marched to the front with Edouard Manet, but has declined to go any further in the company of Paul Cézanne. For him the art of Cézanne was a distinct retrogression, and, recalling the stern admonition of Charles Baudelaire — truly a clairvoyant critic — who had warned Manet that he was the last of his line, en plein décadence, my painter friend pointed out to me that the camp followers of Cézanne, the sans-culottes of art, the ragtag and bobtail regiment would end by disintegrating the elements of art, all beauty, nobility, line, colour, would be sacrificed to a search for "truth," "decoration," and the "characteristic," said qualities being a new name for ugliness, ignorance, vulgarity.

"They want to do in a year what Cézanne couldn't accomplish in a lifetime," wailed my friend. "They are too lazy to master the grammar of their art, and they take Cézanne as a model, forgetting that he, like Manet, had diligently practised his scales for years before he began to play on canvas." And Henri Matisse? I asked. Well, perhaps Matisse was a "talent," but he had received a very sound education, and knew what he was about. If he chose to pitch his palette over the moon he must abide by the consequences. So Matisse, despite his fumisterie, is admitted on all sides as worth while, though he is bitterly attacked for his volcanic outbursts and general deviations from the normal. But you can always tell a human figure of his from a cow, and the same can't be said of the extraordinary productions of Picasso or Picabia.

The catalogue of the Tenth Autumn Salon shows the astonishing number of one thousand seven hundred and seventy works, which does not include the two hundred and twenty-one in the retrospective portrait exhibition, or several other minor exhibitions. Out of this formidable number there are few masterpieces, much sterile posing in paint, any quantity of mediocre talent, and in several salles devoted to the Cubists and others of the ilk any amount of mystification,

150

charlatanry, and an occasional glimpse of individuality. I am in sympathy with revolutionary movements in art, but now I know that my sympathies have reached their outermost verge.

I confess that I can't unravel the meanings of the Cubists, though I catch here and there a hint of their decorative quality, while shuddering at the hideous tonalities — strictly speaking, there are no tonalities, only blocks of raw primary colour juxtaposed with the childlike ingenuousness of Assyrian mural decorations. Massive as is Matisse in his wall painting, he sets up no puerile riddles to be demolished by the critic. New formulas these young men have not invented. To recapture the "innocence of the eyes" they have naïvely gone back to the Greek frieze, to the figures on Greek vases, to Egyptian tombs, to archaic bass-reliefs; they are desperate in their desire for the archaic. Picasso proudly asserted the other day that there are "no feet in nature," and some of his nudes seem to bear out this statement. Not to be natural, that is the new law. Not to represent, but interpret; not to show us the tangible, but the abstract. New mathematicians, seekers after a third dimension in paints, these young men must not be all set down as fakers. They are deliberately flouting the old conventions and missing thick butter on their daily bread. Sincere some of them are, apart from the usual wish, so dear to the budding students, of startling the bourgeois. And this same bourgeois goes to the exhibition and holds his sides with laughter, never buys a canvas, and disports himself generally as did his father before the pictures of Manet. Meanwhile some art dealers are sitting up and taking notice.

Such accomplished artists as Desvallières, D'Espagnat, Mme. Marval, Flandrin, Bonnard, Villéon, Frantz Jourdain, Dezire, Picart-Ledoux, Albert André, Mlle. Charmy, Lucien Stoltz, Valloton, Maufra, Maxime Dethomas, and others do much to redeem the weariness aroused by the contemplation of the Cubist section, the galleries set aside for the "Searchers," as they are called. What of that terrifying Woman in Blue! What of Mountaineers Attacked by Bears! Matisse is not at his best, though his work is comparatively clearer than last year. Those three flame-coloured nudes dancing against a blue background are very rhythmic. They bring into relief a red bottle entwined with nasturtium leaves and flowers. A pail of blue water in which swim goldfish is decorative. However, I was slightly disappointed in this slim showing, only to be consoled later in London. Mme. Georgette Agutte presents a remarkable Japanese interior, very effective in both colour and composition. Attractive are the plaster heads of René Carrière, who models the head of his mother with the same divining touch which his father manifested in his famous portraits of his wife.

II

The Post-Impressionist Exhibition at the Grafton Galleries last October in London was the second. There are British, French, and Russian groups. Two years ago the first show of the so-called Post-Impressionists — unhappy title! — scandalised and amused all London. Clive Bell says in the catalogue that the battle has been won, and to-day Cézanne, Gauguin, Van Gogh are the "old masters" of the new movement. Roger Fry, well known to New York as art critic, was in charge and he told us that the idea of the present exhibition is to show Post-Impressionism in its contemporary development not only in France, its native place, but in England, where it is of very recent growth, and in Russia, where it has liberated and revived an old native tradition.

"It would, of course," continues Mr. Fry, "have been possible to extend the geographical area immensely. Post-Impressionist schools are flourishing in Switzerland, Austro-Hungary, and most of all in Germany. In Italy, the Futurists have succeeded in developing a whole system of æsthetics out of a misapprehension of some of Picasso's recondite and difficult works. We have ceased to ask: 'What does this picture represent?' and ask instead: 'What does it make us feel?' We expect a work of plastic art to have more in common with a piece of music than with a coloured photograph. These Eng-

'lish artists are of the movement because in choice of subjects they recognise no authority but the truth that is in them; in choice of form, none but the need of expressing it. That is Post-Impressionism."

But in practice the English Cubists and Post-Impressionists do not bear out his hopeful words. A Mother and Child, by Wyndham Lewis, may be at once a "simplification," but its plasticity of design is far to seek. With The Dead Mole, by Etchells, it shares honours in the domain of the grotesque. A large wooden doll holding in its wooden-painted arms a wooden baby, to which this wooden mother is giving ligneous nourishment from a wooden bust, is as "emotional" as a basket of chips. As for The Dead Mole, it will be a joy for ever. It is so comical that all notion of an artistic formula is forgotten in what Henry James would call "the emotion of recognition." The looker-on recognises the absolute imbecility of the design and smiles accordingly.

Symbolists would be a better title for Matisse and his fellow-artists than the meaningless phrase Post-Impressionism, for, despite Mr. Fry's belief that they aim at reality rather than illusion, they are essentially symbolists, and, like the Chinese, by a purely arbitrary line seek to express their idea of decoration. I once described music as a species of "emotional mathematics," and Mr. Fry's "visual music" is but emotional geometrising. At the best, in the hands of a big man such experimenting is a dangerous thing; when employed as a working formula by lesser artists, such as Derani, Braque, Herbin, Marchand, L'Hote, Doucet, and others, the results do not justify the means. Even Mr. Fry in his landscapes does not go too far; they wear a gentle air of the Italian Primitives. The portrait of his wife by Picasso did not shock me, for only the day before I had seen hanging in the National Gallery a head by Piero della Francesca, pure gold against a hard terra-cotta background. The colour contrasts of the new men, while harsh as to modulation, do not offend the eye nearly so much as do those involved mosaics by the Cubists. What does Braque mean by his Kubelik-Mozart picture? Or Picasso by his Buffalo Bill? The Woman and the Mustard Pot is emotional enough, for the unhappy creature is weeping, no doubt, because of the mustard in her eyes; certainly because of the mustard smeared over her dress. A pungent design, indeed.

Matisse is at his best — also at his most terrific. One nude sits on a chair drying herself with a bath-towel. You look another way. Degas at his frankest never revealed so much. Nothing occult here. All plain sailing for the man in the street. Presently you cover your eyes with your hand; then you peer through your fingers. All is bald. The Eternal Female, and at her ugliest. What's the symbol? There is none, only volume and planes. Matisse models in paint. But you catch a glimpse of his

Dancers — a design for a decoration in the Palace
of Prince Tschonkine at Moscow — and you
admire the bacchantic rhythm, the pattern of
rose, black, blue, the scheme of contrasted
colour, the boldness, the vivacity of the design.
It is wonderfully rhythmic, this arabesque.

There is strong modelling in his La Coiffeuse;
indeed, it is impossible to deny the power of this
painter or deny his marked individuality. His
designs (there are several in the Metropolitan
Museum) reveal his creative rhythms, and if, as
has been said, genius is mainly a matter of energy,
then Henri Matisse is a genius. But, alas! your
eye alights upon that grotesque Conversation,
and you murmur: "No, not a matter of energy
but pajamas." Again the risible rib is tickled.
Picasso's Nature Morte is dead, not still life.
His master, Cézanne, knew how to portray po-
tatoes and onions which were real if not precisely emotional. Two pictures are by Auguste
Chabaud, a young Paris painter who lives all the
year in the country.

His exhibition at Paris last spring won for him
attention and praise. His design is large, simple,
virile; his sincere feeling for landscape is not to
be doubted, though his colouring is rather sombre. A road scene in the hills, with its firm silhouette, and his sheep leaving the fold after the
rain, is rhythmic, especially the figures of the
shepherd and his dog. At first I fancied the
sheep were moles, then tapirs, then cockroaches,
but they soon resolved themselves into sheep

Chabaud is not given over to paint metaphysics. He writes, it is true, but he writes sensibly. In art, he says, we invent nothing. Art is not of yesterday, nor of to-day, nor of to-morrow; it is eternal. He mocks at the words classic, romantic, ancient, modern. Some of the new crowd might pattern after his wisdom. The Russians give us Byzantine figures in hieratic attitudes. They are monotonous. And in the octagon room are four Cézannes, a painter who, with all his departures from tradition, nevertheless respected the integrity of his design, respected his surfaces, was reverent in the use of his medium. Cézanne is a classic. It is difficult to predict if even Henri Matisse will become one.

V

LITHOGRAPHS OF TOULOUSE–LAUTREC

A human ass — and his tribe does not decrease — once made the profound remark that he never read Dickens because so many common people circulated through the pages of his novels. We call this remark profound, for it illustrates in the clearest manner what has been named "the heresy of the subject." The majority of persons do not go to the theatre for the sheer joy of the acting, do not read books because they are well written, or look at pictures because they are painted artistically. The subject, the story, the anecdote, the "human interest," "little touches," all the various traps that snare the attention from poor or mediocre workmanship — the traps of sentimentalism, of false feeling, of cheap pathos, and of the cheap moral, these the greater public willingly embraces, and hates to be reminded of its lack of taste, of its ignorance. The man who first said "Give the people what they want" was probably born close to the tertiary epoch, though his fossil remains as yet undug; but we are assured that he was a mighty chief in his tribe. So are his successors, who have cluttered the market-places with their booths, mischievous half art and tubs of tripe and soft soap. Therefore we select for his courage the snobbish chap who found Dickens ordinary; to him Millet would have been absolutely vulgar.

The cult of the subject is warmly worshipped in America and England. It nearly ruined English painting half a century ago, and even to-day you must go to the Glasgow or the Dublin galleries to see contemporaneous art naked and unashamed. In New York we are more lucky, though here the public, always prudish, prefers the soapy surfaces of Cabanel's Venus or the oily skin of Henner to the forthright beauty and truth of Manet's Olympe — now known as Notre Dame du Louvre. If Dickens had made his "low" characters after the style of Italian opera peasants; if Manet had prettified his nudes, censors would have called them blest. We have selected these names at random; Dickens is the idol of the middle class (the phrase is not of our making), while Manet fought for recognition in a Paris not too easily startled. In reality he was a puritan in comparison with his predecessors and successors, not to mention such contemporaries as Gérôme, Boulanger, Cabanel, and Lefebvre, men who painted nudes their life long. But they knew how to mix saccharine on their palettes; Manet did not.

But what would our friend the snob say if he had seen the original lithographs of the ill-fated Count Henri de Toulouse-Lautrec? Either faint or fight; no middle course in the presence of these rapid snap-shots from life by a master of line. The subjects would be revolting to our possible case, and no doubt they will prove revolting to most people who mix up art with their personal preferences for the stale, the sweet, the musk moral. Lautrec's favourite browsing ground was Montmartre, the Montmartre of twenty years ago, not the machine-made tourists' fake of to-day. You will get a prose parallel in the early stories of Huysmans in Les Sœurs Vatard, though not in the tinselled glory of Charpentier's Louise. Lautrec, born in an old family, was literally slain by his desire for artistic perfection. Montmartre slew him. But he mastered the secrets of its dance-halls, its purlieus, its cocottes, its bullies and habitués before he died. In Meier-graefe's little book on the impressionists Lautrec gets a place of honour, the critic asserting that he "dared to do what Degas scorned." This is a mystification. Degas has done what he cared to do and has done it in an almost perfect fashion. A pupil and follower of Ingres, he paved the way for Lautrec, who went further afield in his themes and simplifications. If Degas broke the classic line of Ingres, Lautrec has torn to shreds the linear patterns of Degas. Obsessed as we are in America by the horrors of magazine illustrations, by the procrustean conventions of our draughtsmen, by cow-boys of wood, metallic horses, melodramatic landscape, it will be long before we can sympathise with the supple, versatile, bold drawing of Lautrec, who gives movement, character, vitality in a curve.

It is not only that he portrays his women of the streets without false sentiment (profoundly immoral, always, in its results), but he actually shows a solicitude for them. He is not the entomologist with the pinned bug, as is often Degas, as was often Flaubert, but a sympathetic interpreter. He doesn't make vice interesting, he makes it hideous. His series Elles is worth a volume of moralising commentary. And there is a certain horse of his — it's as good as a real horse. His lithographic method is personal and effective. He is one of art's martyrs, and for that reason has always been discredited by those who conceive art to be a sort of church for morals and the sweet retreat of the perfectly respectable professor.

VII

NEW PROMENADES OF AN IMPRESSIONIST

I

ART IN COLOGNE AND CASSEL

In Cologne of course you go to the cathedral; every one does, even the Colognese on Sundays and holidays. If you ask: What after the cathedral? the answer invariably is: The Zoological garden. Thus one day at least is safely tided over. It is the second that sends you to the river Rhine, there to quote Coleridge, and later to the Gurzenich, and if you are industrious enough you may gaze upon the Moltke monument and peep into the Church of St. Martin and the Church of the Apostles. There is then nothing else to do but drink Pilsner at the Ewige Lampe and rejoice that you left Düsseldorf and its ugly mid-nineteenth-century German art. But there is another attraction in Cologne besides the desire to escape from it on the big boat that takes you to Mainz. It is the Wallraff-Richartz Museum, where the German Primitives may be studied to your heart's content, for no traveller seemingly ever visits the neat little gallery.

Meister Stephan Lochner is there in all his glory, though both at the cathedral and in the Archiepiscopal Museum (the Madonna with the Violets) there are specimens of his best work. The Madonna in the Arbor of Roses is fairly well preserved by sheets of shiny varnish, but there is not enough of the latter to obscure its pristine beauty. The galleries are arranged so that the student may go in at one door and come out at another. You begin with the triptych of a Cologne master, a Crucifixion, cruel, bald, and terrifying, and note the date, the middle of the fourteenth century. These masters of the Ly-versberg Passion, masters of St. Bartholomew, with their harsh colouring and angular drawing were the veritable realists and not their succes-sors, who introduced the qualities of lovely colouring and pulchritude. But the old fellows have the feeling, the poignant note, the faith unfeigned. There is a Madonna with a Flower, by an unknown who is called the master of the Holy Veronica, which might have come across from far-away Italy, so mellifluous are its senti-ments and execution, though this sort is rarely encountered.

Stephan Lochner — his Dombild is considered the finest painting of the school — is addicted to Last Judgments of the same horrific character as Hell-Breughel's fantastic writhing composi-tions. Comical and astounding as is all this creaking mediæval machinery of redemption and punishment, we prefer the serene beauty of the

Madonna in the rose-garden. But a Jan van Eyck it is not; indeed, these chillier Germans of the Upper Rhenish school limped perceptibly in the rear after the Flemings. Works by the master of the Life of Mary, truly a noble crucifixion piece, the Crowning of Mary, the Madonna and St. Bernard, the Descent from the Cross — same master — another triptych of intense power and extreme ugliness, a Martyrdom of St. Sebastian, and specimens by the master of St. Bartholomew and the master of St. Séverin — alas! for glory these be but shadows of former fame — enchain the attention because of their native sincerity despite their gaudy tones. When we reach the portraiture of Bartholomew Bruyn there is less elevation of spirit but a more satisfying prose in the matter of realism.

Bruyn (1493-1555) is best represented in Cologne, though he flourishes in Frankfort at the Staedel Institute. Holbein had no greater sense of reality than this solid painter with the bourgeois vision. His portraits are charged with character, even if he misses the finer issues of the soul. A Lucas Cranach, a Mary Magdalen, captures the eye with its quaint costume of the lady, who is modestly covered almost to her slender neck. She stands in a strong landscape with a few distant hills, and the hair of her is in ringlets and of an abundance. Her face is tranquil. In her left hand she holds the historic box of ointment. It is a charming masterpiece. Another famous specimen is the portrait of a young man by the master of the Death of Mary. Hieronymus Bosch is represented, but the most striking work in the gallery after the Madonna of Lochner, and to our taste much more wonderful, is the bust portrait of a man by Jan van Scorel (1495-1562), a Flemish master who is beginning to come into his own in the estimation of connoisseurs. You conjure up the august name of Holbein when looking at this solemn-eyed old man with the pursy cheeks and the pet dog whose little head protrudes from the coat of the sitter. A learned pundit this with marvellously painted hands.

Albrecht Dürer, Paris Bordone, Tiepolo, Francia, Murillo, Rubens, and Jan Steen are represented, and there is a singularly attractive Johann Anton Ramboux, a double portrait. Among the later Germans are the names of Julius Schnorr von Carolsfeld, whose son was the first Tristan in Wagner's poetic music drama; Karl Begas, Overbeck, Bendemann, Boettcher, and other mediocrities; Piloty and Boecklin are not missing. A strong portrait by Wilhelm Leibl and Max Liebermann's finely felt self-portrait are among the moderns; Slevogt, Peerat, Von Hoffmann, Eugenio Lucas, and the rest. An unusual note is furnished by Vincent Van Gogh, the unhappy young Dutchman who cut his throat in 1890 during an attack of madness. The head and bust of a young man which is in this collection proclaims the painter a superior artist to his friend Paul Gauguin, a portrait by

whom hangs hard by. There is power in this
Van Gogh, and after so many insipidities of a
by-gone school his vision of a robust reality is
very refreshing. Altogether a visit to this
museum is recommended to those tourists whose
interest in the city is dominated by the extraordinary Gothic pile. For the art amateur there
is no other place so plentifully endowed with
examples of a certain phase of northern Rhine
art as Cologne.

The railway journey to Cassel is very interesting, quite as interesting, though not as full of
dramatic surprises, as the Rhine trip. After
leaving Cologne the train winds through the
valley of the Ruhr, crossing and recrossing that
river, going uphill the greater part of the time
and surrounded by scenery that recalls New
Hampshire. You pass town after town, busy
thriving towns, with such unfamiliar names as
Arnisberg, Warburg, Marburg, and if it were
not for the occasional ruined castle perched on
distant peaks you could easily fancy yourself in
northern New England, especially if it is a brac-
ing October day. Cassel reached and superficially promenaded is bound to extort a cry of
admiration. Americans visit this delightful town
in the hills of Hesse-Nassau, but not in numbers.
Berlin with its theatres, hotels, and noisy out-
door life, and Dresden with its more domesticated
airs, are the objectives of the majority. And thus
it is that a gem of a city, one of the prettiest in
Germany, is best known by the Germans. For

one thing, it is out of the beaten track; New
York folk go to Frankfort, to Munich, and not
enough to Prague and Vienna, and seldom think of
alighting at Cassel when en route to Nauheim or
Wiesbaden from Cologne. Nearly seven hundred
feet above the sea, Cassel is pre-eminently a
summer city. The air blows crisp, dry, and cool
across the mountains, and the view from the
Schöne Aussicht is one of the most captivating
in Europe. Again you are reminded of the White
Mountains, without such a giant as Mount
Washington towering over the scene. Naturally
Cassel is not archaic, as is Lübeck or Rothenberg
or Nuremberg. It is, on the contrary, very
modern, very spick and span, very spacious and
comfortable, with its Hotel Schirmer, as good for
its size as any in New York; its big Tietz department store, its Royal Hof Theatre and opera
house, one of the finest in Germany, far in advance of the dingy old opera at Berlin. These
and the numerous palaces, the magnificent Wilhelmshöhe palace and gardens, only half an hour
away, make this place on the river Fulda with
its one hundred and fifty thousand inhabitants
a magnet to those who like modest little cities
and not overcrowded advertised monsters of mu-
nicipalities.

Your Baedeker tells you that Cassel is an important railway centre, which is no news to the
student in search of the picturesque. For him
the Karls meadow and the enchanting panorama
of Wilhelmshöhe suffice. The vaunted beauties

of the Nymphenburg at Munich and the trim,
aristocratic elegance of Versailles are forgotten
in the vast ensemble of Wilhelmshöhe palace,
temples, parks, terraces, fountains, cascades,
forests, and lakes. It is all in the grand manner,
this royal abode; and you reflect, not without a
sigh, when the fair picture unrolls at your feet,
upon the awful results that would follow if it
were thrown open to the mercies of our own
choice Sunday citizens. But the public knows
how to savour life slowly in Germany, particularly in Cassel. At five o'clock every afternoon
the knitting brigade is seated drinking coffee; every table is occupied in the cafés, and gossip is
running at full speed. From one to three P. M.
the Casselians take dinner and a nap. No need
to go to the bank, you will be gently repulsed
by warning signs. At night the theatres and restaurants are crowded. Leisure is understood in
this spot. And best of all is the picture gallery.

Let us suppose that you were not acquainted
with the contents of the solid-looking though not
large gallery surrounded by flowers overlooking
the Karls meadow. Let us suppose as a lover of
art you go up-stairs and suddenly find yourself
in the Rembrandt room. What joyous amazement! What a clicking of the tongue and rolling of the eyes as you enumerate the list, note
the quality. And then your waxing wonder when
you behold the Frans Halses. There are seven
in number, as against twenty-one Rembrandts.
There are eleven Rubenses, twelve Van Dycks,

twenty-three Wouvermans, three by Antonis Mor, think of three canvases by this rare master! while there are precious examples by Ter Borch, and a fair showing for the Italians and other schools. Only eight hundred and twenty-five pictures are listed in the catalogue, yet we can recall no gallery that holds so little dross. That doesn't mean that every frame contains a masterpiece, but we do assert that the negligible canvases are fewer in proportion than in most museums.

Among the portraits by Hals is the celebrated Man with the Broad Brimmed Hat, a masterpiece among any of the Hals pictures. Der lustige Zecher is another famous Hals. Then there are two bust portraits and the portrait of a Patrician, also the Two Children Singing, the Boy with a Lute in his left hand. Outside of Haarlem there are no better Halses. The Rembrandts naturally begin with the Saskia van Uylenberg, his wife, which is as notable as the younger Saskia in Dresden and much better than the older Saskia in Berlin; Rembrandt at his top-notch in the matter of the handling of textures, jewels, flesh tones, and character. Then follows an embarrassment of pictorial wealth; the Old Man with the Chain, depicting the beautiful gravity of old age; the study of an Old Man, the Architect, the Sentry, the magisterial Jacob Blessing his Grandchildren, worthy for its style and composition to be hung beside the Nightwatch and the Syndics at Amsterdam;

the head of the painter's father, one **Hermann**
(or Harmenz) by name, with his Hebraic lineaments; then a bald-headed man who looks like
Paul Verlaine, and the portrait of Nik. Bruyn-
ingh, surely one of the most ingratiating presentments of virile beauty in the world; the
Soldier with the Helmet, a self-portrait painted
with magic; the touching though not so artistically important The Family of the Woodcutter.
Here's a list that might make water the mouth
of the art lover. Amsterdam and St. Petersburg
(the Hermitage) excel this Cassel collection as to
Rembrandts, though not in quality. An excellent copy of Der Bürgerfahnreich, the original
of which is in the possession of the Paris Rothschilds, is to be seen.

The Rubenses and Van Dycks need not be
gone over in detail; they are all admirable. The
head of the painter Jan Wildens, by Van Dyck;
his very Rubensesque Child Jesus, various full-
length portraits, and the remarkable portrait of
the painter F. Snyders, quite the equal in quality
and preservation of the same theme exhibited
several years ago at the Knoedler Galleries, are
in the best vein of this artist. Among the
Rubenses are Meleager and Atalanta, Diana and
Nymphs, The Flight into Egypt, Hercules In-
toxicated, Venus, Amor, Bacchus, and Ceres,
and a large portrait of Nicolas de Respaigné in
Turkish costume, a very unlikely Rubens.

We should like to relate further the number
of good things we saw in this jewel of a gallery.

Dürer, Baldung, Grien, Altdorfer, no less than six genuine Lucas Cranachs, Bruyn, Herri Met de Bles, Van Orley, Van Scorel (three), the entire Flemish school, a superb Ter Borch, the Lute Player, and that virtuoso of candlelight Gotfried Scalcken; two Jacob Ruisdaels (one of the best period), Millet, Daubigny, and a Troyon, of all painters, and an alleged Titian. The Carlo Maratta portrait may be better enjoyed at the Metropolitan Museum, for it is the original. There is a capital Ribera, while Tischbein is worthily represented. A Gainsborough landscape more than holds its own, as does a John Constable nocturne, among a lot of German eighteenth and nineteenth century nobodies. A portrait of Arthur Schopenhauer by a certain Engelbert Goebel reminded us that Frankfort was not many hours distant.

One morning after wondering at the bad taste of the giant statue of Ludwig Spohr, king of German violinists, whose monument stands on the Theaterplatz, we drifted into an exhibition of the Kassel Kunstverein, and there got a foretaste of the present desperate condition of modern German art, tainted as it is by French impressionism, Post and otherwise, all inevitably misunderstood. Ernest Oppler of Berlin, Julius Schrag of Munich, Karl Thiemann of Dachau, who has talent as a wood-engraver and pastellist; Georg Broel, Hermann Keuth, H. J. Koenig, and Edmund Steppes were among those present. The etchers were headed by A. Baertson, a Belgian genuinely gifted. Among the dead, Haden and Rops were to be seen; the coloured etchings of the unique Félicien Rops were in excellent state and offered at surprisingly low figures. Zorn too was in the group, a group that made one forget the vulgarity, brutality, and technical ineptitudes of the men who used oil as their medium to express the absence of temperament. But the glory of Cassel is its gallery of old masters.

II

ART IN FRANKFORT

One afternoon we found ourselves in Sachsenhausen hardly knowing how we got there. Sachsenhausen, be it understood, might be called the Brooklyn of Frankfort-on-the-Main, but who ever heard of any one reaching Brooklyn without his knowledge? On the left bank of the placid river Main this suburb is approached by such broad roadways that you are not conscious you are traversing bridges, and only when you find yourself staring at the Dome which rears its spire over the spacious streets and huddled houses of the city do you realise the transposition. This naturally if you take the tram-cars; walking gives a better view. But if the comprehensive tableau gained by our mistake compensated in some sort, the excursion did not help us to discover the house where lived and died that amiable old gentleman and patron saint of the suffragettes, Arthur Schopenhauer. We merely mistook the wrong side of the Main for the Schöne Aussicht, therefore No. 17 was missed. Later a pessimistic policeman put us to rights and we recrossed on a bridge lower down — or is it further up? — and soon found the gloomy old building where the gallant philosopher lived from 1843 to 1859 and died in one next door in 1860. Here the fame denied him for so many decades came to console if not actually to mollify his irritability. We were not duly impressed by the commonplace commercial atmosphere and were more than glad to escape to the Juden-gasse, whence sprang the Rothschilds.

There is no denying the beauty, even splen-dour, of appearances in Frankfort. You easily ap-preciate the popularity of the city with American travellers. It is not so loose-gaited and gemüth-lich as Munich, but it wears a more smiling mask than Berlin, which puts on Prussian airs since some flatterer called it a world-city. Frankfort is amiably hospitable. There is the south in its manners; the climate is more mellow than Berlin. The magnitude of public places and buildings, boulevards, for the Kaiserstrasse is a veritable boulevard, the monumental style of the opera-house, the Römer (Rathhaus), the Royal Theatre, hotels and churches impress one with a sense of solidity, of wealth well spent, of artistic taste. Life after all is not a frantic struggle in crazy excavations, with a dynamite obbligato, a medley of dirt and din. That Germany is prosperous is demonstrated by the way its inhabitants spend money in the cafés, theatres, and opera. In Frankfort, as in Berlin or Cologne or Cassel, you fight for your table in the famous Kaiser Keller, and no wonder! About one thousand of your fellow-beings, chiefly Teutonic, are imbued with the same desire as you, and at the same time. The only time we ever saw a German excited was when he tried to get a seat in a restaurant ahead of some one else, and at Hamburg when he struggled like a football virtuoso to force his presence into the opera-house where Caruso was singing in a novelty written by a young chap named Verdi, the opera Ballo in Maschera. Talk about love of art!

The first act of piety of the sentimental voyager is a visit to the Goethe house at Grosse Hirschgraben 23, in the centre of the town. Here the poet was born, here he spent his boyhood. He was reared in comparative luxury, though according to our modern notions the house seems rather bare. After visiting Weimar and the garden-house and the museum there seems paucity of personal interest in the collection at Frankfort, rich as it is in memories of the youthful Goethe. The same old guardian, who over twenty years ago was precisely as loquacious, said that he remembered our name but forgot our face — he must have heard this bon-mot of Oscar Wilde's — and did not fail to remind us that he had served nearly forty years as cicerone in the historical spot. What lies he has told, what "gulls" he has mystified. A pet anecdote of his is the following, and we give it publicity because we never saw it in print. Goethe's son was fond of wine and his grandson followed suit. Once in the memory of the keeper this grandson of an illustrious poet came to the Grosse Hirsch-graben but stopped at a certain hotel across the street. When urged to visit the birthplace of his granddaddy he shrugged his shoulders and ordered a fresh bottle. The curious part of the story is not the wine but the ineffable laziness, or call it Olympian indifference, of the man. He didn't care a hang whether his ancestor lived in Frankfort or Weimar. To Weimar he returned, where he died from thirst, or was it the remorse of indigestion?

In Sachsenhausen, about ten minutes from the heart of Frankfort, is the Staedel Institute (please read guide-books for the history of Herr Staedel, who founded the institution in 1816-17). It is an art gallery pleasantly situated, overlooking the river, and it contains many noteworthy pic-tures, not so many Rembrandts and Halses as at Cassel, nor yet is it such a tremendous gallery as is the Kaiser Friedrich Wilhelm at Berlin. There are, however, Rembrandts, Halses, Velas-quezes, Rubenses, Dürers, Botticellis, Cranachs, a Veronese, a Jan Van Eyck — unequalled the world over — a Holbein, a Vermeer, and a fair sprinkling of the Flemish Primitives. Modern French art has not been neglected, and alto-

gether the seven hundred and odd numbers of
the catalogue make a brave showing. It would
be manifestly a thankless task to enumerate the
various "best" canvases of the Staedel Institute.
A glance must suffice. Let us begin at the beginning, æsthetically at least. Despite Dr.
Benkard's sketch of the Rembrandts it may be
acknowledged that neither in quality nor in
quantity do they approach the Cassel collection.
But they are interesting, and in one instance rare;
for surely such violence and cruelty as are manifested in the Triumph of Delilah are seldom de-
noted in the works of this master. There are
cruelty and obscenity combined in his etching
of Joseph resisting the abysmal advances of
Potiphar's wife, and we could if we had the
space mention some other examples, yet none
approaches in writhing and tumult and riotous
colouring this Frankfort picture.

The Blinding of Samson is horrible to gaze
upon; you shudder and turn with relief to
the portrait of Margarete von Bildersecq, with
its sumptuous modelling and its homely attrac-
tiveness. In this composition, dated 1633, the
painter meets Hals on his own field and almost
vanquishes him. The note is bourgeois, commonplace; there is mystery in the atmospheric
envelope. Whoever Margarete may have been
she was above all else a practical housewife, addicted to large clean ruffs and lace caps; furthermore, she tramped the earth with solemn,
solid feet, and she loved substantial food and

drink. Rembrandt is her historian and every stroke of his brush depicts a trait of character. His Saul and David is not as eloquent as the same subject at The Hague. Now that Dr. Bredius is seeking to rob Rembrandt of the glory of being the creator of Elizabeth Bas at the Rijks Museum, Amsterdam, — the most wonderful old lady in the world of dreams and paint, — it would not be a bad idea for the worthy director of the Mauritshuis at The Hague, where he has placed several peculiar Rembrandt discoveries (?) of his own, to visit Frankfort and study the Margarete von Bildersecq. He above all other experts of old Dutch art ought to know that Rembrandt had more than one string to his bow of styles. Elizabeth Bas is one, the Night Watch another, the head of the cavalier at Cassel a third, the etchings a fourth, his landscapes a fifth, — and no Hercules Seegher ever approached them; think of the mystic chiaro-oscuro of The Mill, — his Biblical themes a sixth, and so on — a Shakespearian versatility indeed.

Of the two examples by Velasquez at the Staedel Institute the portrait of Cardinal Borgia is the more significant. This ecclesiastic, whose full name was Casper Borgia y Velasco, was also Archbishop of Sevilla and Toledo (1582-1645). His is not an unkindly countenance, if you are not afraid of facing the consequences. It is one of the painter's masterpieces of psychological observation without unfriendly comment on the facts of the features. Borgia, according to contemporary accounts, was a man of intellect, a lover of the arts, a sober, God-fearing man and one not averse to boiling oil for contumacious heretics. Señor Beruete throws cold water on your mounting enthusiasm for this masterly characterisation by proving to his own satisfaction that the original work has long since vanished, the pair of portraits at Frankfort and in the Cathedral of Toledo being copies. This may be true, but we hasten to state that the Toledo specimen is a poor affair compared with this vital canvas in the Staedel Institute. If Beruete had said that the portrait of the Infanta Margarita Theresa was not a genuine Velasquez one could well credit him. It does not approach the Louvre portrait or the one in the Vienna Imperial Gallery, and suggests, despite the passages of paint, silvery in tenderness, the brush-work of that precious son-in-law of Velasquez, Señor Mazo.

But let the heathen rage, there are two portraits by Frans Hals that throw into the shade everything else in the gallery except the Van Eyck. A man and a woman, the latter equals in sharpness of veracity though not in charm the Elizabeth Bas of Rembrandt, and makes pale the memory of the elderly dame accredited to Hals at the Metropolitan Museum. The Staedel Holbein is the portrait of Sir George of Cornwall, a stirring composition in which the blacks and whites struggle, although with harmonious results. As is always the case with this master, the humanity overshadows his technical methods, which only means that he is a consummate technician. Two Botticellis are not of overwhelming importance; one doesn't visit Germany altogether for its Italian art; nevertheless we wish our museum boasted such a pair, particularly the Madonna and Child. There is a Veronese, a studio piece, Mars and Venus the subject, the Venus being the same model as the Venus given to Veronese in the Metropolitan Museum. The posture of the god and goddess is different, though the Cupid is there. Perhaps this is one of a series of panels. We admired the slim virginal figure of the Lucas Cranach Venus; the forthright sincerity of the Matsys portrait of a man; the purple splendour of the astronomer's robe in the Vermeer; the Veronica of the Master of Flemalle, Jacques Daret: Dürer's Job subjected to the mercies of his wife — the first advanced woman in Biblical history; a luminous interior by P. Janssens, nearly equal to the best De Hoogh; a Crucifixion by the Flemalle master, positively pathetic in its expression though dangerously near that pathological point so powerfully illustrated in the Crucifixion by Mathias Grünewald at Colmar, and the Jan Van Eyck Madonna with Infant, formerly known as the Madonna of Lucca, after its former owner, the Duke of Lucca. It was acquired by the Staedel Institute at The Hague from the collection of King William II of Holland in 1850, and it is the noblest Van Eyck in Germany, notwithstanding the superior historic and artistic interest attached to the two panels in Berlin from the great Ghent Adoration of the Lamb. The Frankfort Van Eyck glows with a rich rubylike warmth. Its decorative quality almost matches its devotional character.

In the same gallery as The Virgin by the Master of Flemalle, celebrated with undue praise, we think, by the late J.-K. Huysmans, is the mysterious portrait of a young woman which so intrigued the attention of the French writer. For Huysmans she was both exquisite and vicious, androgynous and enticing. Who was she? He hazards that it might be Giulia Farnese, called Giulia la bella, "puritas impuritatis," who became the favourite of Pope Alexander VI, mayhap his daughter. By whom was she painted? The catalogue says Bartolomeo da Venezea or Veneziano (?). According to Lanzi there are at least eleven of the tribe. And according to our humble opinion the portrait might have come straight from the brush of Botticelli. Every line, the epicene expression, the hair, head, flat bust, hand, above all the delicacy of the fingers and the shape of the nails, proclaim the Botticelli studio. The dominating tonality is a wonderful white. Huysmans was correct in calling to the attention of the critics the enigmatic character of the head, which would have fascinated Walter Pater.

We have but superficially praised the contents of this very attractive museum on the Main, where one encounters a George Inness or a Keith cheek by jowl with a Sisley, a Monet, or a Hobbema. Catholicity rules, and it is exceedingly refreshing in its results. It is hardly necessary to add that there are several excellent Tischbeins, a splendid Terborch, and a capital portrait of Schopenhauer by Jules Lunteschütz, dated 1855.

When in Frankfort a trip to Darmstadt, half an hour away, should be a labour of love to art amateurs, for there in the archducal palace in addition to a rather mediocre art gallery is the most treasured of Hans Holbeins, possibly painted in 1526, representing six members of the Jakob Meier family kneeling on either side of the Virgin and the Child Jesus. It is a more finely conserved work than its former rival in the Basel Museum, the Madonna of Solothurn, though for years it was considered a copy and the excellent copy in Dresden the original. The restoration by Hauser in 1888 cleared up all doubts as to the identity of the Burgomaster Meier (or Meyer) Madonna, as it is entitled, and you may account yourself one of the lucky to have studied it. The excessive heat and drought of 1911, which endured seven weeks in Darmstadt, warped the panel, and the lower folds of the robe of the Virgin bulge a little. Otherwise the work is free from the corrosion of time and the detestable additions of the restorer.

There is no evasive handling here, yet the human soul transfigured by religious awe and fervour and in all its subtlety shines forth from

these solidly modelled countenances. No caper-
ing chromatics distract the looker-on from the
beauty of the few large tones soberly soldered
one to the other without a hint of either emptiness or huddling. Humanity is present in the
breadth of feeling and simplicity of expression,
and the religious sincerity is indubitable. Der
Dichter spricht, and also the master painter
enamoured of lovely surfaces and supreme sentiment. Impeccable Holbein!

III

NEW YORK — COSMOPOLIS

I

When Merlin the Magician visited Prester
John, as related in the veracious chronicle of
Edgar Quinet, he discovered that potentate
dwelling in an abbey of fantastic and conglom-
erate architecture; the building was a mixture
of pagoda, mosque, synagogue, cathedral, Greek
temple, Byzantine and Gothic chapels, basilicas,
with domes, spires, turrets, minarets, and towers
innumerable. To complete the intellectual confusion of Merlin, he saw Prester John alternately
reading from the Vedas, the Bible, and the Koran.
With what consternation would the victim of
Vivien greet the picture of New York if we could
fancy Merlin on a Staten Island ferry-boat?
Once within the zone of lofty buildings would he
not snap his magic wand in the impotence of

sheer envy? And that great cosmopolitan, Stendhal — can we not imagine him viewing with angry, contemptuous eyes the towering triumphs of a democracy he so loathed? The master-builders! They are of our city, building not only homes for humans, but dizzy hives for supermen — the American business man is your true superman nowadays; his idealism is deflected from the region of poetics to the plane of reality; his reality the subduing of Things, and the making of them a symbol. The kings who erected the Pyramids, the satraps who helped fashion Babylon's mighty hanging gardens and palaces that reared their heads to the skies like swans, those rulers with monumental undertakings from Karnak to Stonehenge are paralleled, nay, outdone by the designers of modern New York.

Twenty years ago the skyline was hardly inspiring; though from the heights of the Hudson the view was then, even as it is now and ever will be, magnificent. Above Wall Street, on the east side of Broadway, was a congested business district. A few spires, Trinity Church, the Tribune Building, and the World Building were the conspicuous objects from the lower bay. To-day you search for Trinity between cliffs of marble; the World Building may be seen from East River or Broadway, and in New Jersey you catch the golden gleam of its dome. The Woolworth Building has outdistanced it in the race skyward, while the Tribune Building by comparison seems of normal height.

NEW PROMENADES

What a difference, too, there was on lower Manhattan! The Battery, a clot of green as you saw it from ferry-boat or steam-ship, was surrounded by a few buildings, imposing enough, yet to-day mere pediments for their loftier rivals. Here and there a church looking like a sharpened pencil protruded from the background. You could see churches then. Now one makes pilgrimages to them through cañons.

Survey on a clear day our new skyline. The low sandy spit of Manhattan Island which our grandfathers knew is thronged by extraordinary palaces and topped by the Woolworth Building. The position of the Singer campanile is inevitable. It lies at the centre of your vision on the return trip from Staten Island. The huge ramparts of marble aligning the lower island are waffle-faced because of their innumerable windows. The City Investing Building cranes ambitiously beside the Singer tower; it makes of the pair a hybrid beast of architecture. Yet from the Hudson the two violently contrasted piles blend, and if there is a mist the combination sets you to dreaming of a far-away exotic aerial *palazzo* in some city conceived by a John Martin or a Piranesi. The Hudson Terminal buildings overwhelm; their vast spread suggests not alone the city population daily harboured in their offices, but also a sense of tremendous density, size, weight. Following the eye we see the Washington Life, the West Street, American Surety, United States Express, Empire,

Manhattan Life, St. Paul, American Tract, and Municipal buildings. At first the general effect is grotesque, denticulated, a jagged row of teeth, with an isolated superb snag on the Hudson River side. Honeycombed with eyes are all these habitations, eyes that watch the Old World as it enters the New. War from without would mean warring upon marble cliffs. Nineveh had not their match, and on their miles of roofs are gardens which make the description of Babylon childish. What a fabulous entanglement of styles, with structural lines effaced, of bold gross masses, not unlike Benezzo Gozzoli's quaint Babylon. To shut out the overmastering vision you turn your back and the sights of Governor's Island, Ellis Island, and the Goddess of Liberty reassure you. The statue is still as ugly as ever and her torch a menacing club in a mailed fist. It commands: "Work!" Over the portals of Ellis Island might be inscribed — (Dante *à rebours*) — "All despair abandon, ye who enter here" — for New York is not a city of Dis; it is the mouth, the melting-pot of America, and in America there is ever hope for the hopeful.

On days when the wind is benign, the iron-coloured clouds a-curdle, erect steam-plumes cut the sky, the sun stains the waters, then the sinister battlements no longer appal, nor does the city huddled and perched behind them unpleasantly excite the imagination. Again it is atmosphere that tells, atmosphere that makes from the shrill architectural dissonances and lace-like façades a new harmony the diapason of which hums through your consciousness — the muted thunder of New York. Already by virtue of its happy symmetry the Singer tower has caught the tone of time. That its sovereignty of position and height has been wrested from it was to have been expected; implacable to sense of beauty are the needs of a growing city. Let us hope a newer architecture will throw double sixes as has the lucky Singer. I recall the days when Walt Whitman's "mast-hemm'd Manhattan" had an actual meaning. Now it is funnel-encircled Manhattan, and in a few years it may be a Manhattan of aeronauts. Tullio Lombardo, Bernini, and Christopher Wren could not in a triple fantasia evolve such a *pasticcio* as this island town. It stuns. It exalts. It is inconceivable; yet there it stands, unashamed, with its absence of rhythmic architectural values and its massive extravagances.

Up crowded expressive Broadway we go, resolutely avoiding arrests before reincarnations of classic Greece and Rome; before the vision in shallow side streets of public exchanges that would not have shamed the Acropolis; before the gleam of sculptured frieze, golden cornice, Corinthian columns, acanthus wreaths and libertine arabesques. Oh! the pity of it, the pity of Manhattan's shape, with its head of a monster saurian showing from the Jersey side. All this polyphony of steel, stone, and marble is so cramped that it will never sing its glorious music with a free throat. Space has conditioned these structures, as structure has conditioned their material. A breathing-spot formerly was old Trinity Church. Alas! it fights for breath, encompassed by marble giants. Some of them might have been transported from a Brobdingnagian Venice. Their capitals are exquisite, and only these stony precipices pierced by windows tell you where you are. Nevertheless, Trinity, facing Wall Street as it does, retains more than a moiety of its spiritual charm. One might hope that the busy brokers and the hustling little manikins in the streets would halt their chaffering when the quarters chime from the steeple — as halted the mirth-makers in Poe's shuddering tale, The Masque of the Red Death. But no, you hear the lisp and silvery clangour of the bell in the steeple; Wall Street pays no heed. Only the dead in the churchyard receive this benison of tone.

Let us pass on, noting the Trinity and Empire buildings and finding ourselves midgets with upturned dizzy gaze at the foot of the Singer. Ernest Flagg, its architect, has put into practice his theory that the new type of buildings should be pyramidal and terraced at a certain height; the tower, thus set back, gives both light and air to its neighbours as well as to itself. Whether or not a halt will come in the upward progress of this city one dares not say. About 1886, as I remember it, there had been a decided lull in building for some years. A few years later saw a boom, 1900 another; to-day it is difficult to tell

where our Babel will end. Already the Metropolitan Life tower is threatened by the plans
of the nine-hundred-and-nine-foot tower of the
Equitable Life. No sooner are fifty stories
achieved than sixty-two are contemplated. And
what of the projected tower one thousand feet
high of the new Mills Building! Or of that im-
pious proposal to build two thousand feet in the
air! Is the fate of Babel forgotten! Certainly
Mr. Flagg has the root of the matter, for, what
with the crowding of tall structures on narrow
frontages and the increasing risk from fire, the
future comfort and safety of greatest New
York may be problematical. The attempt to
vary the tone of the new buildings is successful.
Terra cotta façades of colourful sorts are employed with enhanced richness, and the purity
of the atmosphere, an Italianate purity, brings
out with a sharp definition the clear lines and
tints of these new structures.

Another breathing-spot, and the City Hall lies
pearl-like in its square. What a joy to gaze upon!
What a cool draught to the spirit parched by the
tophet of stone from which we have emerged!
It is hemmed about by many wonderful structures, the Hall of Records not being the most
beautiful, while the Home Insurance is the most
graceful; not to mention the Municipal Building.
Then follow the wriggling vermicular street and
the white suavities of Grace Church — why
waste time lower down on mediocrities? Union
Square is achieved. Of the far West Side or

the far East Side we need not speak. Our ingenuous friends the sociological novelists and benevolent "slummers" have told us all about the horrors of the East Side. And that distinguished observer, Henry James, has called the Ghetto, Jerusalem Disinfected. He should have chosen rather Tasso's title, Jerusalem Delivered, for on the much despised, little understood, fairly comfortable East Side the Chosen Race is safely anchored. It is natural that the present stupendous New York offends visiting Rip Van Winkles; but the Socialist prophets, why has it failed to please them? What more perfect phalanstery for your latter-day Fourierites than those big buildings housing thousands and tens of thousands! Why doesn't H. G. Wells see that here his dreamer's dreams are come true? Nothing is lacking but the landing-stages, the big aviators, and the "all aboard" for Europe or Asia on the sky-steamers. How long will these be missing? There is also realised his dream of a population toiling in the depths for a privileged few and a unique "boss." Yet the English seer when confronted by actuality was aghast, possibly because the fulfilment of his prophecy appeared in such questionable shapes.

New York is not beautiful in the old order of æsthetics. Its beauty often savours of the monstrous, for the scale is epical. Too many of our buildings are glorified chimneys. But what a picture of titanic energy, of cyclopean ambition, there is if you look over Manhattan from Washington Heights. The wilderness of flat roofs of London, the winning profile of Paris, the fascination of Rome from Trinità dei Monti, of Buda from across the Danube at Pesth: these are not more startling or dramatic than New York; especially when the chambers of the West are filled by the tremulous opal of a dying day, or a lyric moonrise paves a path of silver across the hospitable sea we call our harbour.

II

Union Square is altered beyond recognition. In our town memories like rats are chased away by the ever-rising flood of progress. There is no room for ghosts or landmarks in New York. Thus Union Square to-day is less interesting than that pretty coign, Stuyvesant Park. More vital is Madison Square, with its prow of a bizarre stone snow-plough, the Flatiron-Fuller Building, cleaving its way northward; with the Giralda tower on the Madison Square Garden, St. Gaudens's Diana of the Cross-Currents, and the memory of the cheery old Fifth Avenue Hotel. Badly posed, nevertheless the marble court-house is still a thing of interest. One of the loftiest buildings in New York blots out a section of the eastern sky: the Metropolitan Life Building with its tower. Another campanile! Beautiful it is, not because of its stature — the still loftier Paris Eiffel Tower is an iron scarecrow

— but because of its lines. I watched it from my uptown eyrie while it was being built; saw its long legs and ribs gradually soar into space like one of Wells's Martians on their tripods. Down the vista of Madison Avenue, its side streets barring with sunlight the tracks of the electric cars, the Singer Building lifts out of the ruck and mass of the crowded skyline; the Flatiron strives jealously for first place in the race to the Times Building; but the Metropolitan is the lord of middle New York.

To enjoy the delicate and massive drawing of the Times Building as etched against a southern sky — now ardent, now fire-tipped, jewelled, or swimming in the bewitching breath of a summer's day — one must study it from the north. A silhouette in the evening — and often like a child's church of chalk lighted at Christmas — it flushes rosy in the morning, and during the afternoon the repercussion of the hot sun waves drowns it in an incandescent haze. The fronds of stone ranging below it support this bell-tower as if it were an integral part of them. It, too, aspires northward where the park blooms an emerald oblong. On its pinnacle the city below wears the precise, mapped-out look and checkered image it has from a balloon or pinned on a land-surveyor's chart. What a New York! Clubs that are palaces, hospitals that are cities, palatial theatres and churches more romanesque than Rome or duelling in terms of Gothic with the ecclesiastical masterpieces of the Old World!

NEW PROMENADES

Why linger on the Great White Way or in the luxurious glass houses lining and lighting this slippery, glittering region; a region of mediocre plays, indigestion, headaches, and the moral herring-bone of dry and dusty to-morrows! Rather let us wonder why Washington Square has in part escaped the rage of the iconoclasts. It still looks, on the north side, like an early novel of Mr. James. Some of lower Fifth Avenue is natural. But woe! When you pass north of Fourteenth Street, where are the mansions of yesteryear? The pave over which once passed the trim boots of a vanishing aristocracy now holds a multitude of Yiddish workers from the ugly factories along this part of the avenue, men who talk in a harsh speech and block progress from twelve to one o'clock every week-day. Occasionally Mark Twain, in white and always smoking, goes by, not a phantom but a reality who makes us believe the past was not a nightmare. [I speak of ten years ago.] However, if Mr. Howells can admire the new Rome and take it in tranquil doses, why should we selfishly resent the destruction of our pleasant memories to make way for such alien shapes? Or despair because the Order of the Golden Fleece is rampant in our business and political world? Or grow excited over the anatomy of the new architecture? Let us be thankful that the old stupid *bourgeois* brown-stone will soon be a thing of the past; that the new business houses are seeking a note of individuality in their con-

struction. Nor need we be shocked because of
the anachronism of a pawn-shop under a basil-
ica. This is the New World; older orders are
changing. Why not architecture — and manners, too, in the fierce St. Vitus dance after
the dollars?

Palaces again fill your eye on Fifth Avenue
from Madison Square to the end of the Park.
Jewellers who transact business in the quarters
of a Venetian doge; shopping palaces; book-
sellers that handle an army of books in a space
as vast as a cathedral; banks that look like
Greek temples; hotels — the Waldorf-Astoria,
Astor, Ritz, McAlpin, Vanderbilt, Plaza, Gotham, Savoy, Netherland or St. Regis — that
are on nodding acquaintance in mid-air with
the Belmont, the Astor, the Singer or the Metropolitan buildings. Wander a block westward and
you will encounter a tiny miracle of early Florentine, the Herald Building, a challenge of beauty
to the big prosaic department stores. Ugly but
useful the elevated railways that go spidering
up and down the city; while in its bowels we
spin through a labyrinth, whether to The Bronx
or Jersey or Long Island or the upper West
Side. Another halt after admiring St. Patrick's
Cathedral is enforced before the Vanderbilt
mansion, a vision of an Old World château.
From Sixtieth Street Arcady begins, the Arcady
of multimillionaires and them that go about in
sight-seeing coaches. Pass the Metropolitan
Museum, the obelisk, Mr. Carnegie's comfortable

house; go over to Riverside Drive and from the Soldiers and Sailors Monument look down the river and ask yourself where there is a lovelier or more impressive sight. Or, gazing northward, note that first jut of the Palisades, like the profile of a sullen monster with the river broadening, hurrying, glistening, and the wide fling of the panorama — little wonder your vocabulary makes for extravagance! Sound, colour, form, substance, in what rainbow region is locked the secret of their verbal transposition? We are not overproud of our Palisades. In Germany they would rival the Rhine scenery — but here, in America, we haven't the time to visit them or bestow more than a passing word of praise. The much-mocked Hudson River School of landscape-painters had at least the courage of good taste.

It is a pretty idea to see New York as a symbol either of cruelty, waste, pain, pleasure, or as a haven for the persecuted; in the concrete, not merely the New York of the impressionistic brush, she is tremendous. Yet we may view her symbol-wise if for naught but mental economy. The city lies sprawling encompassed by three rivers, a monstrous Gulliver, overrun by busy Lilliputians who, the surer to subjugate her, have builded bridges about her, making her a part of Long Island and — underneath the river and the gliding and the conquest of boats — of New Jersey. Soon bridges across the open Hudson will make our neighbour State next door. Bridges! Washington, High Bridge, over the Harlem;

Queensboro, Williamsburg, Manhattan, and the Brooklyn bridges across the East River. Yet not enough. Some day both rivers will be spanned by broad-bosomed roadways; New York will have ceased to be an island.

On Sunium's heights, on that enchanted plateau known as the Acropolis of America, where are Columbia University, the Teachers and Barnard colleges, where the Cathedral of St. John the Divine already commands the city — as does the Sacré-Cœur at Paris — we breathe another atmosphere. The sense of greater space, of air untainted, of a *milieu* in which broods the sentiment of the grave and academic, of repose and absence from the strain and roar in the streets beneath — these rare qualities endear the spot to the contemplative mind. The College of the City of New York is a noble group of dark field stone and white terra cotta, the central tower of which burns curiously in the sunlight or fades in the shade of the clouds. And the New York University on University Heights, The Bronx and the Hall of Fame, stir the pulse. Of the Bronx Park, the Speedway, of the immense tracts of developed territory and wide boulevards in upper New York, soon to become the homes of the thousands who jam the subways, surface roads, and elevated railways — a monotonous mob going south in the morning, north at night, a mob of which we are all members — over this region we cannot speculate. We expect some time to see streets and terraces in the air to re-

lieve the crowded surface traffic. Cosmopolis!
A Cosmopolis never dreamed of by Stendhal.

When the softer and richer symphony of the
night arrives, when the jarring of your *ego* by
innumerable racking noises has ceased, when
the city is preparing to forget the toiling day-
time, then the magic of the place begins to operate. That missing soul of New York peeps forth
in the nocturnal transfiguration. Not on Broadway, however, with its thousand lights and lies,
not in opera-houses, theatres, or restaurants, but
on some perch of vantage from which the nocturnal scene in all its mysterious melancholy
beauty may be studied. You see a cluster of
blazing lights at the West Side Circle, a ladder
of fire the pivot. Farther down theatreland
dazzles with its tongues of flame. Literally a
pit, white-hot. Across in the cool shadows are
the level lines of twinkling points of the bridges.
There is always the sense of waters not far away.
All the hotels from the Majestic and Plaza to the
Belmont and Manhattan are tier upon tier starry
with illumination. "The night hath a thousand
eyes" surely applies to Gotham after sundown.
Fifth and Madison Avenues are long shafts of
bluish-white electric globes. The new monoliths
burn, as if to a fire god, votive offerings; while
the Metropolitan tower is furnished with a light
high enough to be seen in New Jersey. Fifth
Avenue mansions seem snow-driven in the moonlight. The synagogue at Seventy-sixth Street
and Fifth Avenue, half Byzantine, half Mo-

resque, as it lies sleeping in the rays of the moonlight might be mistaken for an Asiatic mosque.
The Park, as if liquefied, flows in plastic
rhythms, a lake of velvety foliage, a mezzotint
dividing the East from the West. Sudden fur-
nace bonfires leap up from the Brooklyn side;
they are purely commercial; you look for Whistler's rockets. Battery Place and the Bay are
operatic, the setting for some thrilling fairy spectacle. Oh! the dim scattered plain of granite
house-tops, like some petrified cemetery of immemorial Titans. New York at night loses its
New World aspect; it wears the patina of time.
It is a city exotic, semi-barbaric, the fantasy of
an Eastern sorcerer mad enough to evoke from
forgotten seas the lost Atlantis.

III

It may be pure fancy, but many feel as in no
other spot that the planet upon whose crust we
move and have our being revolves faster under
New York. The tempo of living is swifter, the
pulse beats more rapidly. The tumult and
alarums of the day are more exciting than a cycle
in Cathay — or Paris or London. Vitality is
at its hottest. We are like a colony of ants disturbed by a stranger. We are caught in eddies
and whirlpools and on the edges of foaming
breakers; we are dumped on densely populated
sands. A national mill seizes the newly landed
emigrant and like a sausage-making machine

turns him into a citizen. But it first washes his face; in America cleanliness is next to patriotism. As if they drink from some well of forgetfulness, the newcomers cease to suffer from nostalgia. Money does lie in the streets, despite contradiction, for those who know how to pick it up; at the end of any thoroughfare a fortune may await the bold-hearted. Childe Roland if he came to New York would not be heard, so many other knights are blowing their horns; besides, he would be puzzled to find that Dark Tower. Our surfaces are glittering, hard, boastful; the rhythms of our daily life abrupt, overemphatic. We appear to be seeking some unknown goal, as in the streets we seem to be running to a fire which we never reach. Alternately repellent and hypnotic, New York is often a more stony-hearted mother than the Oxford Street of De Quincey.

Of course it is money New Yorkers are after, that mercenary madness reproved by Europeans though indulged in by them on their arrival here — also on our arrival in Europe. New York is the note dynamic in the world's concert, perhaps too much brass and cymbals for the balance of the orchestra. But overtones count. We sound a few, even if we don't wear our souls on our sleeves. It may be the fault of the climate and perhaps the fault of the millions of people ceded us so freely by Europe; yet the city has a soul, even though it is as yet invisible to European critics. We are not too nice in the conduct

of a clouded cane, though we make good citizens
rapidly. The bite of the salt air is responsible
for our too responsive nerves; sun-bathed half the
year, our very thoughts are coloured by the sun.
We may have too much temperament. We are
more optimistic than London or Paris; optimism
is our natural vice. As in Paris or London you
may step aside here from any of the main-
travelled highways and soon become lost; worse,
you are forgotten. We have not much time for
social intercourse — remember, we speak of the
majority. Individuality is gained, but at the
loss of many desirable things. That is an old
joke, though more fact than fiction, about New
Yorkers living in the same apartment house and
not discovering until years afterward that they
are old friends. There is little leisure to cultivate the minor graces. We fly at our music, at
our theatres and pictures as we fly after a tip on
stocks. We bolt new ideas and invent new relig-
ions every season to match the gowns and hats
of our wives. We swallow Beethoven and cry
What next? Wagner is speedily engulfed and
we cry for Richard Strauss. After he has gone
we try French and Italian sweetmeats. Ibsen
is an old story, Maeterlinck a mere fable. Debussy begins to tire. What next? There must
always be a "next" in New York.

The crowd ever marching on heedless heels
passes in all its motley. Possibly a man with a
green face might make it pause, but we doubt it.
Poor Baudelaire with his hair dyed green would

not have had a chance. Every nationality on the globe traverses our streets — every national-ity, with the native-born New Yorker in the minority. Are there any more New Yorkers? The Italian, Slavic, Hebraic types predominate where once Irish, German, and American ruled.

You can't lounge in a treeless city. The in-tensity of life, its futile intensity, prevents a man from assuming the attitude of a looker on in Vienna. We boast no dilettanti. To catch a glimpse of one's submerged soul one must enter some church where, away from the heat of the race, you can overhear yourself. Do I exag-gerate? But then every one does in New York. It is part of the game to be in a terrible hurry to go somewhere, anywhere out of the quiet. The temper is the ironically gay rather than the cheerfully cynical. You see no old women; no grandmothers make a sweet picture for tired eyes. All the women have grown young; all ex-cept the young women.

There are few timid backwaters left for sen-sitive persons who dislike the glare of modern traffic — backwaters such as you discern in old Chelsea or on the other side of the Seine. Young America insists on eating to the accompaniment of a brass band and in the open market-place. The antique and intimate chop-houses, the half-way uptown stopping-off places, the cosey liquid life-saving stations have been swept away — gone with the crooked streets and beckoning trees. The nuance is missing in our crushing life

— the nuance which alone makes existence tolerable. With an over-developed sense of national continuity we assume ourselves to be "Central" in the cosmos. Ring us up from Persia and we will answer you quicker than a call from Philadelphia; which is a trait of vanity undeniable. On the other hand foreign fault-finders no longer annoy. We may grumble good-naturedly over them, but they are soon forgotten. New York is as terrible as an army with banners for the man who has the desire of the moth for the millionaire. In that she is pragmatic. Work, that you may earn money to spend recklessly! Otherwise go your ways. Yet, despite all our hot zest in the acquisition of money, who really cares for the unimportant millionaire here? An enormous fund of indifference exists at the base of the local consciousness; at times it borders on inhumanity. New York is a Sphinx which always asks questions but forgets to listen to the answer. The Time Spirit sports the guise of a building contractor. In Europe the old humbug and Janus-faced illusionist is supposed to be more poetic. Hydra-headed is this monster as an Asiatic deity, but in America it moulds itself to popular opinion instead of controlling it.

Yes, we lack shadow in our local picture — spiritual shadow; though on the physical plane, as our theosophical brethren would say, there is too much shade — especially in those windy downtown borings called streets. We are all foreground, without much middle distance and hardly any perspective. Our tones are too brilliant, but our national cânvas is sound.

At present our architects have hitched their house to a star. They plan upward. They see their art as a tower, and a city of towers we are bound to become. The *leit-motiven* of the New York architect are wind velocities and bearing strains rather than Attic beauty. His head is figuratively in the clouds. The ideal building is conceived under the rubric of base, shaft, capital; in a word, the tower. Our architecture is stately, graceful, crazy, and mediocre; but whether Palladian or Baroque, or German, English, or French Renaissance, modified Gothic or like the eclectic abbey of Prester John, it is as it must be. A hundred styles are in the air clamouring for recognition; a reckless architectural improvision, heaven-storming at times, evokes the image of a demon-like Rops's Sower or of that frolicsome devil from Madrid called Asmodeus, who stalks across the island dropping here a note, there a chord, here a scale, there an arpeggio, the full fulminating battery; yet when the smoke and noise made by his dissonant splinters of tone clear away we discern a strange harmony in the scattered designs. So it is with our city — ugly, heterogeneous, disquieting, and huge.

And since the foregoing was written, a few years ago, what changes! The Woolworth structure, tallest of all; the two magnificent stations of the Pennsylvania and New York Central railways; the Municipal building; the new Po-

lice Headquarters; the New, now the Century,
Theatre; new bridges, new hotels; the night
skyline, too, how it has altered so that no municipal spectacle in Europe can vie with the
vast numbers of lights atop of hotels, theatres,
in the parks, on the bridges, and blazing in
open squares. The Art Museum has a new front-
age. The obverse side of the picture is the daily
destruction of venerable buildings, the trans-
formation of private residences, literally palaces,
into hideous loft buildings, and the consequent
spoiling of that once royal street, Fifth Avenue,
now become the strolling ground for an anonymous herd of toilers from the Old World.

Notwithstanding its exuberance, its crudities
and cruelties, this city is the core of the universe for those who have once submitted to her
sorceries. And might not James Russell Lowell
have meant New York when he sang:

"Strange new world, that yit wast never young,

. . . .

Nussed by stern men with empires in their brains."

IV

ENGLISH MASTERS IN THE COLLECTION
OF JOHN HOWARD McFADDEN

The psychology of the art collector has been
studied by great writers from Balzac to Henry
James. Benvenuto Cellini wrote himself down a

virtuoso as well as a scoundrel in his incomparable memoirs, and we recall a half-forgotten tale
by Philip Hale (not the painter, but the music-
critic of Boston) in which a sort of Jack the
Ripper figures as a passionate amateur of art.
Murder and suicide as fine arts have had their
possibilities exploited by De Quincey and Robert
Louis Stevenson. Balzac's collectors are either
semi-maniacs or demi-idiots; the Frenchman
always believed in high lights and heavy shadows. In the many stories of Mr. James which
delineate collectors these personages are for the
most part natural and reasonable. Each one has
his particular *tic*, but he does not wear his mania
abroad. Nevertheless the lover of art is a normal
being. He should not be classed among those we
call in America "cranks." If he buys from sheer
vanity there are worse ways of parting a fool from
his money. If he collects from sheer love of a
master, as does nowadays M. Pellerin in Paris,
or of a period, like Archer M. Huntington, then
he is to be envied. Such collections as the Mor-
gan, the Frick, the John G. Johnson are catholic
in their variety; different schools are represented.
Such a collection as that of John Howard
McFadden, of Philadelphia, is small, choice,
and aims at the assemblage of one school. To
have succeeded thoroughly in one thing is to
have achieved success. Mr. McFadden ought
to be a happy man. He has succeeded in his
artistic adventure. We once declared, we hope
not cynically, that in the heart of every collector

there might be found a bargain counter. But this Philadelphia collector is an exception.

He lives in his own gallery, the pictures of which are practically scattered over the walls of his home facing Rittenhouse Square, and few men enjoy the companionship of beloved canvases more than he. We dislike that smug phrase of the art dealer who, after showing you some sentimental smudge, insinuatingly adds: "Ah! Now there's a picture you could live with," meaning that its poor, puling colour and outlines will not offend the eye simply because they make no impression upon the retinal memory. Show the average potential picture purchaser a strong, a masculine work of art and he shivers. What, he asks himself, that harsh, ugly Manet on my walls, hanging near my beloved Bouguereau or my Jules Breton? Never! And my new pink draperies — the harmony of my drawing-room would be destroyed for ever. This type of collector is quite right in his surmise. Manet, a taste for whom is a touchstone for imbeciles, brings a breath of fresh air into those abodes of musk-scented art. Millet earlier in the century aroused the same protest. He was too natural and loved powerful uneducated shepherds instead of Venuses or Madonnas painted in cold cream with a fat voluptuous brush; or else the eternal tittle-tattle anecdotage of the studio genre picture. The impressionists met with the same reception, and as to-day they are already "old hat" the neo-impressionists are become the sacrificial goats of contemporary art. The truth is that you can live near all good art and literally grow with it as you understand and love it.

Now we do not know whether Mr. McFadden cares very much for latter-day manifestations in paint, but we assume he does not from the very nature of his beautiful collection of English masters. He frankly avers that he does not understand early Florentine and that there is much in Whistler that does not appeal to him. Some Celtic blood in him makes him more at home with the characters of Sir Walter Scott or Sir Joshua Reynolds than with those of Dante or Botticelli. So you are not surprised to find in his dining-room a famous canvas by Turner, the Burning of the House of Parliament, which was shown here for a short time at the Knoedler Galleries. It is one of the masterpieces of the great Englishman and not in his rotten-ripe manner; the incandescent conflagration, the bridge, the river are in Turner's opulent vein. How much French impressionism owes him, beginning with Monticelli and not yet ended, may be noticed in this work. The new McFadden Raeburn, dated 1756, is a portrait of Master John Campbell of Saddell, a youth said to have possessed a genius for lightning calculation. Another novelty is a large landscape by John Linnell showing a storm about to break over a heath; the lightning zigzags down the threatening sky, some belated people accompanied by a dog are rushing to shelter, the animal well in the van. An honest work of a conscientious artist.

But the Gainsborough landscape in the centre of the room is something far better. Characteristic Gainsborough, it is almost matched in interest by George Morland's Manchester Coach, though not quite. Miss Nelthorpe and Miss West, depicted by Sir Thomas Lawrence, do not exhaust the treasures of this room, for over a door is a study by Romney of Lady Hamilton, one of the many — there are said to be forty-six pictures of her — he hastily brushed in, an inspired presentment, not lacking a touch of the tragic with the flying locks, eyes dramatically upturned, the modelling firm and sweet. We have seen other presentments of this friend of Nelson, but few more sincere or more skilful.

Around the halls, which could house a church, we note two tall William Dobsons, a Richard Wilson, a lifelike bust portrait of Sir Walter Scott by Sir J. Watson Gordon, Romney's John Wesley, the head and face of whom, with its gentle, meek expression, might pass for Abbé Fénelon's; a dashing Raeburn, a Lawrence and the portrait of Edmund Burke by Reynolds. You encounter two David Coxes of fine quality on the way to the library, in which latter place you will be embarrassed by riches. There hangs the sumptuous Constable entitled The Lock, a glorious reproach to certain experts who have labelled an inferior copy in this city as a genuine Constable; there is an old Crome of rare interest, The Blacksmith Shop, near Hingham, Norfolk, exhibited 1808 in London. Mrs. Dorothy Champigny-Crespigny is portrayed by Romney, and there is Lady Rodney by Gainsborough, also Mrs. Crouch by Romney; Lawrence and Copley are in this mellow concert of singing canvases. And remember, in reeling off these names so glibly we do not mean the Raeburns, Romneys, Gainsboroughs, Lawrences, Sir Joshuas, or Turners of commerce. Every example is a masterpiece. Mr. McFadden has guarded his Old World prejudice in favour of quality over quantity.

He has converted his drawing-room into a portrait gallery, and the presence of a Steinway Grand pianoforte suggests the idea of Franz Liszt, who once declared that his ambition was to give a concert in the Salon Carré of the Louvre, where amid the questioning glances of the Da Vinci, the Giorgione, the Rembrandt, the Titian, the Paolo Veronese, the Raphael, and other miraculous creations he would discourse as equally miraculous music. But in the McFadden gallery a pianist would be restricted to playing the music of a single school; neither Beethoven, Wagner, Chopin, nor Schumann would be wholly appropriate. Rather John Bull, Gray, Byrd, Gibbons, Arne, Tallis, Purcell, above all the noble and ever-fresh piano music of Handel — the gravely graceful dance suites; the menuetto sarabande, courante gigue, passacaille, chaconne, allemande, and not forgetting the fire-fugue for the Turner — would interpret the stately coquetries, the delicate attitudes, the delicious archness of these

English belles and beaux of by-gone days.
There are two Hogarths recently acquired, A
Conversation at Wanstead House, rich and
slightly sombre in tone, and a portrait group,
the Fontaine Family. Hoppner is represented
by the portrait of Miss Stamper and one of his
wife, that might have been painted yesterday,
so in the mode is it, with its lyrical blues and
whites. An unfamiliar master is George Henry
Harlow (1787–1819), a follower of Sir Thomas,
but not a slavish one, as the portrait of a mother
with her children proves. She is a Mrs. Weddell,
and the picture is extremely brilliant. Lady
Elband by Raeburn, Lady Belhaven by the
same, Miss Finch and Miss Nicholl by Romney
gaze down at you with the veiled vivacity or
sweet disdain these masters knew the secret of
imparting to their subjects. But the clou of the
gathering is Master Bunbury, by Reynolds, a
masterpiece in miniature, for it is not a large
canvas, the paint of a lovely richness, the
theme treated in a human fashion without the
accustomed rhetoric of the sometimes pompous
Reynolds. Certainly this time the son stood still
when Joshua commanded.

V

HOW WIDOR PLAYED AT ST. SULPICE

Of course I don't mean an entire night at
Maxim's, because the place isn't alive until mid-

night. It closes its doors at dawn or mid-day just
as circumstances order. I was sitting in the par-
terre at the Grand Opéra when Churchill crowded
past me. His name isn't Churchill, but it will do
here. He is a young American composer studying in Paris. He had the orchestral score of La
Valkyrie under his arm, so I rejoiced when he
sat beside me. I never knew how absurd Wagner could be when Gallicised, so naturally enough
I was thirsty after the curtain fell, leaving
Brunhilda automatically sleeping on the steam-
and-fire rocks of Walkuere-Land, with Wotan
humming sonorously in the middle distance.
Back of the Opéra, just at the junction of the
streets called Gluck and Halévy, is the Café
Monferino. Therein may be discovered the
best Pilsner beer in all Paris — this was in
1896. Naturally I discovered the beer when
I had been in this delectable town a few hours,
so I asked Churchill if he was athirst. He said
he was, and soon the beer of Bohemia was
before us in big steins. For two hours we
talked Wagnerian *tempi*, and it was two hours
after midnight when we were told that no more
beer could be procured.

"Let's go to Maxim's," said Churchill.

"Any place in Paris," I answered, meaning
any place where recollections of Wagner could be
drowned in amber, as is the fly of fable. So we
drove to the Rue Royale and to Maxim's, which
is not far from the Place de la Concorde. As we
forced our powerful personalities through a mob

of men, women, waiters, and crashing, furious music I said:

"Lo, art thou in Arcady!"

Churchill, who knew the place well, soon spied a table surrounded by a gang of young fellows all yelling: "Constant, Constant!" I wasn't foolish enough to fancy that this combination of imprecation and cajolement meant an adjective, yet I couldn't at first locate Constant. I was speedily introduced to six of my countrymen, hailing mostly from New York, and after solemnly bowing and staring suspiciously at their friend Churchill, they quite as solemnly shook hands one with the other, and yelled in unison: "Constant!" And again I rejoiced, for I knew in my heart that I had met the right sort.

Then appeared Constant, known to all good Americans, and as he bowed his round, sleek head for the order, I tried to untangle the fritilant delirium about me. In front of me waltzed furiously a red-headed woman who looked as if Chéret had just thought her out on a big salacious poster. She sprawled, and she slid in midair as the Hungarian band played vertiginously. The red-headed one had in tow a small fellow whose eyes bulged with joy and ambition. He possessed the largest lady in the building, and what more could one expect? The Hungarian band was wonderful. It ripped and buzzed with rhythmic rubato rage, and tore Wagner passion to tatters. It leered, sang, swooned, sighed, snarled, sobbed, and leapt. Its leader, a dark

gipsy with a wide, bold glance, swayed as he
smote the strings with his bow, and I was quite
hurt when he went about afterward, plate in
hand, collecting thankful francs. At tables sat
women and men and women. The moral tone
was scarlet, but the toilettes were admirable.
Occasionally there strayed in a party of tourists,
generally British. They fled in a moment if they
had their women folk with them; yet I saw nothing actually objectionable. The whole establishment simply overflowed with good-humoured
devilry, and there was that scarlet moral tone; it
was unmistakably scarlet, and as the night wore
apace it became a rich carmilion!

Churchill suddenly cried aloud and our table
ceased singing.

"Let's get a room with a piano."

"Constant, Constant!" we howled, and soon
the active, indispensable Constant conducted us
up-stairs to a furnished apartment, in which stood
a mean-looking upright piano. Beer had become
a watery nuisance, so champagne was ordered,
and my voice trembled as I gave the order, for I
knew Young America in Paris — and we had already absorbed enough to float a three-masted
schooner. Constant left us with a piteous re-
quest not to awake Napoleon in his stony palace
across the river, and then Master Churchill, who
is an organist, sat down to the instrument, and
without any unnecessary preluding began playing — what do you suppose?

Oh, only negro melodies, and those boys

started in to sing and dance with frantic and national emotion. A bearded fellow, who wore his hair and whiskers *à la* Capoul, sang Irish songs with an accent that any song and dance comedian of Tony Pastor's would have envied. He is a pupil of the Beaux Arts, but it was his Saturday night off, and he proposed to spend it in American fashion. Two young men students at the Sorbonne got together and "said" some cold, classic things from Racine, but broke into a wild jig when sounded the stirring measures of that sweet African lyric, " My Gal, My Gal, I'm Goin' for to See."

We fought double-handed. We improvised tugs of war with a richly brocaded table-cloth serving as a rope. We galloped, we pranced, and we upset furniture, and every time a dark-eyed boy said in a fragile voice: "Oh, I want to dance," we smothered him in the richly brocaded table-cloth. It was not a time for blandishments, but the hour for stern, masculine rioting; and accordingly we rioted. I have since marvelled at the endurance of Churchill who braved the ivory teeth and cacophonous bark of a peculiarly evil French piano. Once when I asked him to resign his post and give my aching fingers a chance he refused. But he was pulled from his place and a magnum of wine poured down his neck. Then I sat down and started, bravely, with a Study of Chopin. Darkness supervened, as I was ruthlessly lassoed by that awful avenging table-cloth and dragged over the floor by the strong

arms of seven Americans. I long nursed three
violet-coloured bruises, a triple testimony to the
Chopin-hating phalanx of the Beaux Arts and
Sorbonne.

We relaxed not for a second in our athletic endeavours to chase merriment around the clock.
After more big and cold bottles a new psychical phase manifested itself. For rage and war's
alarums was substituted a warm, tender sentimentalism. We cried to the very heavens that
we were all jolly good fellows and that no one
dared deny. Constant came up a half-dozen
times to deny it; but corks, crackers, napkins,
and vocal enthusiasm drove him from the room.
Only when the two young men from the Sorbonne went out upon the balcony and informed,
in stentorian tones, the budding dawn and a lot
of coachmen that France was a poor sort of a
place and America God's own country, then did
the counsels of the trusty Constant prevail and
order temporarily restored. But the glimpse of
awkward daylight told on our nocturnal nerves.
Our inspiration flagged and a beer thirst set in,
and beer meant dissolution; some among us
were no lovers of the fruit which grows in brew-
eries; besides the pace began to tell. Our maes-
tro Churchill came to the rescue. Drinking a
celery glassful of wine he sat down at the little
dog-house — I mean the piano — and began
with deep feeling those mystically intense measures of the prelude to Tristan and Isolde. Another psychical storm arose. The jesting, hulla-

balooing, rough horseplay ceased, and a genuine delirium set in. Wagner's music is for some people emotional catnip at times. These boys wriggled and chanted, and enjoyed to the full the opium-charged harmonies.

Wagner was our Waterloo.

Maxim will stand anything but Wagner. Churchill proved a master trance-medium, and as six o'clock sounded we tumbled down-stairs and into the daylight. Eight American citizens blinked like owls and a half-hundred coachmen hovered about them. It was a lovely Sunday morning. Huge blocks of sunlight, fanned by soft breezes, slanted up the Rue Royale from the Place de la Concorde. A solitary woman stood in the shadow of a doorway. Her elaborate hat, full of fantastic dream-flowers, threw her face into shade. Her costume was rich, her style Parisian. She stood in shadow and waited. Her eyes were black wells of regard and her mouth sullen, cruel, crimson. Her jaw was animal and I faintly recalled the curious countenance with its blending of two races. (Ah! how sinister this sounded ten years ago.)

"It is the Morocco Woman," said one of the boys.

It is the "Woman from Morocco," they all repeated shudderingly and we moved across the street. I never discovered who she was, this mysterious and sinister Woman of Morocco. (Probably some *bonne* going to church.)

After two of the crowd narrowly escaped arrest for trying to steal a sentry-box we tumbled into

a carriage and told the driver to seek for beer,
anywhere, any place, at any cost, beer. The
Madeleine looked grey and classically disdainful as we turned into the Grand Boulevard, and
in the full current of the sunshine we lifted up
our voices on the summer air and told all Paris
how happy were we. At Julian's we stopped.
Up two heavily carpeted flights of stairs we
travelled to find only banality. There were a
few belated night-hawks who preened as we
entered, but we were Sons of Morning and sought
not the Aviaries of the Night. No beer, but lots
of coffee. Of course we scorned such chicory
advances and once more reached the open after
numerous expostulations. Our coachman, who
had been with us since we left the Café Monferino, began to show signs of wear and tear.
He had had a drink every quarter of the hour.
Yet did he not weaken, only whispered to me
that every place except the churches was bolted,
and this too, despite the fact that the name of
Raines had not been heard in the land. We had
melted from eight to six not absolutely reliable
persons, so we hated to give in. After some
meditation the coachman called out encouraging words to his rusty old horse and then I lost
my bearings, for we drove up side streets, into
back alleys leading into other back alleys, down
tortured defiles and into empty, open, clattering
squares. At last we reached a café bearing in its
fore-front the information that the establishment was a rendezvous for coachmen.

Alas! it was too late to pick our company; besides, our withers were still unwrung and the general sentiment of the crowd was that to the devil justly belonged the hindmost. We pell-melled into the building and found, indeed, a choice gathering. Coachmen, cocottes, broken-down English and Americans, the rag-tag and bob-tail, the veriest refuse of Parisian humanity found we, and our entrance was received with a shout. Degraded Paris knew a "good thing" when it hove into view. We looked like a " good thing," but we weren't; we were quite exclusive. After we had treated every lost soul in the place twice over we sobered up, and one scion of America made the original remark:

"I never knew that Paris held so many thirsty people before."

I don't believe that it ever did, so we manfully squared financial matters, and after fighting off the preluding of twenty-nine awful persons we escaped out of doors. There our coachman, who had succumbed, introduced us to an old boot-black from Burgundy, who had wept, laughed, and fought with the First Consul. We believed all he said for ten centimes, and with another View Hallo! drove down an anonymous alley, cheered to the zenith by the most awful crew of blackguards ever dreamed of by Balzac. But the sun set us thinking of life and its duties. One man spoke of his mother, another of a break-fast with an impossible cousin. Then Churchill reminded me of an engagement that I seemed to have made years ago. It was relative to hearing the great organist, Widor, play at St. Sulpice and at the eleven o'clock service that very day. It was only eight o'clock and of course it was an easy engagement to keep. Churchill left us and I was foolish enough to say that I had a letter of introduction in my pocket to a young American architect living in the Latin Quarter.

"Name, name!" was cried. I gave it, and a roar was the response.

"Why didn't you say so before? He lives in our house. We'll drive there at once." We did.

Never to my dying day shall I forget that introduction. We were five strong, and there lived on the fifth floor of the apartment to which I was escorted about sixteen young architects. I can swear positively that two young men bearing the same name as my letter of introduction arose to salute me, although the crowd only spoke of one person. Perhaps it was the result of atmospheric refraction, some beery Parisian mirage. The devils in whose company I found myself went from bed to bed shouting:

"Hello, old son, here is a man from New York with a letter from your brother," and many pairs of pajamas got out of drugged slumber bowing sleepily but politely.

All lovely things must end, and soon I found myself in front of the Gare Montparnasse, talking to a trainman about comparative wage-earning in Paris and Philadelphia, and then I hailed a carriage and drove across the river to the Café Pilsen, for I was thirsty and the day still young.

The café was closed, and I suddenly remembered
that engagement to hear Widor. My watch told
me of two hours in which to dress and furbish
up my morals. Home I went and took a short
nap, for I had made up my mind to hear the
great Widor at St. Sulpice. Then I awoke with
a guilty tongue and a furred conscience. It was
quite dark and eleven o'clock precisely.

But just twelve hours too late for Widor, and
I was hungry, and I went forth into the night
blinking with the lights of cabs, and as I ate I
regretted exceedingly the engagement I had
missed with Churchill, and I regretted, exceedingly, not having heard the Great Widor of St.
Sulpice.

VIII

THE CELTIC AWAKENING

IRELAND

"Ireland, oh Ireland! Centre of my longings,
  Country of my fathers, home of my heart!
Over seas you call me: *Why an exile from me?*
  Wherefore sea-severed, long leagues apart?

"As the shining salmon, homeless in the sea depths,
  Hears the river call him, scents out the land,
Leaps and rejoices in the meeting of the waters,
  Breasts weir and torrent, nests him in the sand;

"Lives there and loves, yet, with the year's returning,
  Rusting in the river, pines for the sea,
Sweeps back again to the ripple of the tideway,
  Roamer of the waters, vagabond and free.

"Wanderer am I like the salmon of the rivers;
  London is my ocean, murmurous and deep,
Tossing and vast; yet through the roar of London
  Comes to me thy summons, calls me in sleep.

"Pearly are the skies in the country of my fathers,
  Purple are thy mountains, home of my heart.
Mother of my yearning, love of all my longings,
  Keep me in remembrance, long leagues apart."
                                —STEPHEN GWYNN.

How dewy is the freshness and exquisite
flavour of the newer Celtic poetry, from the more
ambitious thunders of its epics to its tenderest

219

lyric leafage! It has been a veritable renascence. Simultaneously, there burst forth throughout Ireland a trilling of birdlike notes never before heard, and the choir has become more compact and augmented. Fiona Macleod told in luscious, melting prose her haunting tales; beautiful Dora Sigerson sang of the roses that fade; Katharine Tynan-Hinkson achieved at a bound the spun sweetness of music in her Larks.

> "I saw no staircase winding, winding,
>   Up in the dazzle, sapphire and binding,
>   Yet round by round, in exquisite air,
>   The song went up the stair."

A pure ravishment of the ear this lyric. Lionel Johnson, an Irish Wordsworth, intoned graver harmonies; Nora Hopper caught the lilt of the folk on the hillside with her Fairy Fiddler; Douglas Hyde, a giant in learning, fearlessly wrote his poems in Erse, challenging with their sturdy splendour the ancient sagas; George Moore made plays with W. B. Yeats; Edward Martyn his Maieve, Heather Field; Mr. Yeats his Countess Cathleen; Fiona Macleod The Hour of Beauty, and Alice Milligan a piece founded on the stirring adventures of Diarmuid and Grania.

Some English critics who went over to Dublin were amazed at the many beauties of this new literature, a literature rooted in the vast, immemorial *Volkslied* of Erin. Then Lady Gregory published her translation of Cuchullain of Muirthemne, and we saw that as Wagner sought for rejuvenation of the music-drama in the Icelandic sagas, so these young Irishmen, enthusiastically bent upon recreating a national literature, went to the very living sources, the poetic "meeting of the waters," for their inspiration. Dr. Douglas Hyde was, and is, the very protagonist of the movement, though its beginnings may be detected in the dark, moody lyrics of James Clarence Mangan, in the classic lines of William Allingham.

Matthew Arnold spoke of the "Celtic natural magic" inherent in the great poetry of England. Here we get it in all its sad and sunny perfections from the woodnote wild of Moira O'Neill to the beautiful phrases of Yeats. The Celt and the Sarmatian are alike in their despairing patriotism, their preference for the melancholy minor scale of emotion, their sudden alternations of sorrow and gayety, defiance and despair. And the Irishman, like the Polish man, is often merry at heart even when his song has cadences dripping with mournfulness. We hear it in the Chopin mazurkas, the really representative music of Chopin, and we hear it in those doleful tunes sung by the Irish peasantry. Even their expressive "keening," touching, as it does, the rock-bed of earthly calamity, can be turned to a rollicking lay with a mere inflection. The Slav and Celt are alike — they fall from heaven to hell in a moment, though they always live to tell the tale.

What Celt whose feet are set in alien streets

can hear unmoved the plaintive Corrymeela of Moira O'Neill?

> "Over here in England, I'm helpin' wi' the hay
> An' I wisht I was in Ireland the livelong day;
> Weary on the English hay, an' sorra take the wheat!
> *Och! Corrymeela an' the blue sky over it.*"

And the singer varies the refrain with "Corrymeela an' the low south wind," "Sweet Corrymeela an' the same soft rain," until you feel the heart-throb of the lonely exile, and Corrymeela with its patch of blue sky, out of which the Irish rain pours — for even the rain is witty in Ireland — becomes the one desirable spot on the globe. Here is a veritable poetic counterblast to Robert Browning's "Oh, to be in England, now that April's there."

And "A. E.," who is George W. Russell in the flesh — what a flame-like spirit, a pantheist who adores Dana the mother of the gods with the consuming ardour of a Roman Catholic before the image of Our Lady. He can sing:

> "In the dusk silver sweet,
> Down the violet-scented ways
> As I moved with quiet feet
> I was met by mighty days."

And you hear as in a murmuring shell the music of Keats, Verlaine, and — Ireland. Russell is a true poet.

This same Celtic melancholy, with an heroic quality rare since the legendary days and all

222

welded into music, lyric, symphonic, and dramatic, is to be found in the work of William Butler Yeats. From the Wind Among the Reeds to The Seven Woods, from the Wanderings of Oisin — incomparable in its lulling music, truly music that like Oisin's eyes is "dull with the smoke of their dreams" — to that touching Morality, The Hour Glass — all of Mr. Yeats's poems and plays create the feeling that we are in the presence of a singer whose voice and vision are new, whose voice and vision are commensurate with the themes he chants. Above all he arouses the image in us of a window, like Keats's magic casement opening upon perilous seas and strange vistas wherein may be discovered the cloudy figures of Deirdre, Dana, Cuchullain, Diarmuid, and Grania; Bran moves lazily in the mist, and in the threatening storm-clouds we see the dim shape of Aoife, the best beloved woman of that mighty chieftain Cuchullain, who slew the son of her body and his own loins. This window is the poet's own; it commands his particular domain in the land of dreams; and what more dare we ask of a poet than the sharing of his vision, the sound of his voice?

The esoteric quality of Yeats comes out more strongly in the prose stories. A mystic, with all a mystic's sense of reality — Huysmans declares that the mystic is the most practical person alive — Yeats has dived deeply into the writings of the exalted, from Joachim of Flora to Jacob Boehme, from St. Teresa to William Blake.

We recall several of his tales, particularly The Tables of the Law, Rosa Alchemica, The Binding of the Hair. Especially notable are his contributions to Blake criticism, so rare that Charles Algernon Swinburne alone preceded him in the field.

Nor shall we soon forget the two poems in Windle Straws, or the rhythmic magnificence of The Shadowy Horses: "I hear the shadowy horses, their long manes a-shake, their hoofs heavy with tumults, their eyes glimmering white"; or the half-hidden charm of O'Sullivan Rua to the Secret Rose. Pagan? Yes, pagan all of them in their keen devotion to sky and water, grass and brown Mother Earth. Yeats seems to be uttering one long chant of regret for the vanished gods, though like Heinrich Heine, his gods are but "in exile." They peep from behind the bulrush and timorously hide in the calyx of the flower; they are everywhere, in the folds of the garrulous old woman, in the love-light of the girl's black eyes. Ireland is fairly paved with fairies, and Yeats tells us of them in his sweet, languorous poetic speech.

One is struck not so much with the breadth of his work as with its depth and intensity. The Celt is narrow at times — but he touches the far stars, though his feet are plunged in the black waters of the bogs. The vision of Yeats approaches more nearly that of a seer. He sees visions. He is exalted by the sight of the fringe on some wandering god's garment. And he relates to us in naïve accents his fear and his joy at the privilege. After a carnival of Realism, when the master-materialists were defining the limits of space, when Matter and Force were crowned on the throne of reason, suddenly comes this awakening of the spiritual, comes first to Belgium, spreads to France, then to Ireland. After solid brick and mortar — to quote Arthur Symons — the dreams multi-coloured and tragic of poets! It has been called pre-Raphaelism, symbolism, neo-Catholicism, and what not— it is but the human heart crying for other and more spiritual fare than the hard bread of reality.

The Irish Independent Theatre has its literary organs in *Beltaine*, in *Samhain*, and other publications edited by Mr. Yeats. Therein one learns of its ideals, of its accomplished work. The Countess Cathleen was first acted in 1899 at the Antient Concert Rooms in Dublin. Mr. Martyn's The Heather Field and Mr. Moore's admirable play The Bending of the Bough, and Mr. Yeats's Diarmuid and Grania, were, with plays by Dr. Hyde and several others, successfully produced.

Yeats says: "Our daily life has fallen among prosaic things and ignoble things, but our dreams remember the enchanted valleys." He remembers his dreams, tenuous as they sometimes are, and many of them troubled. As he has grown, the contours of his work are firmer, the content weightier. A comparison of The Land of Heart's Desire and On Baile's Strand will prove this.

One is the stuff out of which visions are woven; the other, despite its slight resemblances to Maeterlinck — notably at the close, when the fool tells the blind man of the drama — is of heroic mould. The mad king thrusting and slashing at the tumbling breakers, after he has discovered that he has slain his own son, is a figure of antique and tragic stature. We hear more of the musician, the folk-lorist, the brooding Rosicrucian — is Yeats not his own Michael Robartes? — in the earlier verse; but in this image of hero and king quite as insane as Xerxes and Canute, we begin to feel the dramatic potentiality of the young Irish poet. In The Hour Glass there is a note of faith hitherto absent.

The artistic creeds of Mr. Yeats are clearly formulated in his collection of prose essays, Ideas of Good and Evil — a very Nietzsche-like title. In this book Blake and Nietzsche are happily compared. We learn what he thinks of the theatre, of the Celtic elements in literature, of "the emotion of multitude," and there is a record of the good work of Mr. Benson and his company at Stratford-on-Avon. One idea, among a thousand others, is worthy of quotation. In speaking of Matthew Arnold and his phrase, "the natural magic of the Celt," Mr. Yeats writes: "I do not think he understood that our 'natural magic' is but the ancient worship of nature and that troubled ecstasy before her, that certainty of all beautiful places being haunted, which is brought into men's minds." The thirst for the unfounded emotion and a wild melancholy are troublesome things in this world, sighs the poet.

He believes that France has everything of high literature except the emotion of multitude, the quality we find in the Greek plays with their chorus. The Shakespearian drama gets the emotion of multitude out of the sub-plot, which copies the main plot. Ibsen and Maeterlinck get it by creating a new form, "for they get multitude from the Wild Duck in the attic, or from the Crown at the bottom of the Fountain, vague symbols that set the mind wandering from idea to emotion, emotion to emotion." Mr. Yeats finds French dramatic poetry too rhetorical — "rhetoric is the will trying to do the work of the imagination" — and the French play too logical, too well ordered.

It is dramatic technique, however, that counts in the construction of a play. All the imagination in the world, all the poetic dreams, are naught if the architectural quantity be left out. I find Mr. Yeats's plays full of the impalpable charm — he almost makes the invisible visible! — we catch in Chopin, Chopin in one of his evanescent secret moods. But place these shapes of beauty out from the dusk of dreams, place them before "the fire of the footlights," and they waver and evaporate. Mr. Yeats and his associates must carve their creations from harder material than lovely words, lovely dreams. To be beautiful upon the stage, with a spiritual beauty, is a terrible, a brave undertaking. Maeterlinck dared to be so; so did Ibsen — though his is the beauty of characterisation. Mr. Yeats would mould from the mist his humans. In the acted drama this is impossible. Shakespeare himself did not accomplish the feat, because, being in all matters a realist, a practical man of the theatre, he did not attempt it. His dreams are always realised.

Mr. William Archer has written of the movement: "The Irish drama possesses a true and — why should we shrink the word — a great poet in Mr. Yeats; but as yet it has given us only dramatic sketches — no thought-out picture with composition and depth in it. . . . The characters stand on one plane, as it were on the shallow stage, always in a more or less irregular row, never in an elaborate group. The incidents succeed one another in careful and logical gradation, but have no complexity of interrelation. They form a series, not a system."

JOHN M. SYNGE

The early death of a lyric poet is not a loss without compensation, for birds sing sweetest when young; but with a dramatic poet the case is altered. Perhaps Keats and Shelley would have given the world profounder music, music with fundamental harmonies; we are rich with the legacies they left. The deaths of Schubert and Chopin may not have been, for the same reason, such irreparable misfortunes. The disappearance of John M. Synge from the map of life ten years earlier would have spelled nothing to the world, his death ten years hence might have found us in possession of half a dozen greater plays than the slim sheaf of six he left us when he passed away a few weeks ago at Dublin. A dramatist must know life as well as art: those "little mirrors of sincerity" which are the heart of the lyricist must in a play mirror the life exterior before they can stir us to the core. Life, life felt and seen and sung, these are the true architectonics of great drama; all the rest is stagecraft. Now John Synge was a poet who spoke in clear, rich-fibred prose. The eternal *wanderlust* that was in men like Bamfylde-Moore Carew and George Borrow also stung the blood of Synge. He had the gipsy scholar temperament. He went about France and Germany, and in his beloved Aran Islands his fiddle was the friend of the half-wild peasantry. He was not thirty-eight when he died, yet he left behind him the sound of his voice, the voice of a large, sane soul — both the soul of a dreamer and the man of action who is the dramatist. His taking off before his prime means much to Irish literature, though happily his few days suffice for the consecration of his genius.

The chemistry which transmuted experience into art will doubtless be analysed by his future biographers. His life was simple — simplicity was the key-note of the man. He loved litera-

ture, but he loved life better. He was not of the
decadent temperament; he was too robust of
body and spirit to be melancholy, nor did he
ever, on the absinthe slopes of Montmartre,
grasp for the laurels of the "moderns." His
friend Yeats has written: "Synge was essentially an orderly man with unlimited indul-
gence for the disorderly." He did contemplate
a career devoted to criticism. His favourite French writer was Racine — we are far re-
moved here from the decadence — but luckily
Yeats persuaded his young countryman to return to Ireland, there to write of the people and
the land from which he sprang. Seldom has
advice borne better results. Synge went to the
Aran Islands, off the coast of Galway, and in a
book of rare interest and vast naïveté gave us a
series of pictures that may be considered the
primal sketches for his plays. Though The Aran
Islands was published in 1907 it is a record dating
back several years. Over the Western country
he went afoot, living in the cabins, talking by
the wayside with the old men and the girls, and
drawing his bow for the couples dancing. He
loved the people, and his eye was not the measuring eye of the surgeons we expect from novelists and dramatists.

Synge was neither a symbolist nor a man with
a message. His symbols are the sea, the sky, and
the humans who lead the hard, bitter lives of a
half-ruined land, bankrupt of nearly all else except its dreams. Your reformer who puts plays

on the stage to prove something is only half an artist, no matter what his wit or the justice of his cause.

But in the Synge plays "sweet Corrymeela an' the same soft rain" does not interest him as do the words of the headstrong girl by the hedge who wants to marry the tinker; or the blind pair of tramps whose vision returns and with their sight a hell of disappointment; or the passionate woman of the glen, whistling for her lover, or the riders to the sea, scooper of graves. Human emotions, the more elemental the better, are for Synge the subject-matter of his cameo carved work. He is mindful of technique; he learned the art in France; he can fashion a climax with the best of them. There are no loose ends. His story moves from the first to the last speech. Eminently for the footlights, these tiny dramas may be read without losing their essential thrill. Beauty and terror within the frame of homely speech and homely actions are never lost sight of; and what different men and women are Synge's when compared to the traditional stage Irishmen of Carleton, Lover, Lever, Boucicault, and a hundred others. Yet the roaring, drinking, love-making broth of a boy hasn't changed. He may be found in Synge, but he is presented without the romantic sentimental twist.

Perhaps the picture may be unflattering, but it is a truer picture than the older. The Playboy of the Western World was hissed at Dublin, and

New York, and harshly arraigned by press and public. The Irish never could stand criticism. The very same element here which protests against the caricatured Celt in comedy and vaudeville, and with just cause, would probably attack Synge's plays as unpatriotically slanderous. Certainly, this dramatist does not attenuate the superstition, savagery, ignorance, drunkenness, and debasement of the peasantry in certain sections of Ireland. His colours, however, are not laid on coarsely, as if with a Zola brush. There is an eternal something in the Celt that keeps him from reaching the brute. Possibly the New Irishman does not differ at base from his forebears, but he is a shade sadder; he is not as rollicking as the gossoons of Carleton. His virtues are celebrated by Synge; his pessimism, which is ever tipped on its edges by an ineluctable hope for better times; his confirmed belief in the marvellous, his idolatry of personal prowess, his bravery, generosity, hot heart, and witty speech — all these qualities are not by any means missing in the plays. Indeed, they loom large. All Ireland is not the province of Synge. He has only fenced off certain tracts of the western coast — the east as well in The Well of the Saints — the coast of Mayo and a glen in County Wicklow. If he had lived he might have described with the same vitality and vivacity the man who walks in Phoenix Park, or the people of Donegal, "the far down." Judging from his own unpleasant experiences in Dublin he could

have echoed Charles Lever, who once sang of
his country folk as:

" Fightin' like divils for conciliation,
    An' hatin' each other for the love of God."

"These people make no distinction between
the natural and the supernatural," wrote Synge
in his Aran Islands. Nor do the characters of his
plays. Technically buttressed as they are at
every point, the skeleton cleanly articulated,
nevertheless the major impression they convey
is atmospheric. Real people pass before your
eyes; there is not the remote and slowly moving
antique tapestry, as in the Maeterlinck or Yeats
fantasies. Stout-built lads whack their father,
or the tinker and his trull knock over the priest:
there is loud talk and drink and bold actions; but
the magic of the Celt envelops all. This is more
notable in Riders to the Sea, which has a
Maeterlinckian touch — the modulation of the
suspicion of death into its culminating terrors;
but it is Irish. It is Synge. What could be more
Irish than the last speech of *Maurya*, the mother
bereaved by the greedy sea of her husband and
sons: "No man at all can be living forever;
and we must be satisfied." The very pith of
Celtic fatalism! The grim humour of the supposed dead man in The Shadow of the Glen is
Irish too; and also the tramp who fills the ears
of the banished wife with his weaving eloquence.
She goes with him into the wet and wind of the
night, knowing that a "grand morning" will

surely follow. This humour is pervasive and does not reveal itself in the lightning flash of epigram. It is the same with the tender poetry that informs Synge's rhythmic prose. His dialogue goes to a tune of its own, a tune in the web of which music and meaning are closely spun in the same skein, while beneath hums the sad diapason of humanity.

Consider the speeches in The Playboy of the Western World, the most important of the dramas. Each line is illuminating. Such concision is refreshing. Character emerges from both phrase and situation. This play, while it is not so shudder-breeding as Riders to the Sea, is more universal in interest. *Christy Mahon*, the young hero who is not heroic, is an Irish *Peer Gynt*. He lies that he may create the illusion of heroism; a liar of the breed artistic. He boasts of murdering his father (didn't the cultivated Charles Baudelaire actually boast the same noble deed?) for he knows the simple folk will regard him with mingled horror and admiration. The two rivals for his love, *Pegeen Mike* and the *Widow Quin*, are etched by the needle of a master; the fierce, passionate girl is real, but the cunning widow is delightful comedy. She crosses the page or the footlights and you touch her flattering hand, hear her blarneying voice. The minor characters are excellent, and they are subtly disposed on the various planes of interest and action. The piece moves briskly or languidly, the varying lines fit each human with

consummate appropriateness. The story itself
is as old as Troy, as is also the theme of The Well
of the Saints. Synge is never esoteric. His
argument never leaves the earth, yet few dramatists evoke such a sense of the Beyond. He
is a seer as well as a manipulator of comedy.
The vigorous sketch of his head by John B.
Yeats (prefacing The Playboy of the Western
World) shows us a fine strong profile, a big brow,
and the gaze of the dreamer, but a dreamer for
whom the visible world existed. "The Synges
are strong," answered a relative to the inquiry:
"Was J. M. Synge's death hastened by the hostile reception accorded his play in Dublin?" It
was not. His view of life was too philosophical
for criticism to hurt; he had the objective temperament of the dramatist, the painter of
manners, the psychologist. Nearing the matu-
rity of his splendid powers, on the threshold of a
love marriage, he disappeared like the mist on
one of his fairy-haunted hills. But the real John
Synge will endure in his plays.

A POET OF VISIONS

William Butler Yeats is a young man — he
was born at Dublin, June, 1865 — but he is
already famous, and for those who only know of
his name through Dame Rumour's trumpet his
fame will be further assured by the sight of his
collected works in prose and verse, eight volumes long, published at the Shakespeare Head

Press, Stratford-on-Avon. Mr. Bullin has spared no pains to make these substantial volumes agreeable to eye and touch; quarter vellum backs and gray linen sides, bold, clear type, and paper light in weight. The price, too, is not prohibitive for the collector. A bibliography of the various editions, English, American — Mr. John Quinn has privately printed many plays of Yeats in New York — is all that could be desired. The poet is pictured in frontispiece by such artists as John S. Sargent, Mancini, Charles Shannon, and by his father, John Butler Yeats; the reproductions are excellent. Volume I contains the Sargent head, from a charcoal drawing, the original in the possession of Mr. Quinn. It is Yeats seen by Sargent and definitely set forth in the terms of the Sargent daylight prose — a young man wearing a Byronic collar, the silhouette as firm as iron, the eyes in the shadow of the heavy overhanging hair. A splendid bit of modelling, yet not the essential Yeats, who is nocturnal, or trembling on the edges of the twilight or dawn. Volume III shows us Charles Shannon's conception: a three-quarter view, the cerebral region markedly accentuated, the expression contemplative. A vital rendering. The Mancini drawing in volume V looks like an improvisation by the brilliant Italian colourist on themes from Yeatsian moods. The poet faces you, he wears glasses, his eyes are almost effaced, his mouth is quizzical; he is perhaps looking at Celtic hats conversing with the dhouls of

midnight on some cosmical back-fence. We like
the drawing of the elder Yeats prefacing volume
VII; it is the poet Yeats of Rosa Alchemica,
and the Tables of the Law; Yeats the student
of the Rosy Cross, the mystic Yeats of 1896,
who, immersed in the occultism of the Orient,
was peering through the mists of Erin in search
of a symbol to fully express his love for her. He
is a trifle uncanny, a dweller on the threshold,
and for us nearer the real Yeats than the other
presentations. In this instance blood tells the
tale, notwithstanding the glory that is Sargent's,
that is Shannon's, that is Mancini's. One fact,
however, stares you in the face: all four artists
have seen their subject as he is, an authentic
poet. His gamut is one of fantasy; he is less at
ease among the sonorous sagas than amid the
fantasy of misty mountains, bracken lights and
the sound of falling waters.

The bibliography tells us that Mosada, a
dramatic poem, was the first published work.
It was reprinted in 1886 from the Dublin *University Review*, and in company with other poems,
plays, and prose does not appear in the definitive
edition; among other omissions we note The
Pot of Broth. Yeats has the courage of a surgeon. Does he sing at the beginning of the
bibliography:

> " Accursed who brings to light of day
> The writings I have cast away!
> But blessed he that stirs them not
> And lets the kind worms take the lot! "

What a motto for all writers! The various volumes are about equally divided between verse and prose, and we do not pretend to assert that the interest is unflaggingly maintained. For the last ten years the poet has been doubled by a propagandist, and in the too few intervals left the latter the dramatist began to bud. The neo-Irish literary movement, literally a cry of back to the people, back to the soil, back to the Gaelic myths, is now history. Suddenly the sleepy old city on the River Liffey became the centre of a poetic renascence, a renascence of wonder, as Theodore Watts-Dunton would say. Further, the spirit of Paris, of the romanticism of 1830, invaded Dublin. Several Yeats plays were placed under the ban of public displeasure, Countess Cathleen for one; as for J. M. Synge, it was a case for the police when his Playboy of the Western World was produced. (Mr. Yeats assures us that there were 500 at the second performance.) Evidently Dublin awoke to the knowledge that a new art was being born and that the travail was not without its pangs.

Yeats has been at both the centre and circumference of this artistic wheel, the hub of which is unquestionably Dr. Douglas Hyde. With such colleagues as Lady Gregory, the late Synge, Russell ("Æ") Martyn, George Moore, Father Peter O'Leary, and a host of other writers, playwrights, poets, critics, the experiments in the smaller auditoriums and at the Abbey Theatre attracted the attention of not only England but of the world. How much the lyric poet who is William Butler Yeats has lost or gained by his devotion to what seemed a hopeless dream we dare not say, but after rereading his collected works one may not doubt as to their contemporary importance and future permanency. The rich undertones of The Wind Among the Reeds, full at moments as are those songs of the echoes of the dead poets, are the key-notes after all of the later Yeats. He is always following a vision or hearing a voice, a "sweet everlasting voice," hearing "the Shadowy Horses, their long manes a-shake." These songs he perhaps thinks slight and dim to-day, but they are not. They are redolent of wind and sky and the souls of the forgotten things far away and the desire for the dead women with locks of gold and the terrible war that is to be waged in the valley of the Black Pig, where all will bow down to the "Master of the still stars and the flaming door." There is less metaphysics, too, in the early verse. Often we feel the weight of the cerebral whiplash in his later verse; also the tones of sophistication. In the Seven Woods holds such jewels as The Folly of Being Comforted, Never Give All the Heart, and that lovely The Hollow Wood, with its Elizabethan lilt, "O hurry to the water amid the trees, for there the tall tree and his Leman sigh." And "O do not love too long" — has the poet ever since recaptured such tender, plaintive notes? Youth is a time for living and singing and loving, and a poet is not young forever. The pipe of Yeats may not compass the octave; but his pipe is pure, its veiled tones hide the magic of the Celt.

We need not dwell now on The Wanderings of Oisin, with the stern responses of St. Patric; or on the Fenians, or those whose eyes were "dull with the smoke of their dreams," a little epic of disenchantment of the vanished pagan gods. In volume II will be found the four favourite plays: The King's Threshold, On Baile's Strand, Deirdre, and The Shadowy Waters. They are known to American readers. While they do not always prove that the poet has the fire of the footlights in his veins, they are nevertheless of great imaginative beauty and of a finely woven poetic texture, and the dramatisation not alone of a moving tale but of moods that seem just beyond the rim of the soul. We can imagine Claude Debussy or Loeffler suffusing these plays with mysterious music. On Baile's Strand, and its mad father duelling with the waters, evokes an elemental thrill; the dire reality when the Blind Man cries to the Fool: "Somebody is trembling, Fool! The bench is shaking"; but it is Cuchulain shivering as he learns that he has slain his son. Such touches as these convince you that Yeats has a dramatic pulse. It is Deirdre that drives home this contention. To us it seems the best grounded, best realised of his work for the theatre. It has the element of awe and the elements of surprise, fear, great passion, and noble humanity. And after Tristan and Isolde, that perfect dramatic poem, is not the tale of Deirdre the most sweet and pitiful? Conchubar is a sinister King Mark, Naisi a second Tristan, and Deirdre an undaunted Isolde. What if Wagner had known this touching legend! There is emotional stuff in it for a music drama. Yeats has handled his material simply and directly — the tale goes on swift, relentless feet to its sorrowful end. There is enough poetry in it to furnish forth the reputation of a dozen minor poets. The Shadowy Waters is a theme for the Irishman; he swims in an atmosphere where others would hardly respire. He himself is Forgael, with the luminous and magical harp. He has tasted that crust of bread of which Paracelsus spoke, and therefore has tasted all the stars and all the heavens.

The Land of the Heart's Desire, with its supernatural overtones, The Hour Glass, The Countess Cathleen, Cathleen Ni Houlihan, and The Unicorn from the Stars — "where there is nothing there is God" — are familiar. Whether Yeats is as near the soil as Synge or as happy in catching the gestures and accents of the peasant we are free to doubt. Yet in The Unicorn there is realism enough to satisfy those who long merely for veracious surfaces. This poet knows the "boreens," the bogs and the "caubeens," the "gloom" and the "doom" of his native land. He is compact with sympathy. If he is a symbolist in The Golden Helmet he can repro-

duce with fidelity the voice of Teig the fool in
The Hour Glass; or he is both poet and painter
in Cathleen Ni Houlihan and its finely wrought
climax. He has not, let us add, attempted to
domesticate the banshee in the back yard of
Irish poetry. Through his "magic casement"
we may always see the haze of illusion.

Yeats reminds us a little of that old Irish-
woman he quotes in one of the western villages
who believed hell an invention of the priests to
keep people good, and that ghosts would not be
permitted to go "traipsin' about the earth";
but she believed that "there are faeries and little
leprechauns and water horses and fallen angels."
He has so saturated himself with the folklore of
Ireland, with the gossip of its gods and fighting
men and its pagan mythology, that we are caught
within the loop of his sorceries in a dream as he
conjures up the mighty deeds and ancient super-
stitions in The Celtic Twilight and the stories of
Red Hanrahan. This is an attractive volume
(V) and should be first read by those readers to
whom all this wealth of legend may prove new.
The plays will then be better understood.

Ideas of Good and Evil (volume VI), essays on
sundry subjects, like volume VIII, Discoveries,
reveal the poet as a prose writer of assured
ease and a master of modern ideas. He knows
Nietzsche, Flaubert, Ibsen, and he knows William Blake. We need not agree with his various dicta on dramatic art, on the technique
of verse, or on that chimera the speaking of

verse to the accompaniment of monotone music; nor need we countenance his statement that music is the most impersonal of the arts; the reverse is the truth. Mr. Yeats, like so many poets, seems to be tone-deaf. Music tells him no secrets; words are his music; at the best, music and words combined is an unholy marriage. But why should he envy the musician? His own verse goes to a tune of its own, a loosely built, melancholy, delicious tune, as Celtic as is the evanescent music of Chopin Polish. We do not hear the swish of the battle-axe in his verse; the heroic is seen as in a bewitched mirror, the cries of the dying are muffled by the harmonies of a soul that sits and wonders and faces the past, never the present.

In Volume VII are those two prose master-pieces — for such they are — of the esoteric: Rosa Alchemica and The Tables of the Law. For the mystically inclined, Michael Robartes and Owen Aherne will be very real; the atmospheric quality betrays the artist. As for the various essays in propaganda, which appeared in *Beltaine*, *Samhain*, the *Arrow*, and elsewhere, they arouse the impression of an alert, sensitive, critical mind, fighting for the acceptance of ideas of national importance. Mr. Yeats the critic is different from Yeats the poet. He is a virile opponent, and as sincere as he is versatile in argument. He must have been a prime figure in the general war waged on the indifference and animosity of his countrymen. Will the new

Irish theatre endure? Anything may be successful in Ireland; success is a shy bird that rarely perches on her worn and tear-stained standards, but in the conflict William Butler Yeats found his soul, and that is the main business of a man's life, and all the life of a poet.

IX

THE ARTIST AND HIS WIFE

I

WHEN Théophile Gautier, young, strong, and bubbling over with genius, asked the great Balzac whether artists should marry, he was sternly advised to avoid women altogether.

"But, how about correspondence?" hazarded the timid youth.

Balzac reflected: "Perhaps; that forms one's style."

Naturally, Gautier did not take the advice seriously. He knew, as the world knew later, that the preacher did not practise. The private life of the master of French fiction is, thanks to Lovenjoul, no longer the sentimental legend his sentimental biographers made of it. A Grand Celibate, notwithstanding his brief, unlucky marriage, Balzac had the bachelor-temperament, and he had, too, many feminine-irons in the fire. He was as reckless as Liszt, and much more imprudent than his breeched, feminine contemporary, George Sand.

But was his advice to Gautier impearled wisdom? Should the artist marry? And if he does marry, what kind of woman should he take to wife? Why does the artist at least in the popular belief, make such a mess of matrimony? Are unions contracted between artist-men and women unhappy ones? Isn't there, after all, an immense exaggeration in the assumption that they are? Let us reconnoitre this battle-field, over which are strewn so many gaunt, bleaching bones, so many wrecked lives — according to fact and fiction — and ask: What in the name of all that is holy and hellish is the "artistic temperament"?

One question at a time. Is the artist always unhappy in his marriage?

You may survey the field from Socrates to Robert and Clara Schumann and find that the scales balance about evenly. Socrates had his Xantippe — the shrew is an historical event long before the spouse of Athens's wise man (a shrew is usually a woman who objects to being ill-treated, just as a cynic is a man who sees the truth and says it more clearly than his fellow-men). Doubtless, Socrates, friend of Plato, often envied the celibacy of his pupil. Philosophers should never marry. Thus Schopenhauer: "When wives come in at the door, wisdom escapes by the window." It sounds pretty, this proverb, but again history disproves it. The Grand Celibates do indeed form a mighty phalanx. In later days the list embraces the names of Balzac — his marriage was the one mistake of a bachelor-existence; Lamb, Pascal, De Musset, Keats, Stendhal, Mérimée, Flau-

bert, Beethoven, Swinburne, Pater, Turgenief,
Nietzsche, not to drag in Michaelangelo, Raphael, Franz Liszt, or Walt Whitman. Bache-
lorhood makes strange bedfellows!

We are by no means certain that these famous
men were happy because of their unmarried
state; some we know were excessively unhappy;
most of them were embroiled with women, and
several went mad. Any sleek statistician will
assure you that married life is conducive to
longevity. And often the mother of children,
forgetting for the moment her strenuous days,
speaks slightingly of the monastic vocation. Nor
is the time passed from the memory of the living, when a bachelor who refused to give up his
liberty was socially looked at askance. He bore
a doubtful reputation: A merry blade given to
midnight wassail! Since emancipated spinster-
hood has discovered that it is not necessary to
marry to be happy, or to escape the stigma of
old-maidishness, the bachelor appears in another
light. Perhaps, who knows, he was not wrong?

To sound the roll-call of the happy and unhappy artist-folk, whose works in colour and clay,
tone, and words, have aroused the world to
keener visions of beauty, is not my intention;
but a few names may be reeled off. Do you
remember Alphonse Daudet's charming yet
depressing book of tales about the wives of
geniuses: Daudet enjoyed a singularly happy existence, being wedded to a woman, an artist herself, who aided him in a hundred ways. It was

his whimsical revenge, in a too successful career, to write such misleading stories. Thousands have read them, as millions read the newspapers. If one half-baked fellow with a spongy, viscous soul, whose conceit has made rotten his nerves, treats his wife badly, or one feather-headed female, who has a singing voice, elopes with the coachman, the world shakes its head and waggishly smiles. Ah, this "artistic temperament"! Just as all the crimes of the decalogue are committed, according to the shallow agitator, by the wealthy and only the poor are virtuous, so the artist is regarded as a natural-born malefactor. It is a survival of the suspicious feeling against strolling players, painters, fiddlers, and such vagabonds of yore.

Yet what an array of evidence may be adduced in favour of the opposite view. When two poets like Robert and Clara Schumann, or two scientists like the Curiés, have lived happily, doesn't this fact, even if exceptional, prove the rule? If the fixed stars of the artist-firmament revolve harmoniously one around the other, what of the lesser planets? Unluckily there are more comets and shooting-stars among the mediocre artists. The Carlyles were not happy — not every day. Better, however, their caustic differences than the glitter of a foolish paradise.

Life is not all beer and skittles even for the favoured artist-soul, nor is Art a voluptuous hothouse. Byron raised a hell wherever he passed. He had a wife who was, to put it mildly, hardly suited to him. After only one suicide in the family, Shelley settled down, if that ethereal spirit ever could settle on anything earthly, with the original suffragist, Mary Wollstonecraft Godwin. Hazlitt philandered with women and was not content in double harness. Nor was much-married John Milton, nor Dante, nor Shakespeare, says legend. Coleridge took opium, became a flabby genius, and daily forgot his duties. De Quincey followed suit at a long distance, though gossip avers that he was a mild and loving husband. William Blake, the poet and illustrator, was ecstatically happy during his married life. Whether his wife was, when he proposed to add another lady to the household, we much doubt. Wordsworth cultivated the domestic virtues. Bulwer did not. Thackeray was a model husband and suffered stoically the misfortune of his wife's madness. Dickens didn't draw happiness in his lottery. Disraeli did, also Tennyson. Thomas Hardy is happily mated. George Moore is a bachelor — and writes like one. Jane Austen would not have been the "divine Jane" if she had married. George Eliot, of whom it was said that she was a "George Sand plus science and minus sex," shocked the British public, yet remained ever eminently British herself, conventional to the last. Ruskin tried matrimony and handed his wife over to Millais, the artist. It was a good transaction for all three. Emerson was married. Hawthorne and Longfellow were married. Poe adored Virginia, his child-wife.

THE ARTIST AND HIS WIFE

Across seas the plot thickens. There are as many happy households in France as anywhere. But it is hard to convince English-speaking people of this very potent fact. The Parisian bohemians have set a pace that makes Puritans giddy. George Sand, a contemporary of George Eliot, is a mystery. She left a brutal husband, met a mob of lovers in her journey through life, and ended in a glow of respectable old age. She had not one, but a dozen happy and unhappy love-lives. And she loved to tell the world all about her lovers in her books. Admirable and truthful artist! Rabelais was a Grand Celibate. Montaigne was a happy husband. Chateaubriand posed all his life as the misunderstood genius. He had his consolations and Madame Récamier. There is Madame de Staël, a feminine genius, but she bored Napoleon and got on Goethe's nerves. Goethe! He married, though not before he had burned tapers of adoration before a half-hundred feminine shrines. He is the perfect type of the inconstant lover who in middle life marries some one to look after his material comfort: a Don Juan on the retired list. Fate played him a trick, for he was forced to nurse himself. Lamartine had his Elvira, and Europe wept over the Elegies. Victor Hugo boasted his Juliette, and no one sympathised with him except his dearest enemy, Sainte-Beuve, who promptly consoled Madame Hugo. Alfred de Musset's career was notorious. Absinthe and not George Sand sent him to the grave.

Alfred de Vigny, a greater poet, though not so

well known, cursed women in his verse because of
Marie Dorval, his faithless love. His marriage
to an Englishwoman, Lydia Bunbury, was a
failure. And the elder Dumas carried off La
Dorval. Baudelaire never married. Would that
he had. Verlaine married and his wife divorced
him. Dumas was a veritable pasha. His son
was a model. Mérimée, for a week George Sand's
lover, later broke a woman's heart, and the account thereof is good reading for both cynics and
sentimentalists. Flaubert loved his mother too
much to marry, but for years was entangled by
the wily Louise Colet. The Goncourt brothers
were born old bachelors, and if, as Bernard Shaw
asserts, the romantic temperament is the old-
maid's temperament, then these two were spin-
sters. They abused women on every page of
their diary, but spent their days in agonised and
acid-etching of her traits for their novels. Zola
was a bourgeois husband. Maupassant committed suicide, spiritually and physically —
work, women, and drugs. Gautier, impeccable
artist, laboured in the unthankful galleys of
journalism. He was adored by his wife and children. He was a lovable, good man. Ernest
Renan was possibly a celibate by temperament,
but his married life was none the less peaceful.
Huysmans was an embittered bachelor. Anatole France is a man of the domestic sort, like
many scholars.

The musicians are not as a rule considered safe
guardians of the hearth. Some, however, were

and are happily married. Haydn had a scolding wife, but he was always merry. Handel had a habit of throwing ladies out of doors. He was much admired by the sex. Mozart, it is said, was fonder of his sister-in-law than of his wife. Who knows? Mendelssohn and his wife were turtle-doves. Chopin died a bachelor; he had loved George Sand in vain, but his affair with her did him no good. Liszt — oh, Liszt! He ran the gamut of love as he played scales: with velocity and brilliancy. He raised a family though he never married the Countess d'Agoult; she returned to her husband later on and Liszt was exculpated. "He behaved like a man of honour," was the verdict of the family council — meaning, of course, what a surprise to find an artist not a blackleg! Beethoven loved. He had his intimate tragedy. Brahms was also a bachelor. Is it necessary to come down to our days? We see a wedded Paderewski attracting large audiences. Marriage, therefore, is no bar to an artist's popularity.

Painters and actors could furnish plenty of examples did we care to linger in the historical meadows. That Angelo and Raphael did not marry is no argument against matrimony. Andrea del Sarto, as readers of Browning know, had a minx for a wife. Rubens and Van Dyck spent sunny married lives. Rembrandt loved his wife, Saskia; also his later wife, Hendricka Stoffels. Impressionist Claude Monet is married, while Degas has cultivated privacy. Whistler

was a contented married man, and so Rodin.
Monticelli did not marry. He drank himself to
death. Ibsen was a paragon of a family man.
Tolstoy abused matrimonial chains, possibly for
the same reason that prompted Daudet to write
his stories of genius. (But were Daudet's men
of genius real? We doubt it. They seem to parade a lot of used-up, second-rate talents, not of
the true genius variety.) The Russian writer's
home life is trumpeted to the four corners of the
globe by his disciples. Is that why he wrote The
Kreutzer Sonata? On Patti and her marital adventures, it is not in our scheme of argument to
dwell. Nor on Marcella Sembrich — whose serene married life is an object-lesson for young
singers about to commit divorce. Rachel —
thanks to Alfred de Musset and others, was
usually an unhappy creature. Bernhardt and
Duse have traversed soul-scarifying experiences;
but each had the courage of her genius. At a
time when there are no masculine counterparts
in the theatre, wheresoever, of these two extraordinary women, it is not tactful for men to crow
over their superiority in the art mimetic. What
D'Annunzio did to Eleanora Duse was the accustomed act of artist-egotism: he utilised the
experience for his books. He is a poet and a man
of versatile genius. What Duse did was perhaps
not so conscious, yet, nevertheless, the result was
the same; her art reflected in richer tones her
soul's attrition by sorrow. It is a sweet idea this:
That one may gather emotional shells on the

sandy beach of disillusionment and decorate with
them one's art, later to be sold to publishers,
picture-dealers, or sung and played in concert-
rooms. Hail the mystery of these artistic trans-
mutations! These transfusions from the veins of
love, of the fluid that is to prove the elixir of
your art!

Glance backward at the list. The scales tip
evenly. Remember, too, that of artists' histories the top, only, is skimmed. Hundreds of
cases could be dug up. Genius is hard to live
with, even in the casual ways of life. Genius
under the same roof with genius (and of the two
sexes) is a stirring opportunity for a psychologist. The wonder is that the number of happily
married great artists — not the quotidian fry —
is so large. The divorce calendar of butchers,
bakers, and candlestick-makers bulks in proportion quite as effectively. But the doubting
male Thomases may, at this juncture, quote
Goncourt: "There are no women of genius; the
only women of genius are men!"

And that brings us to the crux of the situation.
What is the artistic temperament?

II

We have now seen that artists, like the lion
and the lamb, can marry or mix without fear of
sudden death, cross words, bad cookery, or loss
of artist-power. Why then does the rule work
for one and not the other? Go ask the stars.

THE ARTIST AND HIS WIFE

Where are the love-birds of yester-year? Why doesn't Mr. Worldly Wiseman get along with his stout spouse? Why does the iceman in the alley beat his wife? Or, why does a woman, who has never heard of Nora Helmer, leave her home, her husband, her children, for the love, not of a cheap histrion, but because she thinks she can achieve fame as an actress? It is the call of the far-away, the exotic, the unfamiliar. Its echoes are heard in the houses of bankers, tailors, policemen, and politicians, as well as in the studios of the great artists.

But the news of the artist's misdemeanour gets into print first. The news is published early and often. A beautiful young actress, or a rising young portrait-painter, a gifted composer, talented sculptor, brilliant violinist, rare poet, versatile writer — when any one of these strays across the barrier into debatable territory, the watchmen on the moral towers lustily beat their warning gongs. It is a matter for headlines. Strong lungs bawl the naked facts to the winds. Depend upon it — no matter who escapes the public hue and cry, the artist is always found out and his peccadilloes proclaimed from pulpits and housetops.

Why, you ask, should a devotee of æsthetic beauty ever allow his feet to lead him astray? Here comes in your much-vaunted, much-discussed "artistic temperament"— odious phrase! Hawked about the market-place, instead of reposing in the holy of holies, this temperament has become a byword. Every cony-catcher, pugilist, or cocotte takes refuge behind his or her "art." It is a name accursed. When the tripe-sellers of literature wish to rivet upon their wares public attention, they call aloud: "Oh, my artistic temperament!" If an unfortunate is arrested, she is generally put down on the police-blotter as an "actress." If a fellow and his wife tire of too much bliss, their "temperaments" are aired in the courts. Worse still, "affinities" are dragged in. Shades of Goethe! who wrote the first problem novel and called it Elective Affinities. All decent people shudder at the word, and your genuine artist does not boast of his "artistic temperament." It has become gutter-slang. It is a synonym for "nerves." A true artist can get along without it, keeping within the sanctuary of his soul the ideal that is the mainspring of his work.

The true artist temperament, in reality, is the perception and appreciation of beauty whether in pigment, form, tone, words, or in nature. It may exist coevally with a strong religious sense. It adds new values to grey, everyday life. But its possessor does not parade this personal quality as an excuse for licence. That he leaves to the third-rate artisan, to the charlatan, to the vicious, who shield their actions behind a too torrid temperament.

Now, art and sex are co-related; art without sex is flavourless, hardly art at all, only a frozen copy. All the great artists have been virile.

And their greatness consisted in the victory over their temperaments; in the triumph, not of mind over matter — futile phrase! — but in the triumphant synthesis, the harmonious comminglement of mind and artistic material. Sensualist your artist may be, but if he is naught else, then all his technical dexterity, his virtuosity, will not avail — he cannot be a great artist.

Whether artists should marry is an eternally discussed question. It is so largely a personal one that advice is surely impertinent. George Moore, above all other Victorian novelists, has described the true artist-life — do you recall his Mildred Lawson? Mr. Shaw, in his Love Among the Artists, shows us other sides. St. Bernard holds no brief for the artist; Shaw is more of a Puritan than his critics realise. Certainly an artist is risking much in marrying, for the artist is both selfish and sensitive. He has precedents for and against the act, and probably he thinks that whether he does or does not, he will regret it.

A rainbow mirage, this of two congenial temperaments entering wedlock! When He exclaims — it is June and the moon rides in the tender blue — "It is just as easy for two to live as one on twenty-five dollars a week!" the recording angel smiles and weeps. Nor has the young adventurer "spiders on his ceiling," as they say in Russia. He dares to be a fool, and that is the first step in the direction of wisdom. But She? Oh, She is enraptured. Naturally they will economise — occasional descents into fifty-cent bohemias: sawdust, pink wine, and wit. But no new gowns. No balls. No theatres. No operas. No society. It is to be Art! Art! Art!

So they bundle their temperaments before an official and are made one. She plays the piano. He paints. A wonderful vista, hazy with dreams, spreads out before them. She will teach a few pupils, keep up her practising, and put aside enough to go, some day, to Vienna, there to study with a pupil of Leschetizky. He will manfully paint — yes, only a few portraits; but landscape will be the object of his ambition.

A year passes. What a difference! Gone are the dreams. There are now many spiders on the ceiling. To pay for the food they eat, or to own the roof over their heads is their ultimate desire. She looks paler. He may or may not drink, it makes little difference. There are no portraits painted — an artist must be a half society man nowadays to capture such commissions. She would accept pupils, but their home engrosses every hour of her day. Artists usually demand too much of a woman. She must be a social success, a maternal nurse, a cook, and concubine combined. Women are versatile. They are born actresses. But on ten dollars a week they can't run a household, watch the baby — oh, thrice wretched intruder! — play like a second Fanny Bloomfield Zeisler, and look like an houri. To be a steam-heated American beauty, your father must be a millionaire.

THE ARTIST AND HIS WIFE

The artist-woman is a finely attuned fiddle. You may mend a fiddle, but not a bell, says Ibsen. Yes, but if you smash a fiddle, the music is mute. And every day of discontent snaps a string. How long does the beauty last? Then begin mutual misunderstandings. Pity, the most subtly cruel of the virtues, stalks the studio. Secretly she pities him; secretly he pities her. This pity breeds hatred. At breakfast, the most trying time of the day — even when you haven't anything to eat — he pities her flushed face as she runs in from the kitchen with the eggs and coffee. In his eyes she is no longer a sylph. (The twenty-five dollars a week are shrunk.) She pities him because he is flushed from his night's outing. His appetite, like his temper, is capricious. In her eyes, he is simply the ordinary male brute, which is true enough. Then he is imprudent and flings Schopenhauer at her.

Have you noticed how often well-bred, bookish, and artist men quote Schopenhauer at their wives? The bow-legged, long-haired sex — eh! Aha! He rubs his hands. Women are, all said and done, the inferior sex! What did Iago remark — but he doesn't like to quote that speech of the Ancient's with its chronicling of small beer for fear his wife may turn quietly upon him with the monosyllable — "Beer!" He hates to be twitted about his faults, so he takes up Nietzsche's Beyond Good and Evil and reads: "That because of woman's cookery, the development of mankind has been longest retarded." Or, "Woman — the Eternally Tedious!" Or, "Woman

has hitherto been most despised by Woman!"
It is not in good taste, all this.

But she has no time to quote Ibsen and Shaw
for his discomfiture. The milkman is keeping
her busy by asking for the amount of his bill.
As baby must have pure milk, she compromises
by smiling at her foolish young man and teases
him for the money. He dives into empty pockets
and looks blankly at her. Sometimes this goes
on for years; often in reckless despair he throws
his lamp over the moon and she her bonnet over
the wind-mill. Female suffrage may make such
conditions impossible in the future by forbidding
men the ballot.

Yet, how many happy artist households there
are! Sometimes the couple paint à quatre mains,
as Manet puts it; sometimes the wife is simply a woman and not an artist. Nor dare we
claim that this latter species of union is always
the happier. It may not be. She may be a
nightmare to him, a millstone around his neck,
through sheer stupidity or lack of sympathy.
Men, ordinary males, like to be coddled; artist-
men, in whom there is often a thin streak of
feminine vanity, must be subtly flattered. The
nerves lie near the surface in artist people.
Idealists, they paint with their imagination
everything in too bright hues. Labour, really,
puts them out. It is the same young man and
the same young woman who, under pine-blos-
soms, swore undying love — the same, except
that a year or several have passed.

As is always the case, the rather despised

Womanly-Woman — the woman of the feather-bed temperament, who is neither dove nor devil — gathers the honours. She knows that the artist-man, that hopeless hybrid, so admirably apostrophised by Shaw in the first act of Man or Superman, must be humoured. (Feed the brute!) He is the spoilt child of Fate. If he goes too far from his mamma's apron-strings, he gets into trouble, falls into the mud-puddle of life, and is sure to drag some silly girl with him. So she, being wise with the instinctive wisdom of her sex — the Womanly-Woman, I mean — I have seldom encountered a Womanly-Woman who was also an artist — plays him to the end of the rope, and then he is back at her knees. Such marriages are successful for the reason that the artist-husband doesn't have time to be unhappy.

It is when the lean years are upon the artist, the years of thin thought and bleak regrets, that he will miss a loving wife. Then he will cry in the stillness of his heart: O Time, eternal shearer of souls, spare me thy slow clippings! Shear me in haste, shear me close and swiftly! He is the literary artist, and even in the face of death he wears the shop-mask. His "affinity," whom he has never encountered at the epoch of their earthly pilgrimage, congratulates herself that the latter lonesome years will not be burdened by the whims and ills of an old man. She may possess the artist temperament and be a spinster. Often she escapes that fate by early marriage to a solid, sensible business or professional man, who pays the bills and admires her pasty painting, her facile, empty music-making, her unplayed plays, unread novels, and verse — that are privately printed. Sensible old Nature, as ever, thus hits the happy mean.

It is not necessary to draw any particular inference from the foregoing, save to add that the "artistic temperament" is not what the newspapers represent it to be; that when it exists in association with high ideals and natural gifts, the result is sincere art; that it is hardly a quality making for happiness; that men and women, whether artists or mediocrities, must fight the inevitable duel of the sexes until death do them part; and finally, that the breakfast-room episode referred to is a comedy played daily all over the globe, and the hero need not be a painter — for a rising young plumber can assume the rôle with equal success. A sense of the humorous would save half the family jars in households, artistic and inartistic. The spectacle of two bipeds strutting and fuming beneath the glimpses of the sun, while over yonder the vast cosmic spaces are undergoing the birth of new constellations — surely the very angels in heaven must sit in reserved stalls, ironically spying upon humanity's antics. After all, an artist is a human being; this fact is too often forgotten by writers who see in the man of talent, or genius, a mixture of gorilla, god, or madman.

To the young artist who has mustered his material the spectacle of the world is an alluring one. He stands on the brink and the great stream of life flows by bearing upon its bosom gaily decorated barges, glittering with lights, flowers, with beauty. He is tempted. It is so easy to step on board and be carried away on this intoxicating current. Besides, it means success. He may be a lover of beautiful things. He may even be domestic and desire a home, a family. And the latter reef is often as dangerous to his art as the rocks on the coast of Bohemia. But whatever he does he must make the choice — there is no middle way. All or nothing. The world or art. Paul Gauguin has said that all artists are either revolutionists or reactionists. The former state may mean glory without bread; the latter always means bread. And if our young artist can live on bread alone let him say to his ideals: "Get thee behind me." But if he is true to his temperament then will his motto be — plain living and high painting. All the rest is vanity and varnish.

X

BROWSING AMONG MY BOOKS

GAUTIER THE JOURNALIST

THERE was a popping of critical guns in Paris
for the celebration of the centenary of Théophile Gautier, August 31, 1911, and while there
was much florid writing about Gautier the poet
and Gautier the romancer, little was said about
his career as a journalist. Perforce a final estimate of the man is made from his work between covers, because the greater part of his
vast production is hidden away in the numerous
musty files of newspapers and magazines the
very names of which are forgotten. According
to his son-in-law, Emile Bergerat, the writings of
the "good Théo" would if collected fill more
than three hundred volumes. Not a bad showing for one whose legend was that of Olympian
laziness and a voluptuous impassibility in the
presence of the dear, common joys of mankind!
But it is all a legend as legendary as the indifference and inactivity of Goethe, an untruth
uttered by Heine, when every hour of a long
life was crowded with his activities as statesman, man of science, poet, dramatist, novelist,
and administrator of public affairs at Weimar.

Gautier played the rôle of an easy-going boule-vardier; in private he bitterly complained of his slavery to the Grub street of his beloved Paris. Nevertheless this same journalism was his salvation, otherwise he might have found himself in the wretched condition of his friends Charles Baudelaire, Petrus Borel, Gérard de Nerval, and Villiers de l'Isle-Adam. What distinguished him from these bohemians of genius was his capacity for work. He possessed a giant's physique and his nerves were seemingly of steel. He once wrote:

"There is this much good in journalism, that it mixes you up with the crowd, humanises you by perpetually giving you your own measure, and preserves you from the infatuations of solitary pride."

Baudelaire and Villiers and the rest of the bohemian crew might have profited by this.

And what a crew of bohemians were his friends in 1831, those poor chaps of great promise and little production! Their "Tartar's camp" was pitched in an open space in the Rue Roche-chouart until driven away by the police. Their motto was "Clothing is prohibited." Louis Bertrand, "Gaspard de la Nuit," as he was better known, died in want and his body was thrown into potter's field. Petrus Borel, at one time acclaimed as the true head of the Romantic revolution and superior to Victor Hugo, died in exile, his talents run to seed. How many others did the young Gascon Gautier see come to naught? He was philistine enough to read the handwriting on the wall; besides, he had the illustrious example of his chief, Victor Hugo, who proved himself canny in dealing with money matters, a sort of Jovian bourgeois, in whose romanticism there lurked a practical flavour. He never wore a scarlet waistcoat; perhaps he didn't care for the colour, though he allowed his disciples any manner of extravagance so long as it furthered his own ambition.

Those pseudo-Parisian pagan poets who set such store on Gautier's revolt against the canons of art, society, and religion might profitably pattern after their master in his sane and solid performances in verse and prose. His full name was Pierre Jules Théophile Gautier, and though he was born in Tarbes (Hautes-Pyrénées, August 31, 1811) he was of Provençal origin. But there was little of the conventional southern expansiveness or vivacity in his makeup; a rather moody, melancholic man despite his robust humours, robust appetites. He wore a mask; that mask was romanticism. Nevertheless he never succumbed to the vapours and mouthings of those sons of Belial. He always kept his head, even when he experimented with haschisch in company with Baudelaire at the famous Hôtel Pimâdon. The truth about him is that he was a hard-working journalist, a good husband and loving father; solicitous of the welfare of his family and unrelaxing in his labours. Over his desk hung this grim reminder: "A daily newspaper appears daily." He never forgot it, and from his atelier at Neuilly he sent his daily stint of columns, poorly remunerated as he was for them. He never went into debt like his friend Balzac. If you haven't read his books you may well imagine him an unromantic and honest business man instead of a composer of most fantastic, delightful dreams and romances.

When Gautier first came up to Paris it was with the intention of becoming a painter. He had the painter's eye, the quick, retentive vision, the colour sense; above all the sense of composition. He entered the studio of Rioult for a period and then he read Sainte-Beuve, Hugo, and the Young France school, and he knew that his vocation was not paint but letters. However, he is always the painter in his prose and verse, full of imagery, yet concrete, supple, vivid of hue, brilliant, and harmonious. His oft-quoted saying that he was "a man for whom the visible world existed" is true enough, though in a much more limited sense than his admirers may realise. He was one of the greatest descriptive writers in the French language, ranking immediately after Chateaubriand and Flaubert without the dazzling verbal magic of the former or the subtle harmonious modulations of the latter. The form of Gautier is fixed; he treats all themes with unfailing and unvarying brilliancy. His style is never so sensitively modulated as Flaubert's in accordance with the idea. Flaubert is ever in modulation; Gautier is, as

Huysmans declared, "a gigantic impersonal reflector." We may demur to the charge of impersonality, but there is no denying the occasional monotonous effect of his overcoloured orchestration. He was a "visualist," not an "auditive," as the psychologists have it; the image with him proceeded from things seen, hence he has been accused of lack of imagination and of a dearth of "general ideas." To be sure he did not meddle with politics; his attitude toward socialism was of unaffected scorn, and he could not despite his genius create a live man or a woman, as did Flaubert and Thackeray. He was not as profound as Baudelaire, though less morbid. But he never tried to prove anything; he was a literary artist, not an agitator. That "professor of literature" Emile Faguet, who has so beautifully misunderstood Stendhal and Flaubert, after saying of Gautier that he knew all the resources of the French language and style and that he produces incredible effects, nevertheless believes that he is doomed to extinction; and these two statements, as Mr. Saintsbury points out, are contradictory. Mr. Saintsbury's "ancient lawyer," father of a family, who found Mademoiselle de Maupin a "most beautiful book," would nowadays discover others to assent to his judgment. Mademoiselle de Maupin, written in 1835, is as unmoral as Mother Goose; and in the once notorious preface, as significant for Gautier's generation as was the preface to Hugo's Cromwell, we suspect the poet of impudent mockery, of putting his tongue in his cheek, as he did earlier in Les Jeunes-France. He had a sense of humour if Hugo had not.

But there was another Gautier. The pantheist who could boast that "I am a man for whom the visible world exists" could also confess that reality evoked in him fantastic dreams, that men and women were as a world of pale shadows. His nerves were not always in tune. He is his own D'Albert, suffering from the nostalgia of the ideal. Strange too that this lover of the concrete should occupy himself for so many years with ideas of death, decay, the horrors of the tomb and of mummies and vampires revivified. In his sonorous, rhythmic daylight prose he attempted again and again to pin down the impalpable in a phrase. How many of his tales deal with the spirit, and fail. The Dead Leman (1836), a wonderful piece of art, is frankly materialistic; but what fancy, what verve! There is bold fantasy a-plenty, yet the externals of the soul are only scratched. Gautier strove to sound spiritual overtones and failed. His most successful rehabilitation of a past epoch is Le Capitaine Fracasse (1863), as successful in preserving tonal unity as Thackeray's Esmond. And Une Nuit de Cléopâtre (1845), so sympathetically translated into English by Lafcadio Hearn, rivals Salammbô in its exotic colouring and archæological splendour. The travel books, Spain, Constantinople, Russia,

Algeria, Italy, and others, are models of their genre. Their author headed the vanguard of the new men, though he didn't wear his heart in a sling or his sensibilities on his sleeve, as do those artistic descendants of Chateaubriand, Pierre Loti and Maurice Barrès. Gautier's Spain is as fresh as it was the day it was written. As a poet he is best known by his polished Emaux et Camées (1852), in which the artistry outshines the poetic significance. His first verse appeared in print in 1830. Within a narrow range he is a poet, but it is for the most part verse for the eye, not the ear. This is as might be expected from one who decries the expression of the sensibilities as shown in De Musset or Coppée and who believes so firmly in the supremacy of art, in its immortality. He saw the secret correspondences of things remotely related. He was pantheistic to the marrow. Henry James once wrote of him: "But if there are sermons in stones, there are profitable reflections to be made even on Théophile Gautier, notably this one, that a man's supreme use in the world is to master his intellectual instrument and play it in perfection." This is happily put, and in that qualifying "even" all the secret of the critical art of Henry James may be lodged.

Gautier denied that he wore a scarlet waistcoat at the world-stirring Hernani first performance in 1830; it was a pink doublet, a distinction without much of a difference. Anyhow it was a symbol of his adherence to revolutionary ro-

manticism, though his revolt was less a question
of literary manipulation than of a state of soul, a
manner of feeling. Rousseau and Byron and
Chateaubriand, together with the moonshine
romancers of Germany, Tieck and the rest, set
rolling the movement of 1830. How far Gautier
had outgrown it may be noted in the statement
of Emile Bergerat that his father-in-law toward
the close of his life had grown fond of Stendhal
and was particularly devoted to La Chartreuse
de Parme. There's a curious literary adventure for you, Théophile the gorgeous, reading
Stendhal, the siccant psychologist. Gautier
first wrote for the *Cabinet de Lecture* and *Ariel;*
then for *France Littéraire*. During the scandal
caused by Mademoiselle de Maupin Balzac sent
Jules Sandeau for him and engaged him to write
for the *Chronique de Paris*, at a desolation-breed-
ing salary. He also "ghosted" for Balzac, whom
he had nicknamed "Homère" de Balzac. He
collaborated for the evening journal founded by
Nestor Roqueplan in 1830 entitled *La Charte;*
this was about 1836. With Alphonse Karr he
joined the staff of *Figaro*, writing feuilletons, also
romances that later were published in book form,
Fortunio, for example. In 1837 with Gérard de
Nerval he went to the *Presse* of Girardin, where
he wrote art, literary, and dramatic criticism.
His criticism has been criticised as being too
amiable, an unusual crime in those cutthroat,
swashbuckling days of the Parisian press. In
reality he was too soft-hearted for the ancient

and honourable art of cricitism. But reread, vanished worlds of art reappear. From 1845 to his death, at Neuilly, October 22, 1872, curiously enough the sixty-first birthday of Franz Liszt, who like Gautier was born in 1811, he wrote for the *Moniteur* and the *Journal Officiel*. In 1867 he wrote for the Minister of Public Instruction the report of the poetic movement in France, and in 1900 his other son-in-law, the poet Catulle Mendès, the whilom husband of the gifted Judith Gautier, continued for M. Georges Leygues, Minister of Public Instruction, the report from 1867 till 1900. Gautier was associated in the Parnassian movement with Catulle Mendès and Louis Xavier de Ricard, a leading figure of which was the icy pessimist Leconte de Lisle. Théophile was in his love of formal perfection a Greek at heart.

His life long he was driven by the lacerating spur of poverty. The revolution of 1848 robbed him of his savings and the war of 1870 quite ruined him. The Tableaux de Siège (1871) reveals an unquiet Gautier, his heart bleeding for his native land ruined by the conqueror, his beautiful city blackened, a waste from the torches of the Commune. Sensibility is abundant in this book. He died broken in spirit, he, the once gay journalist who had boasted that he never revised his manuscripts, for he always tossed his periods like cats in the air and they always fell on their feet. Théophile Gautier laboured long and wrote beautifully. There are epitaphs of less distinction.

MAETERLINCK'S MACBETH

The way of the translator is hard. Maurice Maeterlinck tells us this with inimitably gracious style in his version of Macbeth. His introduction to the play is simple and perspicacious. A loving student for many years of the English poet, he is acquainted with the vast commentary that has parasitically encumbered that giant oak; his notes reveal the depth and breadth of his reading. A literary critic asked the other day: Why translate Shakespeare? The answer is obvious: Because it is Shakespeare. No English writer, with the possible exception of Chaucer, is so difficult to transpose to another language; yet Shakespeare has been turned into nearly every language and still remains Shakespeare. Shelley and Keats, Marlowe and Milton evaporate in translation; but Shakespeare even when shorn of his music remains the essential Shakespeare. He is more lyrical in Italian, sturdier in German, more rhetorical in French; yet his essence remains. This cannot be said of Goethe in French or of Ibsen in English. If, as has been contended by modern iconoclastic critics, the philosophy of Shakespeare is borrowed from Montaigne, his humour from Rabelais, and his history from Plutarch, Holinshed, and the Italian romancers, and if his poetry is not translatable, what then is the secret of his power when garbed in foreign language? Maeterlinck does not pose this question, though he is conscious of its complexity.

His introduction poses as a preliminary the question of the trilogy, Hamlet, Lear, and Macbeth. The last is in the world of tragedy a solitary peak which Æschylus alone could have attained. Many critics will disagree with this contention, for Lear has been held to be the Himalayan summit. However, we can but fall in line with the Belgian poet at present, for he is chiefly concerned with Macbeth. He finds the play a sort of biography more or less legendary; it floats on the confines of history and legend. The form is confused, the chief characters not sympathetic. Macbeth is not a *pièce bien faite;* it is too long. Of the more than two thousand verses about one-fifth must be suppressed for representation. This history of two crowned assassins is repugnant, for their intelligence is mediocre, their morals on the other side of good and evil, their show of repentance null; in a word, there is little in the machinery of the drama to win our approbation. All the qualities that do not go to making a masterpiece are absent. Nevertheless, a masterpiece Macbeth is, and one that quite o'ercrows Corneille, Racine, Goethe — we are now quoting Maeterlinck, who sets himself the task of again solving the enigma. For the scholarly Frenchman from Voltaire to Faguet a play must be literature as well as moving drama. It must develop logically according to

canon. If not Greek then Gallic. Maeterlinck, with his Flemish temperament, you are
tempted to add his Gothic *fond*, has no such
scholastic scruples. His own theatre shows him
a poet who first supped on the enchantments,
mysteries, and horrors of the Elizabethan and
later writers. He knows Marlowe as well as
Webster, John Ford as well as Beaumont and
Fletcher. Thus it may be seen that Macbeth,
with its profound painting of sinister souls, *âmes
damnées*, would stir him to his marrow.

He points out the impersonality of the poet,
the conversational diapason, a realistic speech so
often to be found; above all his favourite thesis
that a dramatist of the first order can suggest
the "interior dialogue" (see Maeterlinck's remarks on Ibsen's Masterbuilder) is in the case
of Shakespeare triumphantly vindicated. The
very pauses in Macbeth are pregnant with
horror. The detestable crime is but the frame-
work around which hovers the echo of the supernatural. Voices of the human conscience, soundless overtones of guilty souls, flood the air. Nor
does Maeterlinck revel in transcendental ecstasies. If he is the poet in dealing with Shakespeare, he is also the cool-headed man of the theatre. He realises the miracle of Macbeth, but,
like Goethe, he knows that every great work of
art is immensurable, even to its creator.

And the translation! There's the rub. If,
says Maeterlinck, a landscape is a state of soul
(Stendhal's *état d'âme*), so is a translation. He

rehearses the various attempts to make Shakespeare domesticated in the French tongue from Pierre Letourneur, François Victor Hugo — not to be confounded with his father — Benjamin Laroche, Maurice Pottecher, Alexandre Beljame to his own. (He does not mention the Hamlet of Marcel Schwob and Morand.) Fidelity to the rhythmic movement, verbal music, poetic spirit, local colour, idiomatic or interpretative — how many rocks there are in the road of the conscientious translator, tormented alike by the majesty and humanity of Shakespeare's speech! Maeterlinck gives as an example the lines (Act III, last scene):

"Strange things I have in head that will to hand
  Which must be acted ere they may be scanned."

Hugo thus renders the speech: "J'ai dans la tête d'étranges choses qui réclament ma main et veulent être exécutées avant d'être méditées" — which is clumsy and unrhythmic. Beljame's version is better, so is Pottecher's. Guizot, Montégut, Laroche, and Georges Duval are adduced. We like best of all Maeterlinck's, as follows: "J'ai dans la tête d'étranges choses qui aboutiront à ma main; et qu'il faut accomplir avant qu'on les ait méditées." We are here far from the famous French version of "Frailty, thy name is woman," which appeared as "Mlle. Frailty is the name of a lady."

But Maurice Maeterlinck, with his funds

of poetic sympathy and subtle intuitions, his tact, knowledge, and verbal versatility, can successfully bridge the gulf that lies between the genius of the English language and the genius of the French language. We select several of the famous single lines as specimens and admire the agile resources of the translator. For example: "Quand nous retrouverons-nous?" is the equivalent for "When shall we three meet again?" "Fair is foul and foul is fair" becomes "Le laid est beau et le beau laid." These are not very difficult tests.

The onomatopœia is of necessity missed in the speech: "A drum, a drum! Macbeth doth come." In French: "Le tambour! Le tambour! Macbeth arrive ici!" Nor is "éteins-toi, éteins-toi, court flambeau!" quite akin to "Out, out, brief candle!" "Frappe donc, Macduff, et damné soit celui qui criera le premier: 'Arrête! c'est assez!'" retains some of the primal rhythmic vigour and assonance of "Lay on, Macduff; and damned be he that first cries 'Hold, enough!'" "Hang out your banners on the outward walls" is rendered: "Déployez vos bannières sur les remparts extérieurs," a faithful transcription.

Some of the tirades are admirably paraphrased, strange though they sound to English ears. The ferocity of Lady Macbeth's speech, Act I, scene 5, misses neither in meaning nor in terrible intonations; and Maeterlinck has fairly succeeded, we are fain to believe, with such a snarl as:

> "Hie thee hither,
> That I may pour my spirits in thine ear
> And chastise with the valour of my tongue
> All that impedes thee from the golden round
> Which fate and metaphysical aid doth seem
> To have thee crowned withal."— *Act I, scene* 5.

With Maeterlinck this goes to the tune of "Viens ici que je puisse verser mon courage dans ton oreille et châtier par la vaillance de mes paroles tous les obstacles au cercle d'or dont le destin et un appui surnaturel semblent te couronner," which is bald prose. (Is it not odd that Richard Strauss should have selected this as a motto for his tone poem Macbeth?) The gross humour of the Porter in the knocking at the gate scene is not attenuated, though we must protest against such a supersubtlety as "le trop boire est le *jésuite* de la paillardise" (the italic is ours) for "much drink may be said to be an equivocator of lechery."

We need not quote further to prove that if Maeterlinck does not overcome insuperable difficulties he has accomplished much more than the majority of his predecessors. It is a brilliant performance, this translation, superior to work for which many a man has attained a seat in the French Academy. This version sustained the trial of a public performance at the Abbey of Saint Wandrille with Mme. Georgette Leblanc-Maeterlinck as Lady Macbeth.

PATER REREAD

Rereading a favourite author is very much like meeting after years of absence a once-beloved friend. A nervous dread that your expectations may not be realised overtakes you as you match your old and new sensations. Not every great writer can be reread. The time-spirit sometimes intervenes; and one's own moods are not to be lightly passed over. Especially is this the case with a markèd personality such as that of Walter Pater, a new library edition of whose works, in ten stately volumes, is just completed. Will he survive a second, a third, a tenth reading? you ask as you open somewhat anxiously these pages with their wide margins. Will the old magic operate? And then the disturber appears, some belated antiquarian moralist who exclaims: "Ha! A hedonist!" A disquieting assertion. No wonder Pater rather pathetically complained to Mr. Gosse: "I wish they wouldn't call me a hedonist; it produces such a bad effect on the minds of people who don't know Greek." No doubt calling Pater an immoralist has had its bad effect on people who don't know anything about literature. "In the House of Morality there are many mansions," declared Henley. Pater lives in one of them, despite the mock puritanical attitude of a few critics who still adhere to the naughty-boy theory and practice of criticism, with its doling out of bad marks. The didactic spirit

279

ever fails to interpret. Consider the uneasy moral itch from which Ruskin and Brunetière suffered.

Our personal experience on rereading Pater was pleasant. The bogy man of hedonism did not frighten us off; nor did the palpable fact that Pater is never altogether for Apollo or altogether for Christ. Indeed, in the Aristippean flux and reflux of his ideas we discerned a strong family likeness to the theories of William James and Henri Bergson; a pragmatism poetically transfigured. That once famous suppressed Conclusion to the Renaissance is quite abreast with modern notions of the plastic universe. You are reminded too of Renan — Renan, who, no more than Pater, suffered from the "mania of certitude." But the silken insincerities of the Frenchman are not to be surprised in Pater's golden sentences. He indulged at times in certain affectations, dandyisms of style, or mood; in essentials, however, he is always earnest. His scholarship may not have been of the profoundest, his criticisms of art not those of an expert; nevertheless he wrote open-mindedly and to the best of his ability — and what a wonderful "best" it was! — and always with humanity in his mind's eye. He distilled from art and literature a "quickened sense of life," and in his books is the quintessence, the very ecstasy of experience. He "loaded every rift of his subject with ore," and despite his reputation for priggish erudition, a delicate humour, not untipped with irony, lines the back of many a paragraph. To read him often would be like a surfeit of Chopin or caramels. The figure of Pater the humanist, rather than Pater the verbal virtuoso, is getting more distinct with the years.

His morals are not exposed with a brassy orchestration. He never tries to prove anything, a relief in these days of cruel didacticism. He is both ardent and sceptical, and could have said with Maurice Barrès that "felicity must be in the experimenting, and not in the results it promises." No critic has ever settled anything. Pater played the rôle of spectator in the game of life, disillusioned perhaps, and not much caring for the prizes run for in the sweat and dust of the arena. Neither was he an umpire, but suffered the slightly melancholy happiness of the disinterested looker-on. It is a part which temperament decides. Luckily for the world, there are not many of such temperaments. In his early essay Diaphanéité he has described such a nature, which "does not take the eye by breadth of colour; rather is it that fine edge of light, where the elements of our moral nature refine themselves to the burning point." Whether in his life he succeeded in maintaining that dangerous mood of ecstasy, a mood that we only associate with mystics and poets; whether he burned always with this "hard gem-like flame" we do not know, nor need it concern us; but we do know that he succeeded in infusing a moiety of the ecstasy into his writings. And that is his success in art as in life. Doubtless he reached his goal as other great artists have done through a series of disgusts. That is one way to perfection, and if for some his art is as cold as a star, for others every page is sympathetic; at times he gives you the impression of a hearty human hand-clasp.

The truth is that his followers or would-be disciples have clouded popular comprehension; Pater formed no school. Himself the product of many complex currents of thought and emotion, a man who filed his form to a tenuous degree, there was never in him a compelling creative element, the simple, great idea that would be bound to have progeny. His originality was the result of accretions and subtle rejections; the tact of omission, as he put the phrase. All nuance, he has also a tangible charm, which is not compounded sweetness and light, as is Cardinal Newman, yet is extremely winning. Mr. Greenslet happily calls his style African, as opposed to the Asiatic profusion of De Quincey. African, or Alexandrian, it is a style that is never strongly affirmative. It sets forth his Lydian music and felicitous scepticism in the precise relief they demand. He is essentially a painter of pictures and, as with Flaubert, the image and the idea are always fused. He would have said that a change in a nation's music meant a change in a nation's laws.

But he was not all languor and ecstasy and music. When the rumour was circulated in Ox-

ford that he had a metaphysical sin on his soul
it was because he flaunted a brilliant apple-
green tie and, worse still, because he kept on his
table a bowl of dried rose-leaves. A hedonist
indeed! Yet he was writing at the time such an
involved sentence on style as this: "Since all
progress of mind consists for the most part in
differentiation, in the resolution of an obscure
and complex object into its component aspects,
it is surely the stupidest of losses to confuse
things that right reason has put asunder, to lose
the sentence of achieved distinctions, the distinction between poetry and prose, for instance;
or, to speak more exactly, between the laws and
characteristic excellences of verse and prose composition." A sentence worthy of old Sir Thomas
Browne, and not any more immoral than the
apple-green tie or the dried rose-leaves. Pater
often made arid and complicated prose; when he
dealt with abstract ideas he could write like
Herbert Spencer. He needed a personality to
set humming in him the warm music of his very
human sympathies. How much simpler is his
definition of style in the essay on Pascal: "The
essence of all good style, whatever its accidents
may be, is expressiveness." And expressiveness
is his characteristic charm.

The Imaginary Portraits, Marius the Epicu-
rean — not the best-composed of his works, for
it is rather a sheaf of essays than a closely woven
study; Gaston de Latour, and the loftily conceived Plato and Platonism, are so many rich

gleanings from the imagination and mental experience of this distinguished thinker. True, his pose was largely romantic, but the classical or the romantic we have ever had and always will have with us. As he writes: "The romantic spirit is in reality an ever present, an enduring principle in the artistic temperament." Particularly true is this of music — no matter in what questionable guise it comes to us, whether as debased as opera or as the spiritual symphony, music is the most romantic art of all, and, according to Pater, the art to which the other arts aspire. That he had not the critical temperament of, say, Matthew Arnold, may not be denied, though both men studied at the feet of Sainte-Beuve. Contrary to popular belief, Pater was the less impressionistic critic of the two, and while he had the urbanity he did not possess the superciliousness nor the wit of Arnold, nor the ethical bias; his personal method was as sound as his contemporary's. As Professor Spingarn would say, the province of the critic is to ask: "What has the poet tried to express, and how has he expressed it?" Pater always asks these questions. As a method this is not exactly novel, as some believe, but it is wholly effective. The critical rule of thumb has with the dealer in moral platitudes forever disappeared from the scene.

And yet — ! After we had reread him we came across the exclamation of the Princess in Disraeli's Coningsby: "I wish that life were a little more Dantesque." And we recall the incident in Alton Locke when old Sandy Mackaye takes Alton to a London alley and bids him make poetry out of it: "Say how ye saw the mouth o' hell, and the twa pillars thereof at the entry, the pawnbroker's shop on the one side and the gin palace at the other — two monstrous devils, eating up men, women, and bairns, body and soul. Look at the jaws of the monsters how they open and open to swallow in anither victim and anither. Write about that!" Not even the bait thrown out by Sandy, that classic tragedy was involved in the issue — man conquered by circumstances — would have tempted Pater to handle such a theme. Therefore, when like the Princess we feel in the Dante or sublime mood, it is not Walter Pater we seek, but Dante, Beethoven, Goethe, Michelangelo. Pater, however, stands the test of rereading, because he wrote beautifully of beautiful things.

A PRECURSOR OF POE.

During the heat and dust of the recent critical powwow over Edgar Allan Poe, why was the name of Thomas Holley Chivers not lugged into the conflict? Bayard Taylor declared that "one of the finest images in modern poetry is in his Apollo":

"Like cataracts of adamant, uplifted into mountains,
  Making oceans metropolitan, for the splendor of the
    dawn."

A superb, a mouth-filling couplet! We defy any Western bard or Carolina lyrist to construct a like billowing rhythm. Who was Thomas Holley Chivers? He was born in Georgia, 1807, two years before Poe, and he died in 1858. The son of a rich planter and mill-owner, he received a classical education. He became a doctor, but devoted his time to poetry and science. He knew Poe; his poetry for the most part antedated Poe's. The unhappy author of The Raven once wrote to Chivers: "Please lend me $50 for three months. I am so poor and friendless I am half distracted." It was for a projected magazine — always the magazine mirage! — that Poe wanted the money.

Forgotten after his death, the name of Chivers came to light in Bayard Taylor's clever book of parodies, Diversions of the Echo Club, a book as fresh now as the day it was written. In the chapter entitled Night the Third Chivers and his amazing verse are discussed to the accompaniment of laughter by the various mouthpieces of Taylor. Did Poe ever write anything comparable to these lines? — we mean anything so delightfully lunatic:

"Many mellow Cydonian suckets,
    Sweet apples, anthosmial, divine,
From the ruby rimmed beryline buckets,
    Star gemmed, lily shaped, hyaline;
Like the sweet, golden goblet found growing
    On the wild emerald cucumber tree,
Rich, brilliant, like chrysoprase glowing,
    Was my beautiful Rosalie Lee."

Not only a predecessor of Poe but of Lewis Carroll's Jabberwocky and Edward Lear's nonsense verse. Taylor remarks of Chivers that "Poe finished the ruin of him which Shelley began"; but there seems to be another side of the story, and in justice to both Poe and Chivers it has been adequately told by the late writer Joel Benton in a little book of his called In the Poe Circle. For the first time we learn something of Chivers, of his supernally absurd word-building, and of his relations with Poe. After a brief inquiry into the reason of Poe's hold on the public Benton says: "You cannot harness humming-birds as common carriers," and then he proceeds to tell of the books written by Chivers. There are or were seven or eight volumes; the British Museum has a set of six. Their titles are verbal dreams. Nacooche, or the Beautiful Star, The Lost Pleiad, Eonchs of Ruby (what are Eonchs?), Memoralia, or Phials of Amber, Full of the Tears of Love, Virginalia, or Songs of My Summer Nights, The Sons of Usna, Atlanta, or the True Blessed Island of Love, and a first book (1834) Conrad and Eudora, or the Death of Alonzo; a Threnody. All testify to the lush and silly taste of the times. What is surprising, however, is to find Poe antedated in many of his own mannerisms and extravagances. For example:

> "I went with my Lily Adair —
> With my lamblike Lily Adair —
> With my saintlike Lily Adair —
> With my beautiful, dutiful Lily Adair."

Even the refrain of The Bells was anticipated by Chivers; or this:

> "In the Rosy Bowers of Aïden
> With her ruby lips love laden,
> Dwelt the mild, the modest maiden
> Whom Politan called Lenore."

You rub your eyes; Lenore, Politan! Or one of the closing stanzas from the same poem, The Vigil of Aïden:

> "And the lips of the damnèd Demon
> Like the syren to the seaman,
> With the voice of his dear leman
> Answered, 'Never — nevermore!'
> And the old time towers of Aïden
> Echoed, 'Never — nevermore.' "

Compared with Poe's dignified and artistic poem this is mere buckram, yet it preceded Poe and he read it, was affected by it, at least his phono-motor centres recalled it when he composed. Swinburne greatly relished Chivers, and Benton quotes Bayard Taylor's meeting with the poet: "Oh, Chivers, Chivers," said Swinburne in his peculiar voice, "if you know Chivers, give me your hand." Edmund Clarence Stedman heard Swinburne reel off yards of Chivers's lines. The truth is Chivers had marked rhythmic ability and an ear for pompous, pulpy, sonorous rhetoric. What a long-breathed phrase is this from Avalon:

> "For thou didst tread with fire-ensandalled feet,
> Star crowned, forgiven,
> The burning diapason of the stars so sweet,
> To God in Heaven!"

If there is ever a museum founded in which will be displayed the "awful examples" of bad, nonsensical poetry, Chivers will be king, though we might easily cite lines by Shelley, Poe, Browning, Mrs. Browning, and Swinburne that make for nonsense, though often resounding. Chivers did not rest quietly after reading the Poe poems. He openly accused him of plagiarism, and to the controversy which ensued Benton has devoted a very interesting chapter. Chivers pursued Poe in several magazines, proving that his own Lost Pleiad was published in 1842, therefore several years in advance of The Raven. As may be seen by the above quotation the resemblances are more than fortuitous. Poe, like Shakespeare, Milton, Handel, and Wagner, knew how to appropriate and adapt. Chivers asserted that he, Chivers, was the "first poet to make the trochaic rhythm express an elegiac theme, and the first to use the euphonic alliteration" — we quote Benton — and gives an extract of his own to prove his statement. It is magnificently humorous, though seriously meant by the poet:

"As an egg when broken never can be mended, but must
    ever
  Be the same crushed egg forever, so shall this dark
    heart of mine,
  Which though broken is still breaking, and shall never-
    more cease aching,
  For the sleep which has no waking — for the sleep
    which now is thine."

I prefer The Raven. If Richard Strauss is still without a libretto for a new comic opera the above contains a germ for his genius to develop. The picture of Chivers which Mr. Benton prints in his study shows us a dignified man; with suggestions of the statesman and the poet, he wears a melancholy expression. He was noted for his domestic virtues, suffered greatly when he lost his children; and he must have daily read quaint dictionaries by the dozen.

MME. DAUDET'S SOUVENIRS

After thirty years of married life, Julia, the widow of Alphonse Daudet, could write that she was never bored an hour; she suffered, she worked, and she worried, but not once did she sit down and say: "Life is stupid." How far from the lethargy, venom, the dulness of many artistic households her existence with her beloved novelist was may be found in her newly published Souvenirs Autour d'un Groupe Littéraire. This volume of fascinating interest for the admirers of Daudet also brings with it the reminder that time in its flight has not spared the vogue of that delightful author. Not only is he no longer the mode, but we doubt if his work is familiar to this generation, with the exception of the miserably garbled Sapho, which in its dramatic form is a libel on the novel. The more solid and less spiritual Zola endures the indifference of readers; Daudet, impressionistic, romantic, sensitive, has not aged gracefully. Like his own physical beauty, his books were for the most part doomed soon to disappear. Written without much effort, the effervescence of a man of the south, they were eagerly read by a greedy public and carelessly dropped. The reason is not difficult to explain.

Alphonse Daudet did not belong to the giant race of fiction; to the race of Balzac, Flaubert, Dickens, Thackeray, Tolstoy, or Turgenief. His swift prose, butterfly fancies, and delicate though slightly malicious humour were seen at their best in Letters From My Mill, Tartarin of Tarascon, Numa Roumestan. When he began to reach for the laurels of the realist he went out of his ordered domain. Too much artist to fail, his later efforts betray the struggle. There is too a note of rancour in them, partially the result, no doubt, of his wasting malady. Sapho contains much good workmanship. It may endure, yet we wish Daudet had written something else. Why should he compete with Germinie Lacerteux, or Nana. He was *au fond* the poet, and as Zola so happily said: "Daudet's mind gallops in the midst of the real, and now and again makes sudden leaps into the realm of fancy, for nature put him in that borderland where poetry ends and reality begins."

Madame Daudet is too modest about her rôle in the life of the fortunate novelist. She refers touchingly to the fact that, as she always read her husband's manuscript revisions and proofs, their handwriting was often intertwined. In reality she was the high wall that protected the frail and capricious Provençal flower from the cold wind of Parisian life. As Julia Allard she had in 1865 made her literary début in *L'Art* with verse, signed Marguerite Tournay. No need here to refer to her cultivated prose. She does not allude to her work in these recollections of such men as Flaubert, Edmond de Goncourt, Zola, Gambetta, Leconte de Lisle, Turgenief, Coppée, Théophile Gautier, Catulle Mendès, Sully-Prudhomme, Verlaine, Hérédia, Manet, Whistler, Augusta Holmès the Irish-French composer, Judith Gautier, Victor Hugo, Princess Mathilde, Paul de Saint-Victor, Mallarmé, Juliette Adam, Mistral, "Gyp," Liszt, Théodore de Banville, Henry Greville, and the Charpentier family— people that made history in their time.

She once heard that noctambulist and disordered genius Villiers de l'Isle Adam recite The Raven of Poe. Verlaine she found outwardly ugly, but a true poet. Her chief admiration, after her husband, is reserved for Edmond de Goncourt. While we are glad to get the story, we do not think it should have been made public property — that letter sent by the elder Goncourt to Flaubert — especially as Madame Daudet finds fault with a certain writer for revealing personal secrets. The letter in question, dated June, 1870, tells Flaubert of a mad resolve on the part of Edmond to kill his insane brother Jules. The sufferings of the poor fellow harrowed the feelings of Edmond. He wrote Flaubert he had a pistol ready and a letter to the police, but his courage failed him when Jules looked at him with his soft blue eyes full of childish astonishment and terror. A startling tale, altogether; perhaps one of Goncourt's best fictions.

Madame Daudet saw something of the Hugo ménage, with Julie Drouet at its head. Her description of the aged poet and his elderly charmer who had won him away from Madame Hugo, is the most vivid in the volume. She reprints a letter from George Sand written shortly before her death. She knew Drumont, and she makes pictures of social gatherings in which Ambassador Beust is shown playing trivial valses of his own manufacture. With the Zolas, naturally, the Daudets were intimate. Madame Daudet records that Madame Zola appeared happy. She was happy during the early fight of the romancer, when they both were half starved. Whether Madame Zola was happy in the last years of the novelist's career we cannot say. No doubt Alphonse Daudet had uphill work, but he never had to face such odds as did Zola (both were born the same year, 1840). The exterior man in the case of Daudet was so attractive, his gifts so sympathetic, that it would have been a surprise if he had not conquered. His finely modelled head with the black, silky hair falling over his eyes (unfortunately myopic), and these same eyes of beautiful colour and shape; his beard worn in such fashion as to win for him the sobriquet "the Arabian Christ," his sparkling conversation and piquant temperament — all these proclaimed his southern, oriental blood. (The name of the family was originally David, softened to Daudet in Provençal.)

He had a petulant temper and never forgave or forgot the slightest neglect or injury. There's a feminine character in his *amour propre*, so easily outraged. We cannot recall a writer whose books so bristle with personalities. Daudet spitted his enemies — and friends too — in his pages. His *romans à clef* are only worth reading nowadays because of the slanderous gossip they contain. As art they are nil. Their author never pardoned the Academy, and his wife relates an unpleasant social encounter she had with an old academician supposed to have served as a model in The Immortal. Her tact saved the situation. And there is the eternal Turgenief quarrel. She revives it, as Daudet did in his own Recollections of a Literary Man. After Turgenief's death a book of reminiscences appeared in which the Russian speaks almost contemptuously of the French circle he frequented when living in Paris. With the Daudets he had been most friendly, and the letters he exchanged with the good-humoured Flaubert are now in print. He helped Zola, Daudet, and Goncourt to procure an audience in Russia, even translating their articles for a St. Petersburg magazine; therefore he could hardly have played at the end the traitor. M. Halperine-Kaminsky has dissipated the mystery by proving that the Memoirs contained interpolations or were written by Sacher-Masoch, a Slav writer of unsavoury fame. But the Daudets would accept no explanations, and it is sad to see Mme. Daudet still believing the ancient lie. The trouble is that Alphonse Daudet was excessively sensitive to criticism and Turgenief did write once that he found much of the work of the Parisian naturalistic novelists "smelled of the lamp." This included Flaubert, Zola, Goncourt, Daudet. He often chided Flaubert for his frenzy over his corrections. It was Turgenief's motto, as it was Whistler's, that in art all traces of the mechanical processes should vanish; his own effortless and wellnigh perfect style is an admirable exemplar of this belief. He felt the strain in Daudet's later novels — the strain after qualities he did not possess. The early charm had almost disappeared; but Daudet would not tolerate the idea. Hence his bitterness regarding Turgenief — a man who towers over him as a creator and an artist. And it should be remembered that Alphonse Daudet was a big "seller" when his friends were not. He was childishly vain of his successes.

After Flaubert's death the Sunday afternoon gatherings of poets, painters, novelists, musicians, philosophers, and other celebrities at his little house near the Parc Monçeau ceased, and Edmond de Goncourt's *grenier* at Auteuil became the rallying-point for all the rising talent in Paris. This pretty *maison d'artiste*, the Villa

Montmorenci, may be seen to-day. It has become since Goncourt's death in 1896 the Académie Goncourt, though it must be admitted no imposing talent has as yet emerged from its portals. Madame Daudet was present at these meetings, where art and literature were discussed with an intensity and an acuity that seems almost ludicrous in our days of machine-made plays, novels, operas, and pictures. Fancy these men of the Second Empire—Flaubert, Zola, Goncourt, Daudet, and a dozen others — fighting over such obsolete literary ideals as artistic prose, form, atmosphere, character, and environment. You rub your eyes with astonishment. What an object-lesson is the group of which Madame Daudet writes so lucidly, for young fiction-mongers who typewrite two novels in a twelvemonth and then boast of their "art" and their many editions.

THE DE LENZ BEETHOVEN

The resurrection of a once-famous and long-forgotten book is always an interesting event, but will the present generation of readers enjoy what was the mode over half a century ago? To be sure a classic is always a classic; the book we allude to never pretended to be anything more than a gossipy chronicle boasting of personal charm about music and musicians, and the music of Beethoven especially. Imagine a Pepys of music, a Russian Pepys, saturated with French and German cultures, himself a pianist of unusual ability and the pupil of Chopin, Liszt, Tausig, Henselt — not to mention others of lesser celebrity — and the name of Wilhelm de Lenz may be familiar to some. He was born in 1808, at St. Petersburg; he died 1883. He was a Russian Councillor. He possessed means. He had musical talent; and he was simply a divine gossip. No such intimate book dealing with Liszt, Chopin, Tausig, and Henselt was ever written like The Great Piano Virtuosi of our Time (translated by Madeleine R. Baker). No one has, with the possible exception of Amy Fay, given us such easel pictures of these musicians as men — Miss Fay, of course, was not a Chopin pupil; but she studied under the three other heroes of the keyboard. In the Biographical Dictionary of Music and Musicians, edited by Dr. Theodore Baker and Richard Aldrich, De Lenz's birth year is given as 1804 and his "de" is there a "von." Need it be added that there will be no "conflict of authorities" over the two dates; De Lenz is hardly as important a personage in the world of music as Chopin; besides in Russia they do not fabricate with such ease as in Warsaw baptismal certificates. Chopin has already had three or four. More will follow as each new biography appears. M. Calvocoressi is the authority for the 1808 birth date. He prints it in his introduction to that long-lost volume of De Lenz, *Beethoven: et ses Trois Styles* (Brentano's).

While the book reads as fresh as yesterday, De Lenz is not a profound critic of music, and he too often writes in the inflated romantic vein of his times. Beethoven, a god for the few, was then compared with Homer, Shakespeare, Dante, Goethe, and Victor Hugo. Liszt has written some mouth-filling phrases about him, Wagner went him several better in the way of muddy metaphysics and cryptic burrowings, while De Lenz when he becomes excited could distance either of them. But Bettina Brentano, the mercurial and rhapsodic friend of both Beethoven and Goethe, leads De Lenz in the chase. Calvocoressi, the author of several monographs of composers, has edited De Lenz's French and furnished a brief introduction. Berlioz praised The Three Styles of Beethoven, as Calvocoressi points out; even if he had failed to do so it wouldn't much matter, for De Lenz quotes the French composer's opinion with a delightful smack of the lips. Luckily for posterity our musical Pepys was not a modest man. A very human, however.

The particular charm of the Beethoven [we prefer to call it thus, not forgetting, however, that De Lenz wrote later (1855-1860) *Beethoven: eine Kunststudie*] is its discursiveness. No matter how deeply the author may delve into the technical mysteries of a sonata or symphony, he soon flies away on the wings of an anecdote. It may be said without fear of contradiction that this book did yeoman's service in its day, and why it dropped out of sight is incomprehensible. In 1852 there was no Grove, no Thayer. De Lenz drew on Schindler and other friends of Beethoven and he had this advantage over critics who followed him — he spoke to the men who had been Beethoven's intimates, and as early as 1827. He played the Beethoven sonatas when they were *caviare* to the musical world, and once astonished Liszt with the performance of Weber's A-flat Sonata, a work which no one in Paris had ever heard. We prefer De Lenz's analysis of the pianoforte sonatas to those of Elterleins. He is painstaking and he follows Fétis in the classification of the sonatas; this same rubric of three styles has its merits. It is convenient, a species of critical milestones.

But when De Lenz reaches the last five sonatas he flounders; half praises, goes into ecstasies over the first movement of the noble C-minor sonata, opus 111, yet balks at the Arietta and variations. To him it is the tonal weaving of a man near the edges of an abyss. Nor did he note, though an old pupil of Chopin (1842 he studied with him at Paris), the curious similarity of the first few bars of the Chopin B-flat minor sonata and those of the Beethoven C minor. Both are bold and tragic. The intervals are suggestively alike in *Stimmung*, though not precisely so. But whereas Beethoven built of his preluding bars a massive entrance to his cathedral of glorious sounds, Chopin jumped from his fiery porch into a sombre dramatic narrative. We need hardly be sur-

prised at the inability of De Lenz to appreciate
the grandeurs of the last five Beethoven sonatas.
A greater than he, the greatest composer — and
we may add music critic — of France, Hector
Berlioz, confessed his mental paralysis in the presence of Tristan and Isolde. The introduction
was for him always the riddle of the Sphinx.
Neither its emotional curve nor its extraordinary eloquence and beauty of colouring made an
appeal to Berlioz. Was he sincere in this? Yet,
Beethoven student as he was, he might have
solved the enigma by analysing the introduction
to the Pathetic Sonata of Beethoven. The germ
of the Tristan harmonic progressions and the
plangent eloquence are there compressed into a
few bars. One might apostrophise Beethoven as
did De Quincey when he uttered those matchless
words at the conclusion of his study of the knocking at the door theme in Macbeth.

But over De Lenz there is no need to become
serious. His sketch of Beethoven's life is stuffed
with errors as well as the facts of the day.
Among other things he remarks that the composer passed the greater part of his life in a
cabaret at Graben, outside of Vienna (page 205);
and asks with comic intensity how could the
creator of that immortal masterpiece the C-
sharp sonata (Moonlight, so called) dine at one
o'clock in the afternoon? Scratch a Russian and
you come upon a Parisian. But what *esprit*,
what sheer joy in the telling of stories are to be
found in this book. The anecdotes of pianists

are many; some of them he transferred to his later book on Liszt, Chopin, and Tausig. Who but De Lenz could have discovered that Leopold de Meyer was a "Master of a Pennsylvania Freemason's lodge"? The lively writer calls Bach "that Sorbonne in harmony"; and of Zelter he said that he was the "Fétis of his time," not a superficial comparison. He literally goes for Mozart's biographer, Oulibischeff, for attacking Beethoven and characteristically concludes that as a critic Oulibischeff might be described in the words of the old vaudeville ditty "J'ai été marié, il est vrai, mais si peu, si peu!" Evidently De Lenz as an amateur critic of music realised the force of the Arabian proverb: "One who has been stung by a snake shivers at the sight of a string."

Beethoven, too, was among the supermen. He is reported as exclaiming — and we hear the prophetic rumble of Zarathustra's voice — "A superior man should never be confounded with a bourgeois." This speech, no doubt authentic, the composer matched with his brotherly report to Johann van Beethoven as to the possession of brains.

One of the interesting anecdotes concerns Wehrstaedt. Who was Wehrstaedt? He was a professor of the pianoforte residing at Geneva about 1827. He only knew the first three studies of Cramer (the Venerable Bede of the Pianoforte, as De Lenz happily styles him), the A-flat sonata of Weber (Rosenthal's warhorse to-day) and the sonata opus 26, A-flat, by Beethoven.

This admirable musical maniac spent his long life with musical baggage so slender in size. He had never visited Chamounix, although his sojourn in Geneva was protracted, nor would he pretend to understand how any one could love Mont Blanc while loving the music of Weber. He always kept his hat on when teaching or playing. In 1828 De Lenz met him, played for him, selecting the A-flat sonata of Beethoven. "Why not a galop by Herz?" interrupted the sardonic Wehrstaedt. "Because I love it," responded the brave young Russian; who writes that he had had many good masters and comprehended no more the meaning of this sonata than mice do of the architecture in the grange through which they scurry. Wehrstaedt pushed him from the keyboard and played the sonata as no one else could play it, save Franz Liszt (then seventeen years of age). Over a certain trill on the first page Wehrstaedt declared that he had spent twenty years. Nowadays your venturesome mechanical piano-player can play this particular trill in octaves. Such pyramidal labours for such trifles, you will exclaim. But Wehrstaedt was secretly happy. Every day he did the same thing, watched as the years rolled by his leaps and bounds toward the promised land of perfection.

IDEAS AND IMAGES

It is a holy and wholesale custom with certain French authors to collect and publish annually in book form their fugitive essays. As a rule, the material, notwithstanding its heterogeneous nature, is worthy of a second perusal. It is hardly necessary to add that the essay as a literary exercise, almost as extinct as the dodo in America, is still vigorously cultivated in France. Anatole France, Maurice Barrès, Lemaître, Faguet, De Gourmont, and many other masters of the feuilleton practise this gentle art of reprinting, and there is often as much variety of subject in one of their books as may be found, for example, in Plays, Acting, and Music by Arthur Symons. In the case of so inveterate an essayist as Remy de Gourmont his readers are always assured of a feast of good things. De Gourmont is luckily a master critic who has not yet "arrived" — in the sense of Bourget or France or Lemaître. An aristocratic radical, a lover of paradox, a profound scholar, a Latinist of the first rank, his supple, smiling prose is a mask that conceals much wisdom, much irony, many disillusionments. For the man in the street he is caviar. He sits in an ivory tower, but on the ground floor, from which he may saunter and rub elbows with life. He has been variously denounced as a subtle sophist, a corrupt cynic, a hater of his kind, and a philosopher without a philosophy. He may possess a little of all these terrific attributes, but he is also something else. He is very human, very gay, very tolerant, very charming, and very erudite. He is more sincere than Anatole France — which still leaves him a fair margin of irony — and he is infinitely less egotistical than Barrès. He deals with actualities as well as parchment learning, and if his tales are salty in their Gallicism we can only excuse him with the remark that they order such humour better in France than in England or America. A literary critic of the first standing, De Gourmont is hated and feared by the hypocrites, puritans, and pharisees who have during the last few years made their voices heard and their prejudices felt in Paris. He never spares them — please remember that *Tartuffe* was a Frenchman — though they sit in the seats of the mighty, whether professors, politicians, or editors.

His Promenades Littéraires is the third volume of the series bearing that characteristically Stendhalian title. De Gourmont promenades among a lot of interesting subjects, some *choses vues*, others the record of his browsings in eighteenth and seventeenth century authors. He recites some of the important facts in the critical career of the late Ferdinand Brunetière, and no essay in this volume so reveals the catholicity of its author, for between the saturnine and ill-tempered Brunetière and the urbane author of Le Latin Mystique there was little beyond their love of the classics to make them fraternal. Temperaments, and consequently points of view, were totally at variance. But Gourmont does not hesitate to lay a laurel of praise upon the tomb of the dead critic. He begins by asking the wherefore of the conventional distinction between the creator and the critic. Why the several hierarchies? He does not take refuge in that very banal definition — also hybrid — creative criticism. As if sound criticism could be aught but creative. He demands to know why Taine should be called a critic and Octave Feuillet a creator. If a history of literature is written the author must construct as well as criticise. Both novelist and critic are creators of values; the former in the category of sensibility, the latter in the order of intelligence. Why, for example, should we consider Brunetière inferior to Bourget? Where are the majority of the novelists of yesteryear? The contemporaries of Sainte–Beuve, who created fiction, constituted a unique group. Balzac, Stendhal, Flaubert, De Goncourt presumably will live; but it is difficult to imagine any single man of the lot outliving the reputation of Sainte-Beuve.

Then Gourmont plunges from the general into the particular. He shows us Brunetière absorbed in the Darwinian doctrines which about 1890 began to enter into the general circulation of French literature. Previous to that Brunetière had passed for a revolutionary; he who later became the leader of the reactionaries. His scheme was to fabricate a vast critical edifice on evolutionary lines. Literary history was no longer to be a series of portraits after the manner of Sainte-Beuve, but a co-ordinated work in which each epoch would in Taine fashion (or Darwinian) produce its various genres influenced by the *milieu;* and the evolution of these genres would be traced with an iron pen. Science was a word seldom absent from his pages in those days. A change supervened. Brunetière became religious. Hence his famous phrase, "The bankruptcy of science." A bankruptcy of metaphysics, adds Gourmont. Nevertheless the phrase stuck. Brunetière made capital out of it. He fell to hating his own times, like all idealists and hyperæsthetic persons, took refuge in the literature of the seventeenth century and with admirable results. But his hatred of life revenged itself in attacking living men, whose shoe-strings he was not worthy of unlatching. Nor did he spare the dead. That over-praised study of Balzac is full of grudging spleen and inept criticism, while his abuse of Baudelaire caused many to remark upon his lack of critical urbanity.

Brunetière's method was the historic. He was exact to pedantry. A rationalist, he forgot, as Gourmont finely puts it, that the domain of reason is very limited and that logic, according to Ribot, is nearly always the logic of sentiments. His complete work may be considered as a valuable repertory of ideas and literary judgments; but cold, but dry. The "ferment of idealism"

is missing, the dislike of originality, the worship
of the accepted, bulk too large. He was a learned
student and a small man.

Mr. Brownell has written regarding the old
crux of criticism and creation that "what criticism lacks and what will always be a limitation to
its interest and its power is the element of beauty,
which it of necessity largely foregoes in its concen-
tration upon truth," but "it is only in criticism
that the thought of an era becomes articulate,
crystallised, coherently communicated." We are
back at the contention of Gourmont that in
essentials criticism and creation are alike. Both
are a criticism of life. When you have need of
metaphysics, asserts the Parisian writer, you
have always need of religion. Metaphysic is the
first rung of the mystic ladder — a statement
seemingly calculated to have given William James
great pleasure.

At the end of the year 1889 Remy de Gourmont paid a visit to the Ministry of the Interior.
He held in his hand the manuscript of a story
named Stratagems, and as he wished to dedicate
it to Joris Karl Huysmans he went to the office
of that writer armed with a letter of introduction.
Huysmans was then assistant chief in the Department of Surety and received the young man with
amiability. After they discovered that they both
knew and admired Villiers de l'Isle Adam the
ice was broken. The elder man accepted the
dedication, and when five o'clock came he seized
his hat and with "the joy of a dog that is loosed

from his chain" he began to walk and talk. Gourmont tells us that in his detested office he wrote
nearly all his books. Là-Bas was represented
there by its original manuscript, written in clear
script with few erasures. Huysmans wrote
slowly, deliberately, and little at a time, but
like Zola it was the daily drop of water that
wore away the stone, and like Anthony Trollope
he could resume his page after an interruption
with perfect tranquillity. Gourmont, who is
qualified to speak, declares that Huysmans was
not well grounded in his humanities. The page,
so fascinating for the lover of original style, in
A Rebours, devoted to the Latin poets of the decadence, was condensed after enormous travail-
ing from Ebert's tomes on the subject (Histoire
générale de la littérature en Occident). The
French writer boiled down to a clear essence the
facts he needed and then verbally reorchestrated
them. He was astonished at the genuine classic
erudition of Gourmont and wrote an engaging
preface to his Le Latin Mystique. We quite
agree with Gourmont that A Rebours has literary antiseptic in it to preserve it from decay.
The later religious studies will endure, though
hardly on the book-shelves of the profane world.
A Rebours is a history of an æsthetic period, and
as such, apart from the magnificence of its execution, will be saved as vital literature.

Of interest is the gossip about the habits of
Huysmans. He arrived after his second break-
fast at his office in the neighbourhood of eleven

o'clock. He smoked cigarettes, stared at his
pet posters, read, wrote, and incidentally attended to his duties. The French Government
is liberal in those matters, despite the sordid
pictures of clerical life sketched by De Maupassant. Nor has Huysmans spared the rod. He
was his own M. Folantin, always grumbling at
the dulness of his life, at the wretched quality of
restaurant food. With Gourmont he went every
afternoon to sip Holland bitters at the Café
Caron, which he has celebrated in his vivid prose
etching Habitués de Café. There a singular
atmosphere reigned. Old customers would protest if their favourite corners were annexed by
newcomers; dominoes were not tolerated on account of the noise they made on marble-topped
tables; loud conversation was prohibited; pipes,
too — altogether a café de luxe. The cooking
and wines were excellent and not dear. Several
editors, poets, and politicians were steady at-
tendants. After the place went to smash because
of its exclusiveness Huysmans selected the Café
de Flore as its successor. Again over his bitters,
himself embittered by temperament, he exposed
his views on art and literature to his young
friend. To call them extreme is putting the case
mildly. He was sardonic, ironic, splenetic, rag-
ing. He never spoke well of any one (when his
back was turned Gourmont also came in for his
rating). Huysmans attacked religion, society,
art. His speech was rank in its frankness. He
took a delight in the abuse of shocking vocables.

His Flemish nature detested polite deceptions. His books, relates our author, are chaste in comparison with his conversations, which is saying much. He smashed the reputations of Bourget and De Maupassant, both former comrades, for "arriving" ahead of him. He never had any doubt as to his own artistic superiority. In a word, a "knocker" of the type — if Huysmans could ever be classified — described by Daudet in Jack.

Now for the other side of this rather discouraging picture. A tender-hearted chap, always doing favours, even to the men he abused, going out of his way — and he loathed all physical effort — to promote the cause of some stranger whose work had appealed to him. He was very charitable and always hard up because of this generosity. The women of course plundered his sympathies, and he wasted time over many who were devoid of talent. However, he put them in his books, and with what malice, what verve.

It will doubtless relieve many sensitive souls to know that the episode of the Black Mass, so horrible for either sick or healthy nerves, in Là-Bas is pure imagination. There never was any such occurrence in the life of Huysmans — for a good reason. If Paris had held so absurd and vile a ceremony he would not have hesitated to ferret it out. He was curious about unhealthy things. He was a dyspeptic with a thirst for the infinite. A certain Mme. de C. introduced him to the Abbé Mugnier, who converted him. Great was Gourmont's surprise to hear of this conversion. He had always known that a religious *fond* existed in Huysmans, but his constant mockeries and blasphemies had deceived him. Astonished too he was when he found out that Huysmans was deeply interested in black magic, spiritualism, table-tipping. Indeed, De Gourmont doesn't hesitate to say that his friend entered the church through the rather dubious gate of spiritualism. All roads lead to Rome.

Besides these souvenirs of Huysmans and Brunetière (who died drinking a glass of champagne) this book of Remy de Gourmont is full of suggestive studies written in a captivating style.

THE ETERNAL PHILANDERER

In France contemporary literary piety is devoted to the celebration of a marking date, 1811, the year of the appearance of Chateaubriand's once famous Journey from Paris to Jerusalem (Itinéraire de Paris à Jerusalem), the pattern of all the picturesque travels of the last century. When Goethe said that Hugo and the Romanticists came from Chateaubriand he could have added that Chateaubriand himself was a joint product of Rousseau and Ossian, and a veritable prose Byron. We remember seeing a picture of the Vicomte François René de Chateaubriand (1768–1848), his slim figure wrapped in a melodramatic cloak, his hyperion curls ruffled by the wind that swept from the sea across the bleak promontory where he posed in the face of an approaching tempest. The book of poems inseparable from such a composition was at his feet. Ossianic was the conception, and you could sympathise with the romantic ladies of the first half of the nineteenth century, who read René, read Atala, read The Genius of Christianity, and worshipped their creator.

He was a genuine force in French literature, indeed, in the literature of the world. As sentimentalist and sensualist he ranks after Rousseau, and he much resembles Rousseau in his constant intermingling of sensuality and religion. He invented a new form of morbid sensibility that is in the very bones of French letters to-day — Pierre Loti is its latest exponent — and consider, too, that he wrote Atala in 1801 and René in 1802, and thus set the pace for the fiction of the century. In the region of sensibility it was not difficult for such an accomplished virtuoso to fiddle across the semitone that barely divides the sentimental from the sensuous. Always he sounded with precision the sultry enharmonics of the senses; and the sounds, set in highly coloured and magnificent prose, ravished the ears of the blue-stockings as well as damsels with nodding curls. Chateaubriand was one more reincarnation of the eternal philanderer in life and literature alike.

André Beaunier has just published a study of the loves of the great writer. He calls his book Trois Amies de Chateaubriand, and tells again

the rather dolorous though fascinating stories
of Pauline de Beaumont, Juliette Récamier,
and Hortense Allart. These three distinguished
women exerted a real influence upon Chateaubriand, a man who in love was infidelity itself.
He early discovered, as other historical personages before him — and since — that to succeed
one must take an attitude in life, especially must
one maintain this attitude toward one's self. Be
always a hero before your looking-glass, said, in
effect, Victor Hugo, Lamartine, and Chateaubriand. The designer of the portrait we once
saw had caught the prosateur across the vesti-
bule of his inmost self. He was a poseur, but he
was also a genius, and his career was adventurous.
He secretly detested Napoleon, being a nobleman
born and a legitimist, though the master of
France sent him to Rome as secretary to the
embassy, and later as an ambassador to the
Valais. But he was equally dissatisfied under
Louis XVIII and Charles X, though one mon-
arch made him ambassador to England, the
other to Rome. In fact, his dissatisfaction was
never-ending.

The lion in the pathway of Chateaubriand was
ennui, a monstrous boredom with men, women,
and things, particularly women. His egotism
grazed the fabulous; so massive, so self-centred,
so firmly enclosed in the depths of his soul was
his self-love that he never even deigned to show
it, after the fashion of smaller men. There it
was, in repose, yet disdainful, revolving at ter-

rific speed, yet not showing its velocity. Kinetic stability, we might term such a passion. What a study for George Meredith would have been this temperament, instead of that faddle Sir Willoughby Patterne. Time, with its sly, ironic sense, has seen to it that this overwhelming, this superb paladin, this prince of the vocabulary, is now chiefly remembered by his fellow-countrymen, and all other cultivated nations, as the name of an appetisingly prepared beef-steak while Récamier is better known as the woman who wore so becomingly an Empire gown.

M. Beaunier first asks if a work of literary art is sufficient in itself, and answers in the negative. He might as well have spared himself the pains of putting the question. He sorrowfully confesses that few books are written nowadays without some "useful" purpose, usually sociological. Sociology is a blight on literature; it has given birth to innumerable libraries of sordid grey pamphlets, tracts that masquerade as books, dismal statistics, and to fiction stupid, hysterical, prophetic, and an amassing of inutile "facts" inartistically presented. Say "art" to any of the young writers of our times — with a few honourable exceptions, and these exceptions are pronounced immoral — and a volley of contemptuous adjectives is launched at your head. Art is for verbal voluptuaries. Art is for hedonists, sinister word; art is for slaves of their senses, not for free, self-inflated, socialistic men of commanding intellect. M. Beaunier concludes that Chateaubriand, an artist in prose with few equals in French literature, or any literature for that matter, would be an anomaly if he were alive and writing at the present time.

However, he doesn't devote many pages to æsthetic polemic. He is chiefly interested in the love affairs of the celebrated writer who had conceived his life as a work of art and could say "one must present to the world only the beautiful." But in working out the practical equation of such a theory, a man so finely organised and self-conscious as Chateaubriand may fall either into the pit of selfish satisfaction, an amateur of the emotions, or into the ecstatic gloom of the mystic. In both cases a woman's heart will suffer, and women's hearts did rebound from the stony, selfish cuirass of Chateaubriand. He loved Pauline de Beaumont, but not as she loved him. A brilliant member of a brilliant circle, most of whom went under the knife of the guillotine, Pauline narrowly escaped a similar fate. In Rome she spent happy days, though she was attainted with consumption. The correspondence is interesting. Joubert, a mutual friend, has said memorable things of this romance. He saw clearly that Chateaubriand had allowed himself to be loved, that he played alternately hot and cold, and, experienced grande dame as was Mme. de Beaumont, she was the live mouse in the clutches of this accomplished cat. He became entangled, nevertheless, in other affairs, the most notorious of which was his friendship for Mme.

de Castellane. The police tracked them, we suppose on the general principle that great writers should be watched at all times. To his "Délie," Mme. C., he wrote often; this was in 1823, when he was fifty-five years of age. A certain Mme. Hamelin supervened; like Stendhal he mixed up his amorous affairs. He knew Stendhal, and, naturally, disliked him. So did Hugo for that matter. All three were philanderers. Pauline de Beaumont died of consumption; some say of a broken heart. Chateaubriand in his memoirs bitterly deplores the coldness some men show to the living, and in his gorgeous rhetoric paints the agony of the survivor, who can never repair his ill deeds. What rhetoric! Mme. de Beaumont was buried at Rome in the Church of Saint Louis des Français.

The affair with that enigmatic but beautiful Juliette Bernard, the Lyonnaise, better known to the world as Mme. Récamier, the friend of Mme. de Staël, immortalised by the portrait sketch by David in the Louvre, was the most remarkable in the long life of Chateaubriand; and what a length the intimacy lasted. He first met her in 1801; again in 1814, and after the death of Mme. de Staël in 1817 their relations became friendly, and so continued until his death in 1848 (July 4). Juliette outlived him one year (May 11, 1849). Curiosity has never been stifled on the theme of Mme. Récamier. Her marriage was a mere convention, on that all authorities agree. But what were her real relations with

Chateaubriand? Here we stumble across an insoluble enigma. The truth may be that she was neither the wife nor the mistress of any man. Before the advent of the novelist, whose books are an ill-concealed autobiography, the dominating influence of her life was "Corinne," the masculine, brilliant Anna Louise Germaine Necker, Mme. de Staël, detested by Napoleon, who once roughly told her that a woman's chief business in life was to give the state citizens. Certainly Chateaubriand won no favour with Juliette Récamier until after De Staël's death. However, the case may not be so puzzling to psychopathists. Mme. Récamier lies in the Montmartre Cemetery.

With the passing of the years Chateaubriand became a lean, unslippered pantaloon; stone-deaf and feeble, he daily mounted, with the aid of canes and his valet, the staircase of the Abbaye-au-Bois, where in her declining years lived that sweet old lady Mme. Récamier. She was almost blind. Yet she received him gently, listened to his grumbling, and inevitably played for him a faded piano piece by Stiebelt (of all composers, sugar-water for canary birds). When he died she was at his pillow. He had deceived her, she loved him; he loved himself, and she gave him her whole life.

The episode with the gay Hortense Allart was not so pathetic. She was called "une petite George Sand," because she wrote and loved so much. She did not break her heart over the infidelities of Chateaubriand, for she committed a few herself. M. Beaunier, with the rigorous logic of his race, has compiled a time-table of the lady's sentimental voyages: from 1826-1829, Capponi, a young Italian hero of the risorgimento; from 1829 to 1831, Chateaubriand; from 1831 to 1836, Bulwer Lytton; from 1837 to 1840, "pendant quelques jours," Sainte-Beuve; from 1843 to 1845 she was the wife of M. de Meritens. A friend of Thiers, a fond mother, she died in the odour of sanctity in 1879, and is buried at Bourg-la-Reine. When she first encountered Chateaubriand at Rome he regretfully exclaimed: "Ah! if I had back my fifty years." Thereupon the sprightly lady replied: "Why not wish for twenty-five?" "No," moodily returned the ambassador, "fifty will do." Which recalls the witty design of Forain, representing a very old man apostrophising the shadow of the past: "Oh! if I only had again my sixty-five years."

We forgot the names of Charlotte Ives, Delphine de Custine, the little Countess de Noailles, who in Spain with the novelist called herself Dolores: all friends of the puissant one. He nearly married Charlotte Ives in London in a moment of self-forgetfulness. He had married in 1792 a lady, Mlle. Buisson de Lavigne, who was a model wife for many years. She was well received at Mme. Récamier's weekly receptions. Philanderers usually have good wives, and philanderers are generally anxious that their various feminine friends be on good terms. It makes life smoother. In this respect Chateaubriand was lucky, for he was an ideal philanderer.

THE NEW ENGLISH NIETZSCHE

A new translation of the works of Friedrich Nietzsche is now in progress and seventeen volumes have been issued. The edition will be complete in eighteen volumes and is to range from the five lectures On the Future of Our Educational Institutions, delivered by Nietzsche when professor of classical philology at Basle, to the autobiographical "Ecce Homo," which saw the light of publication (in an expensive edition) last year. This first complete and authorised (by Frau Foerster-Nietzsche of Weimar) translation is edited by Dr. Oscar Levy of London. Dr. Levy is a citizen of the world, author of Revival of Aristocracy. As a follower of Goethe, Stendhal, and Nietzsche his views on England and English institutions are distinctly stirring. Rather than be outdone by Heine and Stendhal, or by Nietzsche, he has said things in print about England which make the famous Egyptian Speech read like mere sophomoric vapourings. In the present series he has renewed the charge in an editorial note and an introductory essay, both of which contain many vigorous ideas. For instance, he utters the timely warning to students of Nietzsche "to read him slowly, to think over what they have read and not to accept too readily a teaching which they have only half understood." "By a too ready acceptance of Nietzsche it has come to pass," continues Dr. Levy, "that his enemies are as a rule a far superior body of men to those who call themselves his eager and enthusiastic followers." Refreshing candour this from a Nietzschean editor.

The truth is that a wave of Nietzscheism is sweeping English-reading countries. Ibsen never had the personal hold on his auditors that Nietzsche now has, but the very brilliancy of phrasing and clarity of expression are pitfalls for the all too human and unwary student. Nietzsche is never more enigmatic than when wearing the mask of mocking Greeklike blitheness (heiterkeit), and already the path of his progress is strewn with the bleaching bones of his reckless commentators. Already the half-baked in philosophy are sending letters to the newspapers and alas! picking out his most poetic and least viable ideas for idolatry. This new edition, containing, as it does, such sterling studies as The Birth of Tragedy and Homer and Classical Philology (his inaugural address delivered at Basle University, May 28, 1869), will show the hop o' the moon "Nietzscheans" that back of the great poet was the sane thinker and man of science. Not that we take exception to the doctrines, if doctrines they are, of the Superman and the Eternal Recurrence, but that we believe these poetic and metaphysical conceptions to be of less value than his ideas on social subjects. Nietzsche, it should be remembered, was a great psychologist, perhaps greater as such than as the formulator of a philosophic system. His Superman is a counsel of perfection; the Eternal Return an old Oriental idea newly presented. As to his escaping metaphysics, there may be quoted his own desire for a new art, "the art of metaphysical comfort." That much misunderstood man Max Stirner once in writing of the economic part that money plays in life declared that "it will always be money." For thinkers it will always be "metaphysics," let them be "realists" as Nietzsche believed himself to be or idealists or even our friends with the smiling modern face, the pragmatists. You can't make bricks without straw, symphonies without counterpoint, or philosophy without metaphysics. Therefore Nietzsche is no more a short cut to the philosophic Parnassus than Kant or Hegel.

The danger of the Nietzschean deluge is this: the very culture-philistines he so heartily despised when alive are going about with tags and aphorisms caked in their daily conversation. They utterly mistake his liberty for license, not realising the narrow and tortuous paths he has prepared for his true disciples. Wagner was for years obscured by the Wagnerians, Browning by the Browning societies. We now know that it is the poetry, not his febrile shrieking at a straw god, that makes Shelley dear to us; we know that in Wagner it is his music that counts, not his preposterous "philosophy"; in Browning his marvellous dramatic power and not the once celebrated Browning "profundities." Nietzsche must take his mud bath of abuse and praise with the others, though he will survive it and emerge, not as so many others have, men of reputation, a mud god himself. The exegetical literature in English concerning him is multiplying apace, and we rejoice that it is thus far of excellent quality. There are H. L. Mencken's admirable study, and Dr. M. A. Mügge's Nietzsche and His Life and Work, a résumé of all that Nietzsche taught and of the criticism he evoked. To our notion the clearest and most concise monograph on the subject is The Philosophy of Friedrich Nietzsche, by Grace Neal Dolson, A.B., Ph.D., formerly fellow of Cornell University. Then there are Dr. Levy's work referred to above, the selections made by A. R. Orage; The Quintessence of Nietzsche, by J. M. Kennedy; Who Is to Be Master of the World? by A. M. Ludovici; On the Tracks of Life, by Leo G. Sera, Englished by Mr. Kennedy. But as Vasari said of the Farnesina Palace, "non murato ma veramente nato" (not built but really born), so must the Nietzsche interpreter have a moiety of the Dionysian spirit coursing in his veins to do the poet and philosopher even slim justice.

The attitude of the English toward the German thinker disconcerts Dr. Levy. If they would only fight him; but to accept him as if he were the "latest" thing in fiction is truly British. They could laugh at him when Shaw served him up in Celtic epigram with sauce socialistic, but

otherwise—! Dr. Levy makes the rafters ring
with his sarcasm. His comparison of Benjamin
Disraeli and Nietzsche is clever. This continental Hebrew good-naturedly avers that it is
now time for a little "Christian baiting" after
the centuries of Jewish persecutions. There is a
Heine-like touch in the humour of this editor.

The introductions to Thoughts Out of Season,
Human, All Too Human, The Birth of Tragedy,
The Will to Power, by the various translators are
brief and illuminating. Above all there is no
"sugaring down," no elimination of the original
thought, which with the Teutonic English was
the demerit of previous English translations. For
Adrian Collins the burden of the first essay in
Part II of Thoughts Out of Season (the first
chapter on The Use and Abuse of History) is
that "with Nietzsche the historical sense became
a malady from which men suffer, the world process an illusion, evolutionary theories a subtle
excuse for inactivity. History is for the few, not
the many. . . . It has no meaning except as
the servant of life and action, and most of us can
only act if we forget." And turning from the
history to the historian he condemns the "noisy
little fellows who measure the motives of the
great men of the past by their own and use the
past to justify their present."

Nietzsche's aim is "the elevation of the type
man," a species of transcendental moral eugenics.
For those to whom socialism is a disgust we
recommend his The Will to Power, now for

the first time done into English by Anthony
M. Ludovici. How well Mr. Ludovici has
grasped the much abused "immoralism" may be
found in his preface: "Nietzsche only objected
to the influence of herd morality outside the herd;
that is to say, among exceptional and higher men
who may be wrecked by it. Whereas most other
philosophers before him had been the altruists of
the lower strata of humanity, Nietzsche may be
aptly called the altruist of the exceptions, of the
particular lucky cases among men"; and how, as
the true poet he was, the idea first came to him
as a concrete image may be read in the account
told by his sister Elizabeth when he conceived
The Will to Power as the fundamental principle
of all life. In 1870 he was serving as a volunteer
at the seat of war in a German army ambulance
corps. "On one occasion," she relates, "at the
close of a very heavy day with the wounded he
happened to enter a small town which lay on
one of the chief military roads. He was wandering through it in a leisurely fashion when suddenly, as he turned the corner of a street that
was protected on either side by lofty stone walls,
he heard a roaring noise, as of thunder, which
seemed to come from the immediate neighbourhood. He hurried forward a step or two, and
what should be see but a magnificent cavalry
regiment, gloriously expressive of the courage and
exuberant strength of a people, ride past him
like a luminous storm-cloud. The thundering
din waxed louder and louder, and lo and behold!

his own beloved regiment of field artillery dashed
forward at full speed out of the mist of motes
and sped westward amid an uproar of clattering
chains and galloping steeds. . . . While this procession passed before him on its way to war and
perhaps to death, so wonderful in its vital
strength and formidable courage and so perfectly
symbolic of a race that will conquer and prevail
or perish in the attempt, Nietzsche was struck
with the thought that the highest will to live
could not find its expression in a miserable struggle for existence, à la Darwin, but in a will to
war, a Will to Power, a will to overpower."

Yet this philosopher of mankind militant, of
the joy of existence, if existence is a conflict not
a concession, this hater of facile optimism and the
smug flatterers of the mob, could turn on his
fellow-countrymen after the victories of 1871 and
tell them that as a race they were hopelessly
uncultured and uncouth. Very different from
Richard Wagner, who insulted the French in
the bitterness of defeat and fawned for favours
at the German court. Altogether this new English edition is treasure-trove for the students of
Nietzsche.

THE LAST DAYS OF VERLAINE

One evening, when nearing the close of his
sad and extraordinary career, Paul Verlaine said
to some of his friends assembled at a café table:
"I wish for nothing better than the existence of

a plain citizen in the Rue Mouffetard"; nor was this a vain boast made by the poet, a hater of the bourgeois and their habits, himself held up as an awful example by decent members of society. Verlaine was worn by dissipation, suffering from rheumatism, from stomach troubles. He longed for the quiet of home, for the care of a good woman. No more absinthe, no more amer picon, no more little glasses of cognac! Temperance and hard work were to be incorporated in his plans for the future, and in effect he did behave himself so admirably for several months that the cafés of the "left bank" wondered if he were dead or in one of his favourite hospitals. The François-Premier, the Soleil d'Or, the Procope, the Escholiers, the Monome, and the Maccha-bées missed him, as did the bars of the Chope Latine and the Académie of the Rue Saint-Jacques; whenever the poet settled down for a prolonged drinking bout, disciples would gather and then business was sure to be brisk. The only news that could be gleaned of his whereabouts was that he was indoors, in a little apartment plying his pen and under the watchful eye of Eugénie Krantz, otherwise known at the Bal Bullier as Nini-Mouton because of her abundant blond woolly tresses.

Not long ago at Paris the annual dinner was given in memory of Verlaine, and afterward the guests went to his monument in the Luxembourg Gardens, which was inaugurated last year. It is a bizarre affair by the sculptor Nieder-

hausern de Rodo; that it suggests an absinthe
flask has not caused much concern among his
admirers, for like Alfred de Musset Verlaine was
a notable victim of the Green Fairy. But the
project for this same monument aroused in certain circles the most violent opposition, which
not even the presence of men the most distinguished in literature and the fine arts at the consecration ceremonies could totally suppress. But
there it stands to the memory of the modern
Villon, to the Pauvre Lelian, whose voice is
sweetest and subtlest in the hoarser and more
rhetorical choir of French poets. He was a
loose liver, with the temperament of a spoiled
child, a genius who never grew up. The world
has forgiven him his vagaries, many of them
largely a matter of pose, for the unaffected beauties of his verse. Let the heathen rage. Paul
Verlaine will not be forgotten, even in an epoch
that saw two such great poets as Victor Hugo and
Charles Baudelaire.

Messrs. F. A. Cazals and Gustave le Rouge
have told all there is worth knowing about the
last days of the poet in their Derniers jours de
Verlaine. He had dragged his rheumatic leg
and exacerbated nerves from hospital to hospital, from the Broussin to Tenon, from Saint-
Antoine, Cochin to the Maison Dubois, Bichat,
Saint Louis, he even had dreamed of retiring
within the mad wards of Sainte-Anne. What
joy, he said, to associate with simple souls who
fancied themselves Christ, Mohammed, Na-

poleon! He would have liked his cards engraved: "Paul Verlaine, Madman, Asylum
Sainte-Anne, Paris." But he confessed that he
was only an accursed poet and such luck was not
for him. His friend Stéphane Mallarmé had re-
peatedly warned him against the abuse of absinthe; Verlaine replied that he drank it to
forget, not for the drink itself, that familiar fallacy of alcoholic victims. Poor Verlaine was
ever seeking to banish the present and evoke
the past, that disgraceful and wonderful past in
which two poets, Rimbaud and Lelian, swam
through golden mists of ecstasy or sank into the
black fogs of despair.

However, he did pull himself together for a
time. The three vultures that fought for his
meagre favours — his poverty was appalling —
Eugénie Krantz, Philomène Boudin, and the
enigmatic creature who simply called herself
Esther, were finally resolved into one, Eugénie,
an illiterate, good-hearted woman of the people,
who worshipped Verlaine as a kind of incomprehensible deity, yet did not refrain from giving
him a taste of her muscular arm when he came
home fuddled. She superstitiously saved scraps
of paper upon which he had scribbled, believing
that they would be worth money after his death.
Had she not seen the publisher Vannier over on
the Quai hand her good man a gold piece for a
few lines? Poetry then had a definite value for
this big-boned guardian of the shrine. After the
passing of Verlaine there wasn't much to seek

in his writing-desk. Though Eugénie Krantz deceived Verlaine with the utmost tranquillity, yet if it had not been for her he would have died in a hospital, a prospect that he had always feared. She did not long survive him. She died from intemperance, which she paid for by the sale of autographs and certain rare papers of the poet, among the rest a fragment of his Louis XVII.

The poet must have led her a merry dance. He was the most irresponsible of men. A wedding, a funeral, a simple trip to church, often resulted in disappearances for days at a time. He had been an assiduous guest at the home of Mme. Nina de Callias, a young woman, talented, vivacious, and a patron saint of artists and literary men. She had private means and kept open house for the hungry and thirsty of the tribe bohemian. A very interesting account of her may be found in The Memoirs of My Dead Life by George Moore, who, a lively young Irishman, was gadding about Paris at the time. Mme. Nina was separated from her husband, M. Hector de Callias, once a brilliant journalist, also a backslider from the principles of temperance. He was practically unknown to her circle, and the astonishment was great when he turned up at the funeral, solemn of mien and garb. He led the cortège as nearest of kin, accompanied by his friend Verlaine. What this pair talked about on the long road to the cemetery, from the Batignolles to the Parc d'Orléans, is not difficult to fancy; but they held themselves in good shape till the obsequies were ended and the little Nina laid in her last resting-place. Then Hector de Callias, his throat dry as a lime-kiln, decamped, leaving to the poet Charles Cros the duty of doing the final hand-shaking with the mourners. Verlaine followed him shortly after, and on the return one by one the men and women who had been the beneficiaries of the dead Nina dropped from the ranks. The day was a warm one and cafés numerous. What that cortège numbered when it reached the Batignolles no one has told; the entire episode reminds us of Gounod's humorous and sardonic Funeral March of a Marionette. Hector and Paul did not reappear in their accustomed haunts for a week. Later, at Fontainebleau, De Callias was put on a milk diet by his physician's order, and he died from the experiment, so they say.

Not even this example proved a warning for Verlaine. He soon slipped into his old wet rut, and as there is an end to all things, even to a thirsty poet, he died January 8, 1896. He wrote his last poem, not inappropriately entitled Mort, January 5. A fever set in; during the night he fell out of bed and was discovered unconscious. A sinapism was applied. "That bites," he murmured; this was his last sentence, after that he merely babbled the names of friends. The state paid the expenses of his burial, which was the signal for the presence of many celebrated persons, Anatole France heading the list. Verlaine died a repentant sinner; he had always been that, always sinning, always repenting. His verse is the record in exquisite music of the contradictory nature of the man. It made him marvellous enemies, this nature of his. And his statue is in the Luxembourg Gardens to-day.

XI

THE PATHOS OF DISTANCE

THE pathos of distance! It is a memorial phrase. Friedrich Nietzsche is its creator, Nietzsche who wrote of the drama and its origins in a work that is become a classic. Distance lends pathos, bathes in rosy enchantments the simplest events of a mean past; is the painter, in a word, who with skilful, consoling touches disguises all that was sordid in our youth, all that once mortified or disgusted, and bridges the inequality of man and man. And to our recollection of favourite actors and actresses, the subconsciousness, in the dark room of which are stored all the old negatives of our life, adds a glow that is positively fascinating.

Recall, if you are a trifle grey and faded, recall now, after your morning coffee, Adelaide Neilson. Eh, my old bucks, have I jolted sweet souvenirs? Was there ever such a Juliet, ever such a Viola, ever such a Rosalind? Emphatically no, our memory cells tell us.

Yet we criticised Adelaide Neilson when she first appeared, criticised her Juliet, and during her later visits to America we criticised her Viola. Every one criticises. Never forget that fact. The only difference between your criticism and mine is that I am paid for mine. That doesn't necessarily make it better. But the statement is well to keep in mind. If you disagree with me, you are only criticising my criticism. By the same token I may challenge yours. Lillian Russell in one of her metaphysical moods — Miss Russell thinks profoundly at times — put the question in a nutshell: "After all," she remarked, "it is only *one* man's criticism." This phrase is magnificent in its anarchic spirit, even if it is not exactly original. She touched a tender spot: it is always one man's criticism. And no man thinks or feels as another. That is physiology, as well as psychology. When dramatic critics disagree, the incident should be acclaimed instead of derided. If they always agreed, then how quickly that stale accusation would be repeated — conspiracy.

Here is a criticism from a Philadelphia journal written when Miss Neilson played Viola in Twelfth Night, I think, but I am not sure, in the season of 1876–77 (and I've forgotten who wrote it):

"There was nothing about her performance demanding extended or minute criticism. It was in most respects a pleasing and amiable representation from a lady who has comeliness, intelligence, and familiarity with all the mechanical processes of her art. She was prettily dressed, and she contrived to express with much nicety the shy coyness of the maiden beneath the half-

hearted boldness and self-assertion of the man.
Her posturing and gesticulation were easy and
graceful, and her treatment of the text was
sometimes good, but very often bad. Frequently
the sharpest ears of her audience failed to catch
her words, and more than once when they were
caught there were mistakes of inflection and em-
phasis which told of carelessness and indifference to study."

Mark what follows: "The part has been taken
as well by actresses of inferior reputation and
less persistent claims to greatness. In one instance it was played by Mrs. John Drew in a
manner which Miss Neilson can never hope to
rival."

Isn't that breath-catching, especially when
the youngsters of to-day are told by their oldsters
that Adelaide Neilson was the perfect incarnation of Shakespeare's Viola? Yet here is a critic
writing in no uncertain tone about the *mediocrity*
of her impersonation. The fact that he may
have lived to repent that criticism does not alter
the still sterner fact of its having been written
and published.

Mr. William Winter speaks of Miss Neilson's
exquisite embodiment of Viola. He wrote of
this actress in 1877. Therefore there was no
pathos of distance in his criticism. When I saw
her, Eben Plympton was the Sebastian, and a
sterling interpretation it was. Strange as it

sounds, Mr. Plympton looked like Neilson in the play. Mr. Walcot, if I can remember aright, was the Malvolio, though perhaps not in the cast with Plympton. McDonough was Sir Toby, Howard the Sir Andrew, Hemple the Clown, Miss Barbour the Maria. But this must have been at an earlier representation. In those days I haunted the Arch Street Theatre, Philadelphia, quite stage-mad, full of the pimply ideals of youth, and I do not regret it now, for I "assisted" at Ada Rehan's début, John Drew's début, the first appearance of his sister, clever, sparkling Georgie Drew Barrymore, and also the first appearance of Edwin Booth as Wolsey in 1876. I detest theatrical memoirs, books about the débuts of actors, and all the miscellaneous chron-icling of theatrical small beer, and yet I am thick in the tide of just such gossip.

Mr. Winter, in his study of Twelfth Night, gives a list of the principal American casts. The only ones that interest us are those we have our-selves seen. In the theatre, nothing is so potent as the sight. Reading of a remarkable perform-ance is getting life at third hand, not at second. So 1820 does not appeal to me as much as 1877, when Mr. Daly revived Twelfth Night at the Fifth Avenue — when it was at Twenty-eighth Street — with Neilson as Viola and Charles Fisher as Malvolio. Edward Compton, Barton Hill, George Clarke, and Henry E. Dixey have played Malvolio, and shall we ever forget Henry Irving? The Malvolio of Beerbohm Tree I witnessed at what was then Her Majesty's Theatre in 1901. Mr. Winter mentions Charles Walcot. He was my first Malvolio, and naturally enough he seemed the best. The Violas we have seen here were Mrs. Scott Siddons, Ellen Terry, Fanny Davenport, Marie Wainwright, Helena Modjeska, — after Neilson's, the most poetic, — Ada Rehan, Julia Marlowe, Viola Allen, and Edith Wynne Matthison. Mrs. Drew played Viola in her palmy days, and Mr. Winter gives a complete array of the old-time actresses who were famous in the rôle. Alas, such is the evanescent nature of the actor's art, an art writ in water, that these names are mere spots of black ink on white paper — unless one has a sympathetic imagination and loves to grub in antiquities and Shakespeariana. I do not. The last play of a Hauptmann or a Maeterlinck gives me more of a thrill than all the musty memories of the days that are no more, and of the dust on forgotten tombs. To-day is more than a million yesterdays or to-morrows! Let the theatrical dead bury the theatrical dead! Yet here I am circling about the past like a fat moth in a lean flame. The pathos of distance!

But halt a moment. As you have seen, there were doubters in Israel even when Adelaide Neilson appeared, a glorious apparition from some hidden Arcady. As I remember, the theatrical small talk of those days set her down as an uneducated woman who was literally drilled into speaking her own tongue. She looked Oriental: but she was English born, without a father's name; her mother, an obscure actress, was named Browne. Her father was said to have been Spanish, and also Jewish. Like nearly all the players, from David Garrick and Mrs. Siddons to Edwin Booth and Mrs. Kendal, from Edmund Kean to Richard Mansfield, Adelaide Neilson perhaps had a moiety of that Hebraic blood in her veins which George du Maurier declared a precious quintessence for an artist. And Neilson showed it, not alone in her royal, dusky beauty, but in her brilliancy of style, her marvellously rapid intuitive processes, her warmth of temperament, and the rich colour of her interpretations.

How did she play Viola? As a poem in the living. One glance of her beautiful eyes confuted a wilderness of traditions. When she walked we heard music. And when she spoke violets and roses fell from her lips——!

What's this? Am I, too, pressing the mainspring of memory? And is it only the pathos of distance? No, a thousand times, no! Hear the voice of one older than I: "Her image, as it rises in memory, is not that of the actress who stormed the citadel of all hearts in the delirium of Juliet, or dazzled with the witchery of Rosalind's glee or Viola's tender grace; but it is that of the grave, sweet woman, who, playing softly in the twilight, sang — in a rich, tremulous, touching voice — the anthem on the man of sorrows acquainted with grief!" Thus William Winter, who can also pour vitriol on his critical sugar better than any man. It shows what a hold Neilson the woman had on all of us in those half-forgotten days.

How did she play Viola? Without a return to juvenile rhapsody I can answer truthfully — better than any other actress that I ever saw — Remember that this is only one man's opinion. She was very unequal, very capricious, and, by an odd contradiction, sometimes mechanical. I saw her once at a matinée when she tore the text to tatters. Being a creature of moods, she recited in a toneless voice her lines until half the play was past, and then electrified us with her arch humour, tenderness, and intense passion. For the delineation of the amorous, the dreamy, melting, sighing, or furnace-hot passion Neilson had no equal in her epoch. Her Viola was more various than the Violas of her contemporaries. Its elegiac, poetic side, was better portrayed by Modjeska — but Modjeska, let it be remembered, had to struggle with a strange language; and despite the music, the most subtle music, — for she was a Pole and a countrywoman of Chopin's, — she breathed into her speech, it was ever a veil between her and her auditory.

No such limitation existed in the case of Neilson. Poetic she was, but poetry realised; not the diaphanous personality of Modjeska, but a real flesh-and-blood woman stood before you bewitching your senses and appealing to your imagination. Her beauty, with all its palpable surfaces, while not exotic, as is Duse's, reached the imagination like a bullet surely sped to its mark. Perhaps it was all a mask, perhaps a sweet, commonplace woman peeped out at her audience, amused at the havoc she played with our hearts and heads. I have heard this said; but I prefer to cherish the illusion, for beautiful illusions are the only reality in a world of ugly dreams. Neilson, starry-eyed Adelaide, we still salute your memory! For our generation you are the first Viola, let the others do what they will. Alas, is it the pathos of distance?

And the others! A superb group! Ellen Terry of yesterday, felicitous, abounding in sweet mad-cap merriment, her melancholy but skin-deep, her love, the joy of life personified. Mrs. Scott Siddons, grave and imperial in her beauty, read Viola. I never saw her on the boards in this character. Marie Wainwright and Fanny Davenport were Violas satisfactory of schooling. Miss Rehan, brilliant and abounding in vitality, did not sound, or did not care to sound, the deeper organ tones of the disguised Cesario. Hers was an assumption that I cared less for than her Rosalind. Its key-note was brilliancy, wit, and aristocratic distinction; above all, personal distinction.

Julia Marlowe's Viola is conceived and played more naturally than others I remember. Few actresses would dare discard the obvious readings and theatrical devices as does Miss Marlowe.

But if she is natural she has much to thank nature for — personal charm, a comely figure and sweet face, and a voice the richest on the English-speaking stage. And brains in abundance direct this unique ensemble of attractions. No one reads blank verse with the simplicity and art of Miss Marlowe. Her conception of the rôle compels by its subtle comminglement of grace and poetry. Some of her speeches are tear-moving; her assumption of boyish youth never disillusions. O rare Julia Marlowe!

And, at last, we reach, after a fatiguing and elliptical route, Edith Wynne Matthison and her Viola. Again let me disclaim, at the risk of protesting too much, that my opinion has no finality. Only fools are consistent, says Emerson; and the Jove of Weimar, Goethe, remarked that only fools are modest. So I hope I shall be accused of neither consistency nor modesty when I wonder audibly why Miss Matthison has not made more of a stir in the dramatic world. She has that rarest of gifts, personality. And yet her Viola did not intrigue me as vastly as I had expected. I still adhere to my first opinion, and will continue to do so until this charming actress plays the part in a different key. She is too sombre, she lacks in buoyancy, lacks in mood versatility — and what is Viola if not buoyant, replete with fleeting moods, a creature of fire and air, caprice, sunshine, and fantasy?

THE PATHOS OF DISTANCE

Miss Matthison, thanks to the funereal atmosphere of the Elizabethan setting, plays within a narrow octave of Viola's moods. She gives us all of her melancholy music, her veiled ardour, her self-effacement. Her horizon brightens in the scenes with Olivia. She essays comedy with a delicate touch. Melancholy, not vaporous as is Orsino's, but pessimistic and modern in its essence, is what I feel as the foundation of Miss Matthison's reading. That she is the greatest Viola since Neilson's I dare not say. She is not so poetic as Modjeska; not so audaciously masterful as Rehan. She is unique in her interpretation, inasmuch as it presents us with a Viola all gracious in her sadness, Viola absolutely in the mode minor.

With that canorous voice, its *triste* and dying fall, the many cadences of her speech, the pensive beauty of brow and sweet mobile mouth, Miss Matthison ought to go far — not as far as Neilson, not so poetically high as Modjeska, yet far. I did not detect evidence of a supreme imagination, but I have only seen her twice on the boards. She seems to have more fancy than imagination. We miss the big, sweeping draught of a commanding personality. She is persuasive, not compelling. And that is one of her charms — that same insinuating personality. For the rest, I can only aver that her hands are beautiful hands, not so pregnant with meaning as Duse's, not so poetic as the pianist Essipoff's, but physically beautiful. Her features are firmly modelled, interest-

*i*ng in their irregularity and effective in profile. With Miss Matthison it is more than — item: A pair of lips, or eyes, or hands; it is the generous and rich nature which shines through her eyes, is manifest in her melodic speech. But a great Viola — no! Again, you will say, the pathos of distance!

XII

IN PRAISE OF FIREWORKS

THE art of the fireworker is pre-eminently suited to summer climes; in the hyperborean regions nature saves man the bother of inventing pyrotechnics, as all know who have witnessed the glory of northern skies at night; but wherever are lands that boast warm evenings there may be seen fantastic-coloured fires aloft and admiring crowds below. Considering the antiquity of this art, which was practised thousands of years ago in China, it has not progressed with its sister arts.

Architecture has come to a flowering and a decay in many countries; sculpture from Phidias to Rodin has met with many victories and many vicissitudes. But since the Greeks has there been great sculpture? Literature, like the poor, we shall always have with us — that is some sort, if not distinguished or original. Painting, according to criticism, reached its apogee with the Italians of the Renaissance, and in Spain with Velasquez. Remains music — for we need not include just now the entire seven arts. Philip Hale has said that since Beethoven music has made no distinct advance; permutations almost innumerable there have been, but original utter-

343

ance there has been little. Men of genius, such
as Schubert, Schumann, Chopin, Berlioz, Liszt,
have each contributed something to the mighty
cairn of music; however, despite their strong
individuality, they, like modern painters, have
only developed certain sides of their art. Creators in the sense that Beethoven was a creator
they are not. Richard Wagner, less original in
melodic gifts, was, thanks to a more potent personality, more successful in erecting a formal
edifice, which, combining — so he believed — all
the arts in one huge synthesis, he named the
music-drama.

Now, in his general scenic scheme light plays
an important rôle. We need not remind opera-
goers of the gorgeous effects he introduces into
the Ring; the dull golden haze of the Rhinegold
in the first act, the infernal smithy of the Nibe-
lung gnomes or the rainbow apotheosis at the
close. Die Walküre, too, is rich in fiery incantations, the mystic light on the hero's sword, the
moonlight, the electric storm in which Siegmund
and Hunding battle, or the forge episode in Siegfried; even flame is vomited from the dragon's
mouth, young Siegfried defeats his grandfather
Wotan amid fire, and fire-begirt he finds a bride.
In fire and smoke at the end of Götterdämmerung the abode of the gods goes up. Yet the
most striking of all the fire tableaux of Wagner
is the finale of Die Walküre, with Wotan singing
to the crisping and crackling of his conjured and
sentinel flames. It is a stirring invocation to

Loki, the fire god, and a magnificent stage picture.

But all this is an art of the foot-lights; it is cribbed, cabined, and confined between a few walls. The genuine art of pyrotechny must have as a background the sky; for a frame the walls of heaven. Its chief merit lies in its inability to express ideas, above all, didactic ideas. It must not tell a story, insinuate a moral, or imitate any earthly form. It is the ideal art of the arabesque. Attempts at portraiture of popular men, politicians and other unimportant persons, are simple burlesques, unworthy of the serious-minded fireworker. His patterns must be varied, his tintings multifarious. He must have the courage of his fiery fugues, and the conviction that if all other arts are moribund, his is still vital and capable of an infinite evolution. In a word, the pyrotechnist should have the eye of a painter, the imagination of a poet, the designing brain of an architect, and the soul of a fanatic.

With his soundless traceries, muted music of fire, he may stand upon the threshold of a universal art, one that will need no preliminary initiations, one immediately understanded of the people. While the sky must not be his pulpit, he may nevertheless inculcate a love of beauty with his multicoloured aerial panoramas. Form and hue, pattern and emotional meanings, may all enter into his incandescent compositions. Professor Pain, virtuoso in the art, delights in showing us historic happenings in a coruscating pragmatic blaze; yet we believe if left to follow his own devices this firesmith would give the world a nobler style of art. And how restful is this art even in its undeveloped state. The eye is gratified without tiring the brain; there are no plots, no dramas of problems; no rude orchestra or vocal howlings assault the ear with modern clangours. You simply sit back and let the professor wend his squibby way, and then you go home to iridescent dreams.

I do not exaggerate when as a regenerating influence I consider pyrotechny far above the teachings of Ibsen, William James, Tolstoy, and Richard Strauss — who should have been a fireworker instead of a musical composer.

XIII

A PHILOSOPHY FOR PHILISTINES

I

PRAGMATISM is in the air. The magazines give the new movement a prominent place. It is discussed on mountain and at the sea-shore as if it were some portentous event like the arrival within our atmosphere of a threatening comet or the advent of a freshly hatched religion. Perhaps some day it may become a religion. The attractive lectures of that extraordinary Professor William James, the growing interest in the writings of Nietzsche, the books of Dewey and Schiller — particularly the latter thinker's Humanism — all point to states of feeling on the part of our reading public which betoken something of genuine import. And it is true that pragmatism offers to the speculative mind plenty of problems. Its ugly title, with its connotations of self-conceit, meddlesomeness, and bumptiousness, is misleading. Professor James wittily calls it an old thing with a new name; in a phrase, old wine in new bottles. But your true pragmatist is the reverse of the dictionary definition. He is as indifferent as the ocean in his views of the universe; a latitudinarian, compared with whom that rapidly vanishing individual the ag-

nostic is a mugwump. The agnostic hopelessly
dropped his hands before the riddles of life, but
the pragmatist does not indulge in such a useless
gesture. Like Peer Gynt, he "goes round
about"; evades the real hard-and-fast issues.
He knows his theory to be good waiting-ground,
and from it he procrastinatingly surveys the
cosmos with gentle curiosity. He is nothing if
not tolerant, all things to all men and all faiths.
He is too sweet to be true. It tickles the
vanity of the man of the multitude who thus
believes that he can think without thinking.
A short cut to Parnassus, philosophy made
easy. To the anxious interrogator of spiritual
uncertainties he says: "Wait! We are on
the wide stream of consciousness. What may
now seem to you inexplicable may be clear when
we drift further down." They do drift. The
landscape on either bank of the river changes
continually. See, says the pragmatist, such is
truth. A chameleon, ever changing. My truth
may not be your truth. As there are so many
humans on the globe, so are there as many
Truths. Comforted, the anxious one may go
on dry land to rob, kill, or outrage if his conscience says him yea. But he is then an extreme case. He has criminal instincts. With
such rude souls Professor James does not deal.
Why should he? But — it may be pragmatism
in the end.

"The true, to put it very briefly," James says
in his first lecture, "is only the expedient in our

way of thinking, just as the right is only the expedient in the way of our behaving." That is, a truth is justified if its consequences are useful to you. In a certain sense we may be pragmatists, just as M. Jourdain spoke prose for a long time without knowing it. The novelty of the idea dates back to the hills, before Protagoras had discovered that man is the measure of all things. Professor James mentions Aristotle as an early pragmatist, but does not speak of Thomas Aquinas, though the angelical doctor "humanised" Aristotle for the Christian world. Terence has been pressed into service with his "Homo sum, humani nihil a me alienum puto." Wasn't St. Paul pragmatic when he spoke of faith and good works? Pragmatic is to be practical — its Greek root so signifies. How about Goethe and his question: "What is the value of this to me now?" Pure pragmatism. And Renan with his Pyrrhonism, and his theory of a world ever in the process of creation, or re-creation — *fieri* is his precise word. And our egoistic friend Max Stirner, an extreme Hegelian, whose motto is "My truth is the truth." Are not all political opportunists pragmatists? Pope Pius X was a pragmatist when he denounced "Modernism," and James would be the first to acknowledge him as such, for modern thought, modern science, are repugnant to the Holy Father; they are not "practical" truths for him — knowing as he does the ever-changing "truths" of science (compare, for example, the evolution of Lamarck and Darwin with the evolutionary theories, the Transformism of Quinton, to-day). Professor James declares that God is not a "gentleman." Villiers de l'Isle Adam proves him a pragmatist in his ironical Tribulat Bonhomet. God asks of Bonhomet: "Quand jetterez-vous le masque?" "Mais après vous, Seigneur!" responds Bonhomet.

Pragmatism, then, while no new thing, is nevertheless propounded as a theory of truth. Truth means agreement with reality, and all truths must be valued for their practical consequences. Nature abhors an absolute. There is no absolute in knowledge or belief. If a man says that he is hot he is hot for himself though the thermometer be at zero. In effect Professor James would deny the absolute of the thermometer, not the validity of the man's assertion that he is hot. All idealism, all rationalism, all ideas based on an absolute, on the infinite, are like the thermometer, *i. e.*, they are relative, though they may do you a lot of good. A Turk, a Hebrew, an atheist, a Christian, may be sound Pragmatists. Indeed, there is nothing so hospitable as pragmatism — which, according to its professors, is not a philosophy but only a working theory, an attitude of utility, a method, rather than a system; a species of sophistical picklock that is to open up all the metaphysical banks and reveal their bankruptcy. James speaks wittily of Kant "as the rarest and most complicated of all the bric-à-brac museums" — that Kant, who is the greatest moral nihilist among modern thinkers, a denier compared to whom Max Stirner is a bubbling well-spring of affirmations.

But man has been called a metaphysical animal. The artistic spider that spins in the dark cells of every thinker's brain is already at work with the pragmatic idea. Its originator, Professor Charles Sanders Peirce (in 1877 and 1878 he first spread the good tidings), confesses that his child got away from him, so he renamed it Pragmaticism. Schiller, a disciple of James, calls his variation on the theme Humanism — also a very old title and something quite different once upon a time.

Other days, other ways. New manners, new modalities. Professors James and Dewey are the American upholders of this boiling down of Locke, Mill, Hume, Bain; in Germany such names as Mach, Hertz, Ostwald, are enlisted, and in Italy Papini, Prezolini, and Calderoni have started a review — at Florence — called *Leonardo*, devoted to the extension of the idea of Pragmatism — which is really not "Pragmatism" but a congeries of pragmatic ideas and theories. In France it is the "Philosophy of action" and has attracted a number of bold spirits. The entire movement is greatly influenced by Nietzsche. Nor need we be surprised if from this humble if arid acorn some amazing trees will grow. You may expel metaphysics by way of the door, yet it will enter through the window or come down the chimney. To be quite frank, pragmatism is old-fashioned utilitarianism with a dollar mark. It has much of the canny Yankee in its ingenious mechanism. And later it may develop into a rule of conduct, for it aims at dealing with the concrete, at giving metaphysical "truths" a new content, at throwing overboard the entire apparatus of metaphysics from Kant to Schopenhauer. Again we beg leave to doubt the possibility of these things occurring, and James would probably tell us: You are quite right. Make your own truths in this very plastic world around you, which is real, as it is your own creation. If not pragmatism, then something else practical.

Upon the beach of life lie glistening in the sun innumerable gigantic wrecks and shards of philosophical systems, washed up by the tides of thought only to be swallowed in the tomb of time. The pragmatists point to these antique remains, once vital, now obsolete, and exclaim: "Behold, to this state must come all truths!" Ibsen expressed the same idea when he said that a truth usually ages after its twentieth year. But pragmatism, not being a system, only a roving comet amid the constellations of philosophers, will, it is asserted, remain eternally young — that is, if some giant planet does not drag it within its orbit and incorporate it as a part — a very small part — of its own system.

In sooth, as it stands now in its nudity there is not much to grasp. It is a thin doctoral thesis. The nature of judgments, most important of

propositions, is not dealt with by James. Or,
to put it thus: deny the perfections of the judgment, and, *à priori*, you impugn the truth of the
system. Deny the truth of the system, and, *à
posteriori*, you infer the weakness of the judgment. Yet the consequences of judgment are
seen in conduct. Pragmatism is not a theory of
truth but a theory of what it is expedient
to believe. No "categorical imperatives" for
James, only expediency — you remember his
major definition: "The true is only the expedient in the way of our thinking." Thus
the nature of belief is never touched, and judgment, "the real problem of truth," is left in the
dark, maintains Mr. Ralph Hawtrey. Professor
James calls the rationalists "tender-minded"
and the pragmatists "tough-minded," *i. e.*, they
do not fear to face reality. It strikes us that
the above crux and the failure of the pragmatists
to come to grips with it prove the new men
"tender," not "tough," minded. A truth that
is only good as a means and not in itself sets us
to wondering what particular kind of falsehood
this "truth" must be. It is putting the cart
before the horse. Life, if lived only for what
we get out of it, would not be lived out by
many men. Bread we can't do without; but
only to have bread ——? We suspect pragmatism to be labouring in the mesh of muddled
verbal definitions.

It calls itself empirical and nominalistic, as
opposed to the ancient realism and the new

rationalism. Despite protestations to the contrary, there is to be detected upon the "new truth" the deadly trail of eclecticism, and when the pragmatic palace is built — and it is sure to be — we may see many old bricks from many old systems used in its construction. The pragmatist is neither a yes-sayer nor a no-sayer to the universe. He is a looker-on, despite his claims to be a worker with viable ideas. His is a critical, not a constructive, attitude. If the centuries preceding him had maintained this pose of indifference what intellectual values would have been transmitted us? To be a cheerful sceptic is much easier than to forge the thunderbolts of affirmation or negation. Moreover, the old ideas, even if "abstract," "obsolete," mere empty frames without "concrete" pictures, were, after all, definite ideas and have served pragmatic purposes. What would have become of our thinking apparatus if back in the womb of Time some genius had not formulated the notions of Time and Space? Working hypotheses, if not realities. Better the bitter thunder of Schopenhauer's pessimism than this limp, waiting-for-something-to-be-proved attitude. Dynamic? The quality that pragmatism does not possess is the dynamic element. William James is a dynamic writer, as is the fantastic Papini — who is more poet than pragmatist — but, between a man and a working system of conduct, gulfs may intervene. For the young pragmatism will always mean: "Nothing is proved, all is permitted." And though Pro-

fessor James admits a belief in God as a working
hypothesis this hypothesis would not long work
in a world where virtue is judged only by its
consequences — pleasant or unpleasant to each
of us, as the case may be. Pascal saw these
things clearly when he told the incredulous man
that it didn't matter much to the sceptic whether
there was a God or annihilation after death, as
the two doctrines were equally indifferent to him;
what mattered very much, however, were the
different consequences of the two doctrines. We
suppose for this speech Pascal will be called a
pragmatist. So are we in this case, for by their
consequences we shall judge the "truths" of the
pragmatists, whether "truths" objective or
"truths" newly manufactured for special oc-
casions.

Curious it is to see bobbing up again that once
fiercely hated word "expediency," with its inevitable corollary: The end justifies the means.
Has the Society of Jesus captured the pragmatists? will be asked by the timid. Yet here is that
same terror-breeding axiom, so sedulously foisted
upon the Jesuits for years, emerging from ob-
scurity and actually used as a catchword em-
broidered upon the banners of the pragmatists.
Expediency! The end justifies the means! Is
Truth (capitalised) a chameleon — or a phœnix?
Professor James in one of his lectures on The
Notion of Truth assured us that, "first, you
know, a new theory is attacked as absurd; then
it is admitted to be true but obvious and sig-

nificant; finally it is seen to be so important that its adversaries claim that they themselves discovered it." We plead guilty to the second count, omitting the word "significant." Obvious is this pragmatism with its "cash values," its vast Gradgrindlike appetite for "facts," "reality," and its sophistical "meliorism." Its "realities" are those of the midriff, not of the imagination. It is all very well to leave the soul — or what is called the "soul" — out of a working scheme of life; but if religion is "the poetry of the poor" it may be also the "reality" of the rich — that is, the rich in imagination and feeling. There are large claims made for the "humanity" of pragmatism; indeed, James includes within its domain all earth and heaven and hell. It welcomes with open arms "the will to believe," the religious spirit. But what special call is there to tell those who seek the truth that it doesn't much matter for practical purposes what the truth is? Here is your invertebrate attitude, notwithstanding the talk of "reality." We know that as far as results are concerned one philosophy is as good as another. To say "philosophy" is only to sum up in a fatidical phrase the physiologic states of the particular philosopher; or, as M. Louis Thomas wittily puts it, "the hazards of my digestions." After all, Plato was platonic and Schopenhauer the first Schopenhauerian. And, judging from The Isle of Penguins, M. France is a Gulliver who has read Anatole France, and, perhaps, H. G. Wells.

A PHILOSOPHY FOR PHILISTINES

Pragmatism is just one more exemplar of metaphysical virtuosity in a world already overburdened with metaphysics and the common plague of mental gymnastic. From pragmatism we turn with relief even to Tertullian and repeat after him: "Certum est quia impossibile est."

II

JACOBEAN ADVENTURES

Almost every great philosopher has been annoyed by his devil. Of this history has assured us. Each according to his temperament has come to grips with his household demon. If Satan once in satanic exuberance threw a stone at the head of St. Dominic, did not Luther fling an inkstand at the dark-skinned gentleman, thereby wasting his temper, good ink, and all to no decorative purpose, though the spot on the wall is still shown to pilgrims? The particular form of devil that entered the *atelier* of Cuvier was of the familiar bovine type. When the naturalist asked him what he wanted, "I've come to swallow you," was the amiable reply. "Oh, no, you haven't. You wear horns and hoofs. You are granivorous, not carnivorous." The evil one departed, foiled by a scientific fact. Now students of demonology know that Satan *Mekatrig* may appear disguised as a maleficent idea. The latter part of his life Ernest Renan despised a devil he described as "the mania of certitude." He dearly loved a concept that couldn't conceive. Nature abhors an absolute, and for Renan the world process was *fieri*, a becoming, a perpetual re-creation. Professor William James has his own devil, a haunting devil, which he has neither named nor summoned, but that sits by his bedside or with him at his study desk. This bright special devil is Monism, and to exorcise it, to banish it without bell or candle but with book, he published his Hibbert Lectures, delivered at Manchester College, on the present situation of philosophy. The book bears the pleasing title A Pluralistic Universe. It is the record of his adventures among the masterpieces of metaphysics; and what an iconoclastic cruise it has been for him!

When pragmatism was discussed Mr. Hawtrey criticised the doctrine — or attitude, or whatever jelly-like form it may assume—thus: The nature of judgments, most important of propositions, is not dealt with by Professor James. Yet the consequences of judgment are seen in conduct. Pragmatism is not a theory of truth, but a theory of what it is expedient to believe. "Precisely so," Mr. James could have retorted; "if it is expedient for you not to believe in pragmatism as a working system, then don't attempt to do so." This advice would have been a perfectly enunciated expression of pragmatism. We confess we do not find him any the less pragmatist in his new volume, as some critics have asserted. He is more protean than ever; but then

the essence of pragmatism is to be protean.
When you attempt to recall the colour of the
mind of William James you are forced to think
of a chameleon. Running fire, he slips through
your fingers, benignly scorching them. The
entire temper of A Pluralistic Universe is critic-
ally warlike. He invades the enemy's country.
Armed with the club of pluralism, he attacks the
bastions of monism, rationalism, and intellectualism. For the seasoned theologian, says a
Roman Catholic theologian, the spectacle must
be exhilarating. That old ice-church, the strong-
hold of rationalism, has long been an objective
for ecclesiastical hot shot. To see a philosopher
of the James eminence shooting the latest-fan-
gled scientific projectiles at the common enemy
must provoke the query *Quo vadis?* What next?
Wohin? That Mr. James employs for hostile
purposes the concepts of rationalism Mr. Paul
Elmer More has remarked; but the philosopher had forestalled this objection in his note to
Lecture Six. Speaking of Bergson, he asks:
"Does the author not reason by concepts exclusively in his very attempt to show that they
can give no insight?" He answers: "What he
reaches by their means is thus only a new practical attitude." *Chi non istima, vien stimato!* we
might add.

Let us broach the Jacobean arguments, with
one intercalation. The enormous power of vis-
ualising a fact, thanks to the author's intellect and literary style, makes of A Pluralistic

World ambrosia for the happy many. Without doubt, beginning with Schopenhauer and down to Nietzsche and James, there has been an attempt to batter the musty walls of metaphysical verbiage. Such clarity of speech, such simple ways of putting subtle ideas as Mr. James's are rare among German or English thinkers. The French have hitherto enjoyed the monopoly in this respect. Indeed, so deft is the verbal virtuosity of James that his very clearness is often deluding and might become for a man of less sincerity a temptation to indulge in sophistry; but this, we feel assured, is not so. Whatever essential weaknesses there are in the ideas presented by our philosopher they are at least presented with the ringing tones of conviction. Or can a man be sincere and a sophist at the same time?

The form of idealistic thinking that postulates an absolute came into English philosophy by way of Germany. "The Rhine has flowed into the Thames," said Professor Henry Jones; "the stream of Germanic idealism has been diffused over the academical world of Great Britain. The disaster is universal." Ferrier, J. H. Stirling, and J. H. Green are to be thanked for this. James thus defines the difference between empiricism and rationalism: "Reduced to their most pregnant difference, empiricism means the habit of explaining wholes by parts, and rationalism means the habit of explaining parts by wholes. Rationalism thus preserves affinities

with monism, since wholeness goes with union,
while empiricism inclines to pluralistic views.
No philosophy can ever be anything but a summary sketch, a picture of the world in abridg-
ment, a foreshortened bird's-eye view of the perspective of events; and the first thing to notice
is this, that the only material we have at our dis-
posal for making a picture of the whole world
is supplied by the various portions of that world
of which we have already had experience. We
can invent no new forms of conception applica-
ble to the whole exclusively and not suggested
originally by the parts. . . . Let me repeat once
more that a man's vision is the great fact about
him (without vision the people perish). Who
cares for Carlyle's reasons, or Schopenhauer's or
Spencer's? A philosophy is the expression of a
man's intimate character, and all definitions of
the universe are but the deliberately adopted
reactions of human characters upon it." James
deliberately renounces the metaphysical apparatus and casts logic to the dogs. He must
of necessity approve of Jowett's "Logic is neither
an art nor a science, but a dodge," quoted by
Leslie Stephen; but when logic goes out at the
door, doesn't faith come in through the window?

With the dualistic theism of Christianity he
does not concern himself. "Theological machinery" is not within the scope of these lectures.
To demolish the monistic form of pantheism,
that pantheism developed by Spinoza, which en-
visages God as One, as the Absolute, is the de-

light of our thinker. In reality we are all pragmatists, all pluralists without knowing it until
now. On the stage of this theatre of ideas the
Cambridge master manipulates the concept pup-
pets, the *"All-form"* and the *"Each-form,"* and
the duel is in this dramatist's hands very exciting. It is not merely a battle of conjunctions,
of the *quâ* and *quatenus*, the "as" and the "as
such"; but a wholesale massacre of "ideas,"
Platonic and their congeners. It is a cheerful
spectacle to witness an intellectual descendant
of Kant, that grand old nihilist of Königsberg,
blow skyward with his pluralistic dynamite the
lofty structure which once housed the *"Ding an
sich,"* and those fat, toddling Categorical Imperatives. Professor James is the one philosophic showman of his day who gives you the
worth of your money.

He does not believe in an objective Truth
with a capital — there are also the "lower case"
truths to be taken into consideration. While he
hints not at having heard Ibsen's statement that
all truths sicken and die about every twenty
years, it is not difficult to conjure our chief pragmatist as chuckling over the notion. Pyrrho
was philosophically begot by Anaxarchus, and
Pyrrho in turn begat pyrrhonism, which begat
the modern brood of intellectual deniers, Kant
and Hegel at their head. In so far as relates
to monism, Professor James is as profound a
doubter as Pyrrho. He would gladly extirpate
the roots of this system, which builds from above

downward. In a suggestive study, L'Absolu, by L. Dugas of Paris, the absolute is studied as a pathologic variation of sentiment. "L'absolutisme, sous toutes ses formes, implique contradiction; il vise un but et en atteint un autre," asserts the French thinker.

"The pluralistic world," continues James, "is thus more like a federal republic than like an empire or a kingdom." Monism, on the other hand, believes in the block universe, in a timeless, changeless condition; "all things interpenetrate and telescope together in the great total conflux." Philosophy, which is a kind of phœnix in its power of emerging from its own ashes, always reflects the Time Spirit. Formerly absolute and monarchical, it is now democratic, even socialistic. Pluralism appeals to Socialists. Only a few years ago J. H. Rosny the elder, the novelist and social philosopher, wrote a book called Le Pluralisme, the first chapter of which, Continuity and Change, appeared in *La Revue du Mois*. Pluralism and pragmatism have been in the air since Ernest Mach and Richard Avenarius published their important treatises. Francis Herbert Bradley of Oxford, with his Appearance and Reality, is the man upon whom James trains his heaviest artillery. Josiah Royce is handled in A Pluralistic Universe more gently than in Pragmatism. We still hear of the "tough-minded" and the "tender-minded," and while transcendentalism (oh, souvenir of Massachusetts!) is pronounced "thin," pluralism is described as "thick." As much as he dares Professor James avoids the conceptual jargon of the schools. His analogies, which are legion, are formed from the clay of every-day imagery. The immanence of god in the universe (lower case god) he admits, but pronounces that god finite, not an All-form. Monism is "steep and brittle" — this for the benefit of Oxford. He has named his empiricism Radical Empiricism to distinguish it from the antique atomistic form. After that wonderful book, The Varieties of Religious Experience, we are not surprised to hear Mr. James discussing the phenomenon of psychic research — "I myself firmly believe that most of these phenomena are rooted in reality."

The truth is that titles such as Monism, Idealism, and Pragmatism belong to the category of Lewis Carroll's portmanteau words, words into which can be packed many meanings. Mr. More has acutely pointed out that "in denouncing Platonism as the type and source of rationalistic metaphysics he [James] had in mind not the Greek Plato but a Plato viewed through Teutonic spectacles." This is well put. The world of thought is not yet through with Plato, Mr. James naturally included. The terrain of mental vision would be terribly narrowed without the Greek.

Two interesting chapters are devoted, one to Fechner and his animism, the other to Henri Bergson, that French philosopher who has attacked the very ramparts of intellectualism.

A PHILOSOPHY FOR PHILISTINES

Read the paragraphs in which are set forth the impotence of intellectualistic logic to define a universe where change is continuous and what really exists is not things made, but things in the making: Renan and his *fieri* again newly instrumented by a brilliant Berlioz of philosophy; also Heraclitus with his fire and flux. While Professor James deprecates the tendency among the younger men to depreciate the originality of our latter-day philosophies, there is no gainsaying the fact that the massive wheel of the World Idea revolves and the systems of yesterday become the systems of to-morrow. Perhaps this is the real Eternal Recurrence of Nietzsche — that Nietzsche who has been the greatest dissolvent in German philosophic values since Kant.

Let us be grateful to the memory of the late William James for his large, lucid, friendly book; for his brave endeavour to establish the continuity of experience. He has worked to humanise rationalism, to thaw the frozen concept absolute. If he had cared to he might have described monism as an orchestra with a violin solo performer, making its many members subordinate to the All-form; while the pluralistic orchestra, each and every musician playing in harmony, would typify the Each-form. Yet despite his sympathy with "pan-psychism" and certain manifestations of "superhuman consciousness," no new Barbey d'Aurevilly would have ever dared to advise William James — as the old French one did Baudelaire and later Huysmans — either to blow out his brains or sink at the foot of the Cross and worship. Faith being the Fourth Dimension of the human intellect, the Cambridge professor dismisses it under the rubric of "Over-belief." Yet mysticism mightily rages down Boston way.

XIV

THE PLAYBOY OF WESTERN
PHILOSOPHY

I

ROBERT LOUIS STEVENSON in an essay on style, charming notwithstanding its discussion of technical elements, describes a conjuror juggling first with two, then three, finally four oranges, keeping them all aloft with seemingly small effort. Stevenson employed this image to explain certain qualities of literature. After rereading the books of Henri Bergson, in the admirable English translation, I couldn't help thinking of the conjuror spinning his four oranges in mid-air, so deftly does the French philosopher keep in motion his images, with a *leitmotiv* which he has named the *élan vital*, the vital impulse. It is no mere coincidence that in every successful philosophy there may be found a boldly coined image which serves not only to stamp the entire system, but also as a handy catchword for its disciples. We know that there is much more in Kant than his *Ding an Sich*, the famous Thing-in-itself; yet shorn of that phrase the Kantian forces would no longer be as terrible as an army with banners. Hegel, that old cloud-compeller, the Jupiter Pluvius of metaphysics, for what would he stand if not for his Absolute and his theory of Negatives; yet they are not altogether Hegelianism. And Schopenhauer, whose Will-to-Live image brought his philosophy safely into port through a muddy sea of pessimism; or Comte and his Positivism, the scepticism of Renan, the agnosticism of Spencer, or the foggy Unconscious of the Berlin thinker, Hartmann — each of these schemes for a new *Weltanschauung* has as a sign, a symbol, an oriflamme, an image that sticks to the memory long after the main lines of the various philosophical ideas are forgotten. A philosopher is often doubled by a poet as an image-maker. And many sport Siegfried's magic Tarnhelm, that not only makes them quite invisible, but invisible too their thought.

Now a happy image captivates. When the poet Nietzsche declared that the gods were dead in the firmament, the world was not particularly shocked, but much more interested when he forged his significant phrase, Will-to-Power. Henri Bergson is a man with exceptional literary gifts. He has an ingratiating manner of saying things, of weaving them into golden loops of prose. As a lecturer he woos the ear with the rhythm of his musical cadences. How persuasively, yet how calmly he juggles his orange-concepts, his Vital Impulse, his Intuition, his Instinct, his Life pictured as a swiftly flowing stream, his Time as a stuff both resistant and substantial, with his Creative Evolution. But, who knows, perhaps the image that will make his philosophy unforgetable is his comparison of human consciousness with the mechanism of the cinematograph. He contrives to make a definite and logical pattern out of his theoretic oranges and literally in the air. I recall a lecture of his at the Collège de France, though the meaning of his talk has quite escaped my memory because I was studying the personality of the man.

The Chinese have a saying that an image-maker never worships idols. Bergson is a mighty maker of images, nevertheless his sincerity, his faith, is unquestionable. He is intensely in earnest, one would say passionately, if it were not too strong a word for a thinker whose bearing and gestures betray perfect equipoise. He is bald, with a beaver-like brow, the brow of a builder born; his nose is slightly predacious, his features cameo-like, his deep-set eyes are dark, the eyes of an oracle though there is nothing of the pontifical in his attitude toward his audience. A modest man, because he knows so much, Bergson is more of the *petit-maître*, the diplomat, even the academician, than the popular notion that all philosophers are bearded old men, their eyes purging amber and plum-tree gum. Alert, even vivacious, M. Bergson is yet self-composed, far from a dreamer, and while he shows his Oriental stemming, he is less Jewish-looking than Anatole France. (It is said that Celtic blood flows in his veins as well as Semitic.) There is an ecclesiastical suggestion; you look for the *soutane*. As he spoke in that *legato* fashion of his, so unlike the average French orator, I thought of him as a Jewish Renan, a master-sophist, more dogmatic than the author of the Vie de Jésus — himself a Hebraicised thinker — and one not averse from the "mania of certitude," which his master did so abhor.

And as Bergson's closely linked argument flowed on the image of his rushing river of apperception arose in my mind. What a wealth of examples. And what a picture-maker. What magic there is in these phrases: "Il s'en faut que toutes nos idées s'incorporent à la masse de nos états de conscience. Beaucoup flottent à la surface, comme des feuilles mortes sur l'eau d'un étang." One is instantly conscious of that pool upon whose languid surface the dead leaves float and in a flash you feel that our half-expressed or discarded states of consciousness are as "dead leaves" that idly drift in the backwaters of our being. Throughout his various books such imagery is not infrequent. What if his *élan vital* be but another "vital lie," of the kind Ibsen believed so necessary to our happiness, that "lie" which the brilliant and original thinker Jules de Gaultier has erected into a philosophical system he calls "Le Bovaryisme" — the tendency of humanity to appear other than it is. People like to be told they are "free"; that life is a spontaneous outburst of optimism; that the intellect is not the chief of the human organism, the brain only being the telephonic "central"; that Intuition is superior to cerebration, and all the rest of the gorgeous bric-à-brac of this Parisian jeweller in philosophic phrases. But he has only set up one more conceptual idol in the metaphysical pantheon — the idol of Time, so long neglected for its fellow-fetish, Space. Time is an Absolute for Bergson, who otherwise detests the Absolute, even insinuating that Nature abhors an Absolute. Time is the *idée mère* of his work. It is also his one noteworthy contribution to contemporary thought. It's magnificent, but it's metaphysics. And it always will be metaphysics — which if expelled from the door comes down the chimney. Paul Bourget says somewhere: "On revient toujours de ses voyages d'oubli," and it is difficult to escape the witchery of Bergson's adventures in the caves of the thought-idols. We are reminded of those old *fantoccini* hoary with age — Time and Space and Causality, or the Ego and the Non-Ego, all capitalised and all recalling the thrill metaphysical of our youth. As William James writes: "conjunctions, prepositions, and adverbs play indeed a vital part in all philosophies; and in contemporary idealism the words 'as' and 'quâ' bear the burden of reconciling metaphysical unity with phenomenal diversity." Bergson plays with his dialectic as does the Playboy of the Western World with his competitors. Not precisely a "vicious" circle of reasoning is his; rather let us say, in medical parlance, a "benign" circle; which simply means

that the *élan vital* is life because it's lively. All
metaphysicians are mythomaniacs, though their
myths are as a rule more verbalistic than conceptual. However, Bergson is not altogether the
victim of his own verbal virtuosity; the faulty
method of appraising him is to blame. He has
been adjudged an absolutely original thinker.
He is not; indeed, the poet and myth-maker that
is in him runs a close second with his metaphysic.
All said and done, he is as much of an idealist as
the next one, and to alter good old Sir Thomas
Browne, he sees men not as trees, walking, but
as images, flowing; and he also declares that
"the mechanism of our ordinary knowledge is of
a cinematographical kind." Truly, a "mechanistic" image!

For the rest, Henri Bergson is a hard-working
professor, born at Paris, October 18, 1859. He
entered the École Normale in 1878, took his
degree 1881, and was made doctor in letters 1889.
Since 1900 he has been professor at the Collège
de France, and in 1901 became a member of the
Institute on his election to the Académie des
Sciences morales et politiques. His Essai sur
les données immediates de la conscience (Paris,
1889), translated into English as Time and Free
Will, is in our opinion the most valuable of his
works, containing, as it does, the matrix of his
ideas on Time and written in a more austere
style than his better-known works. Matter and
Memory followed (in 1896), with, in 1907, the
favourite L'Evolution Créatrice (Creative Evolu-

tion). The success of his writings has been universal, and in the English-speaking world largely due to the praise of the late William James — to my way of thinking a profounder philosopher than Bergson, and the possessor of a simpler and more searching rhetoric.

Mankind longs for a definite "yes" or "no" in answer to the eternal enigmas, and Bergson is a yes-sayer. He tells us in his supple prose that we need not be determinists or believers in the automaton theory, that life is continually creative, that we are in our individual way gods fashioning our own destinies, and much more that suspiciously sounds like old-fashioned teleological arguments. And in our century, "famous for its incoherences," this "spiritualisme en spirale" of Bergson, as Remy de Gourmont wittily puts it, has attracted the amateur philosopher as well as the idle of intellect, cultured women, the crowd without spiritual ballast, the whole flock of mystic, emotional, artistic, and semi-religious folk that are seeking for the unique sign, the objective frame, the message from Beyond. Bergson is their pet planet for the moment that Zarathustra speaks of: "Between two seas, between what is past and what is to come." Mysticism, with a nuance of sentimentality, has poked its nose once more into the crib of philosophy, demanding its share of flattery and sustenance.

II

Imperial-minded Goethe reserved for philosophy but a small province in his vast intellectual kingdom. He loathed "thinking about thought," and made Mephisto tell the scholar: "Grau, teurer Freund, ist alle Theorie," though he did not fail to study Spinoza his life long. Yet his spinning spirit sings to Faust: "So schaff ich am sausenden Webstuhl der Zeit und wirke der Gottheit lebendiges Kleid." That living garment of the deity is composed of Time and Space — and as many categorical imperatives as the ingenuity of philosophers can invent. Those are the convenient — and fictive — forms by which we apprehend the sensuous universe. Bergson lays the stress on Time as the more important factor in the understanding of life. Too long has the world been regarded through spatial spectacles; science recognises Space more than Time. But Time is not abstract, declares Bergson, it is concrete, real. He says: "My mental state as it advances on the road of time, is continually swelling with the duration which it accumulates: it goes on increasing — rolling upon itself, as a snowball on the snow. It is a mistake to tie together our conscious states as manifestations of some ego. Time is all that connects them; indeed, they are time. As regards the psychical life unfolding beneath the symbols which conceal it, we may readily perceive that time is just the stuff it is made of. . . . There is, moreover, no stuff more resistant nor more substantial."

No denial here of objective reality; all is solidly concrete in a concrete world, far different from the "timeless block universe" of the absolutists. Time is a living thing. The original impetus of life is the fundamental cause of variations. This impetus is conscious. Its vital matter is the impediment, and its collision with the living stream, the resistance overcome, causes creation. Wherever this flows it organises matter. The greater the resistance, the more complex the resulting organism. Evolution is continually creative. It is now and everywhere. "Life seems to have succeeded in this by dint of humility, by making itself very small and very insinuating, bending to physical and chemical forces, consenting even to go part of the way with them." Life at the outset — but was there ever a beginning, M. Bergson, you who so dislike the idea of finalism? — was "possessed of the tremendous internal push that was destined to raise them — specks of protoplasm — even to the highest forms of life." The opponents of our philosopher contend that while his erudition is undeniable his inferences from facts observed are faulty; that his employment of analogies is specious — what have a snowball and Time in common? Snow accumulates while rolling, but does Time? Furthermore, he too often sets up a metaphysical man of straw so as to overturn it and triumphantly conclude that because he upsets one theory his own is necessarily truthful. Which statement cannot be contravened. Bergson has mastered much science and presses it into the service of his theories. But he has not proved his case any more than, say, Büchner with his Kraft und Stoff. What is really the difference between Bergson and Büchner? The latter is the apostle of Matter and Force. More metaphysics, as metaphysical as the Becoming (which suggests Renan's *Fieri*) of Bergson. All such phrases are symbols of *là bas* that we shall never know — from the lips of philosophers.

In Matter and Memory he writes: "Truth no longer represents our past to us, it *acts* it." (Italics are his.) "Itself an image, the body cannot store up images; and this is why it is a chimerical enterprise to seek to localise past or even present perceptions in the brain; they are not in it; it is the brain that is in them. . . . My past gnaws into the present." Isn't this mediæval scholasticism *redivivus!* All consideration of Free-Will must be considered in Time not Space. "Can time," he asks, "be adequately represented by space? To which we answer, Yes, if you are dealing with time flown; No, if you speak of time flowing . . . all the difficulties of the problem and the problem itself arise from the desire to endow duration with the same attributes as extensity, to interpret a succession by a simultaneity, and to express the idea of freedom in a language into which it is obviously untranslatable." We prefer to make these quota-

tions rather than risk blurring the brilliancy and
originality of the original thought by transposition. Bergson is obsessed by the idea of a
temporal, not a spatial, universe. Old Father
Time is in the saddle again after being so long
deposed by the Critique of Kant. The image of
a focal point, our normal consciousness, imper-
ceptible, shading into a fringe at the periphery
is arresting, for it is that "fringe" from which
we draw, as from a reservoir — never mind
the mixed metaphor — our vision of life. Consciousness, he asserts, is almost independent of
cerebral structure. He has been challenged to
offer proofs of this existence apart from cerebral structure. His Time is a clock-face that is
always pointing to the high noon of eternity.
Real Bergsonism is cosmic rhythm. He has in
this respect the innocence of the ear, yet he knows
that no two clocks ever strike simultaneously.
The new mysticism is here. The subconscious as
a reservoir for the eternal certitudes is not missing, but the old verbal counters are used in the
interest of a new obscurantism. He seriously
subordinates the intellect to a minor rôle in his
doctrine of Instinct; the intellectual operations
are of less value than Intuition or Sympathy;
yet he rather illogically objects to the agnosticism of Huxley — that humble student of truth
revealed by science. The "new" theory of Free-
Will — which Bergson handles rather gingerly —
as a concomitant of his Vital Impulse, is, frankly
speaking, a more terrifying metaphysical mon-

ster than the old-fashioned and elaborately em-
bellished Determinism. We wonder what Hartmann would say to the subtle recreation of his
Unconscious in the "Fringe" theory of Bergson!
Or, Professor Münsterberg! Curiously enough,
with all his assumption of libertarianism, Bergson's human is much more of an automaton than
the man of the Cartesian formula.

He doesn't subscribe to René Quinton's ingenious contention that birds followed verte-
brates in the procession of evolutionary existence
on our globe; nevertheless he declares the instinct of bees and ants as actually superior to
human intelligence when interpreting the meaning of "life" to human intelligence. With all his
depreciation of the intellect and his charming
plaidoyer for the intuitive process — whatever
that precisely means! — Bergson is the most
signal example of rampant "intellectualism" —
mollified by romantic rhetoric — that has put
pen to paper during the past quarter of a century.
But the seeming pellucidity of Bergson's style is
often dangerously misleading; his ideas are not
always pellucid; indeed, there are phantasms
in this much-vaunted style with its shining
photosphere, and its formidable shadows, in
which lurk all sorts of metaphysical hobgoblins;
the Boyg of Ibsen is there, the old Nominalism
and the "Buffoon of the new Eternities," and a
little rose-water — the Bergson metaphysic is
not lacking in perfume; that is why his philosophy is allied to feminism, with its sympathetic

divinations and intuitive reactions. Sensual mathematics all this, and an Icarus-like attempt to fly into the Fourth Dimension of Space. An excursion to Laputa, there to interview with its philosophers or the Struldbrugs of Swift, might produce more topsy-turvy ideation than Bergsonism, but why should we go further?

"We are rarely free," yet if free-will endures but an instant we are always free. Renan advises us to act as if we were really possessed of free-will. "Duration as Duration, Motion as Motion, elude the grasp of mathematics . . . of Time everything slips through its fingers but simultaneity, and of movement everything but immobility." (Time and Free-Will.) But Bergson could also write: "In the Absolute we live and move and have our being." (Creative Evolution, p. 199.) "In reality, life is a movement, materiality is the inverse movement, and each of these two movements is simple, the matter which forms a world being an undivided flux, and undivided also the life that runs through it, cutting in it living beings all along the track." The image of a prow sharply cutting the stream of consciousness—the waters of life—and creating as it swims, is poetical and apposite. It may survive the Bergsonism of Bergson; but not so novel an idea as one finely expressed. Didn't the late Harald Höffding say that we live forward, we understand backward? From Heraclitus to Newman the student encounters variations of this imagery on the theme of the identity of the living universe. "He who tastes a crust of bread has tasted of the universe, even to the furthest star," wrote Paracelsus. And Leopardi said: "All the ages have been and will be more or less periods of transition; since human society never stands still, nor will there ever be an age in which it will be stationary." Some one has averred that Bergson reasons about Free-Will as the astronomers before Copernicus reasoned on the movements of the sky. His Intuition is not as convincing as the Illative Sense of John Henry Newman. In the Grammar of Assent Cardinal Newman wrote: "His progress — man's — is a living growth, not a mechanism; and its instruments are mental acts, not the formulas and contrivances of language." But didn't Pascal exclaim: "The heart hath its reasons," and the heart — or Sympathy, Intuition — may decide when the intellect can go no further. Ludwig Feuerbach, who occupied the philosophic affections of Richard Wagner, before he lost them to Schopenhauer, once wrote: "God was my first idea, Reason my second, and Man my third and last thought. Man is alone and must be our God. No salvation outside of Man." (Over-capitalisation of words is another vice of philosophers, which Professor James did not include in his list of their defects.) Bergson seemingly would restore Man to his former anthropocentric position in the scheme of things — though shorn of his intellectual primacy. Yet he insists that he is not an idealist. While not being the pronounced Pluralist that was William James, he thinks that the conceptual vision of the Absolute is lacking in the largeness of rhythm, or rhythmic periods, which characterise Pluralism. The consciousness of our present is overflowed by the memory of our past. There is no Now in the old sense of the word. This fluidity of a real Time — not a metaphysical abstract — is the best thing in the Bergson philosophy. It is a vital idea. And what a fairy-land is metaphysics, a million times more romantic and thrilling than any fiction; indeed, the most entrancing fiction in literature, both ancient and modern, is philosophy. Fancy such an astounding assertion as that "instinct brings us into closest tie with the universe." Bees and ants ought then to be the masters of mankind. Even the meticulous guinea-pig has as good a chance to win in the evolutionary race as the Eleatic tortoise had over Achilles. Perhaps the time will come when metaphysics will occupy the same relative position to real thought that astrology does to astronomy to-day. But Pascal's Abysm — the unknowable — will always be at the side of mankind to disquiet or strike terror to his heart. Hence the world will ever listen to the voice of the philosopher who cries aloud in the darkness: "Lo! I, alone, am the bearer of light."

III

Some objections: William James writes in his
A Pluralistic Universe: "Intellectualism has its
source in the faculty which gives us our chief
superiority to the brutes, namely, of translating
the crude flux of merely feeling-experience into a
conceptual order." He admits that, "We of
course need a stable scheme of concepts, stably
related to one another, to lay hold of our experiences and to co-ordinate them withal." In his
The Thing and Its Relations (the volume above
quoted, p. 351), writing of the intellect, he goes
further: "It originated as a practical means of
serving life; but it has developed incidentally
the function of understanding absolute truth;
and life itself now seems to be given chiefly as a
means by which that function may be prosecuted.
But truth and the understanding of it lie among
the abstracts and universals, so the intellect now
carries on its higher business wholly in this
region without any need of redescending into
pure experience again." (1905.) Where does
Bergsonism come in here? "Absolute truth!"
James has confessed that the Bergson philosophy
was not all as a lantern shining on a dark pathway; perhaps he scented its latent "spiritualism." But what does all this verbal hair-split-
ting mean to us in actual life? What an Ixion
wheel! Monism or Pluralism? Idealism or
Realism? Under which king? A comma instead

of semicolon may wreck a philosophic system.
There are those who believe that the misreading
of a certain holy book gave birth to a mighty religion. The very structure of our cerebral organ
forces us to think by associating disjointed ideas.
Nevertheless the mechanistic theory has the
authority of experience, and even if James does
define Empiricism as meaning "the habit of explaining wholes by parts, and rationalism means
the habit of explaining the parts by wholes"
(and strictly speaking, neither one nor the other
explains), we must pin our faith not to metaphysics, but to the more tangible results of science, which moves slowly but surely. Modern
philosophy has always followed science like a
the furrow of a well-sown field, picking here
here a seed. Bergson makes a great show
rently believing the tenets of science but,
st opportunity, flies off on a fiery-winged
to the land of metaphysical Nowhere.
imagination, though not much humour;
ironical presentation of the adversary's
case he lags far behind William James. His system — though he disclaims having any — is impressionistic, it also straddles between the real
and the ideal, and flirts with both the mechanistic
and the metaphysical. In his Huxley lecture at
the University of Birmingham (1911) he concluded that "in man, though in man alone, consciousness pursues its path beyond this earthly
life." Shades of Thomas Huxley!

We find some of the ideas of Professor Berg-

son in the works of Emile Boutroux ("De la con-
tingence des lois de la nature," 1874), and also
of Renouvier. The germs of his leading ideas
may be discovered in Nietzsche — that sworn foe
of metaphysics. When he has given us his projected Ethic we shall see then what bearing his
philosophy has upon the nature of judgments,
as a pragmatic reason about the chief use for the
art of philosophising. His Æsthetic, too, will
surely prove of interest judging from his essay
on Laughter (Le Rire, 1910). In it are swift
if not satisfactory generalisations, and a plenti-
ful lack of humour, together with much polished writing. I prefer George Meredith's less
metaphysical but more illuminative essay
Comedy.

Bergsonism is riddled with paradox, yet
stimulating as just another multicoloured p
of the universe by a man in whom the
sophical play-instinct (in Schiller's sense
vated to a fine art. For him the vast hin
of metaphysics, the "unknowable" of philo
the Fourth Dimension of Space, is a happy hunt-
ing-ground where with his highly burnished metaphysical weapons he pops away at Time and
Space and other strange fauna of that misty and
tremendous region. He exhibits the daring of
the hardy adventurer and he occasionally returns
with a trophy worth while — but always heavily
laden with the flora. All the rest is metaphysics.
As his philosophy is mainly an affair of images —
delicately fashioned mosaics, fairy-like structures

and dazzling mental mirages — its study naturally begets images. That is why I call the image-
maker, Henri Bergson, the Playboy of Western
Philosophy.

XV

A BELATED PREFACE TO EGOISTS[1]

Writing a preface to a book several years old is not necessarily either a matter of prudence or a kind of belated precipitation; it may well be only that fatal itch of the author who is not satisfied to leave sleeping hornets unawakened. Possibly because I was rudely twitted on the appearance of Egoists for its lack of general ideas — as I surely shall be about the present volume—I gently hasten to print an apology for the omission of something I do not believe in, the famous "general ideas"; also missing in my Iconoclasts as I was reminded by a French critic, M. Loyson. That book contained no preface which might have helped the reader across arid and thorny definitions; no friendly footnotes; not even a postlude instead of a preface, in which would be found a neat little theory of a school or a "stream of tendencies"; no special application of the art of plumbing to doctrines held by various dramatists. I confess I am still a sceptic as to the value of "general ideas," believing more in their dissociation, as practised by Remy de Gourmont. A "general idea," for example, is the so-called period of transition used with such

[1] Egoists; published 1909, New York, Charles Scribner's Sons.

386

effect by writers of æsthetic history. Liszt was a "Transitional" composer, according to Bayreuth; a musical John the Baptist sent to prepare the way for the musical Messiah, Richard Wagner. So, too, Berlioz. That these men, the Frenchman and the Hungarian, were each a unicum, a perfectly distinct personality, and the inventor of something never before heard, is but the truth. Manet, Richard Strauss, Ibsen, have already been placed in the "Transitional" class by writers over-eager for to-morrow's crop of painters, composers, and dramatists. How can we say that our period is "Transitional" till it has vanished in the vortex of the past? But M. Bergson says all "Time" is transitional! How do these pundits catch their perspective before they have finished their foreground?

And now what is to be conjured up from the dreams of all the jostling personalities in Egoists — the original title of which was The Ivory Tower — those madmen, wits, saints, and sinners? I could have decked out its pages with an ingenious introduction which would set forth the facts that Stendhal was the first "modern" philosophic Egoist — he, the most unphilosophic of men; that Baudelaire was the Dante of the decadence, a topsy-turvy Catullus to whom the "joy of life" was denied; that Flaubert was a lyric prophet, a philosopher and realistic historian; that Anatole France is a miraculous and tantalising sceptic, who, *au fond*, despises humanity more than any of his cenobites, and never ceases to depreciate moral values, though with the triumphant air of a physician who has discovered an interesting malady. Into what *cadre* must Anatole France be fitted! He is pagan. He is Hebraic. And he adores the Fathers of the Church. Is he not a latter-day expression of the Eternal Mocker, a French Heine *sans* the lyric genius of the Jewish Aristophanes? If he is not, does it much matter? Rather let the question be settled by the reader, in whose intelligence I have firm faith. Remember that I have not suggested this inutile scheme of classification; but there are those who demand it, and in the domain of music they, lacking all fancy, will tell you that it is immoral to put the thumb on the black keys of a pianoforte when playing a prelude of Bach.

Now, there is Huysmans, what more need be said of this extraordinary soul? One morning he awoke and thirsted for God; gods in some shape or other have been always a necessity for mankind; though there were atheists before the invention of mirrors. (It is impossible for a man not to believe in a god when he shaves himself. Tender masculine egoists!) Barrès shows us the importance of being Maurice; a *fauteuil* in the Academy would still be for him a delectable dream if he had not kept this notion well in view. O the starry music of self-esteem! Of the mystics what may not be written? "Soft and terrible, foul and fair," as Yeats has it. To me they seem the sanest folk in a world full of futile sounds and

388

gestures. They write with more precision than rationalistic thinkers, because they have the vision. And most mystics are anarchs. Ibsen is a thrice-told critical tale; like the earlier Wagner works his first plays are in the mists. To-day, Nora Helmer would not slam that front door; her husband would probably be the one to leave, though not for ever — like Hjalmar Ekdal — for a drink or two while away from the doll's house. Women have changed since the days of Nora; they were always realists, to-day they are pragmatists, and, as Jules Laforgue declared, "Stability, thy name is Woman." That is at once her charm and her fate.

Max Stirner is the *enfant terrible* of the Lutheran doctrine of private judgment. Of him I said that ours is the best of possible worlds — if we don't abide in it too long. It is the menace of eternity, whether it is to be spent aloft or in the nethermost region, that is so disconcerting to those who beat against the bars of their prison, the appalling prison of Self. Ernest Renan, oily, sacerdotal, most fascinating of sophists, had an equal horror of paradise, a place of perpetual ennui, as he had of hades, so he diplomatically preferred purgatory. But isn't there an ancient adage to the effect that in hell it is considered bad form to speak of the heat! I know of nothing more sinister than Nietzsche's doctrine of the Eternal Recurrence. To be born ever anew makes Nirvana as welcome as ice to lips parched by the fires of Tophet. Nietzsche, too, how many pages might be devoted to him and his rainbow thoughts. What is one man's gehenna may be the heaven of another. Like Pascal, like Flaubert, like Huysmans, Nietzsche elected the dark and narrow path of pain. Set this down to a neurosis — do not forget he was the first to diagnose his trouble as spiritual decadence — or to any modish psychical fads you will, the fact remains that he saw certain "terrible" truths that would not have been realised if his brain had remained normal. The world is the gainer thereby. Fancy a man mortally wounded registering with rectitude his symptoms. This Nietzsche did. Very often sick souls discover robust truths. Healthy-minded men are seldom pathfinders of the spirit. Nietzsche's sickness was of the soul, and while George Moore has said that "self-esteem is synonymous with genius," the pride of Nietzsche became a monstrous atrophy of the Ego. Yet we must perforce admire the bravery of this giant scholar who burned his books behind him, thus believing to "free" himself. He was a neo-pagan who defiantly cried: I have conquered, Galilean! And in an age that is almost pyrrhonistic Nietzsche at least believed in something, believed that Christianity was on trial and found wanting; whereas his contemporaries in the world of intellect, for the most part, didn't care who ruled, Jove or Jesus, Jehovah or Buddha. The pathetic side of the Nietzsche case is his naïve belief in the power of the written word. He thought that his verbal dynamite had mined Christianity. Perhaps his time-fuse has been set ahead one or more centuries. Nevertheless, his is a grandiose vision of humanity. His Superman, the penultimate evolution of a gorilla into a god, is a plastic clay figure in the hands of this dream-potter; a promise, a Beyond. Who knows, whether long after the last performance of Wagner's Ring and its socialistic sonorities, the august name of Friedrich Nietzsche will not be sounded through golden horns from the belfries of the world? This is not a hazard at prediction, only a chess-play of inference.

Said the wise Goethe — the wisest man since Montaigne — "In der Beschränkung zeigt sich erst der Meister." All these heroes have their limitations; though they may not be Supermen they have attacked the slopes of Parnassus, far above the goose-land of altruism; that land now filled with the discordant sounds of equality quackery. Philosophic Egoism is at least free from the depressing sentimentality of "going to the people." Brotherhood of Man! Brotherhood of fudge and hypocrisy! No one sincerely believes in it; it's a catch-word for gulls and politicians. How much is in it for us? sums up the programme of the professional altruists. Rousseau, not Nietzsche, is the real Antichrist, for he invented that lying legend: Liberty, Equality, Fraternity — that seductive three-voiced Cerberus-like fugue, which has led millions sheep-wise over the precipice of false hopes.

But the accusation that Egoists, like Iconoclasts, lacked "general ideas" did not seem as
curious to me as the insinuation made by certain
reviewers that the writers treated in Egoists
were more or less negligible. I was gently reminded that Victor Hugo, Lamartine, De Musset,
Balzac, and several others were of more importance than my selected heroes of the ink-pot.
Who said they weren't? Only they are not of
the same importance to-day as they were over
a half century ago. The "main-currents" of
French literature, *i. e.*, Continental literature,
were traversed and dominated during the past
fifty years by Stendhal — to whom Tolstoy admits his indebtedness — by Flaubert, by Baudelaire (in poetry and criticism particularly), by
Nietzsche, by Max Stirner (who played a rôle
in the intellectual development of Nietzsche),
and in a minor degree by Barrès, Huysmans, and
Anatole France. To Stendhal the world owes
the analytical novel — he wasn't its creator but
he gave the genre its definite mould — and from
Flaubert stern naturalists, symbolists; even a
new school of philosophy, Le Bovaryisme of Jules
Gualtier. And Baudelaire was the most original
poet of his day. He brought into the domain of
poesy new subject-matter, a wellnigh incredible
achievement. These men quite filled the literary firmament of Europe and to patronise them
as do some critics for not being giants of the stature of Hugo or Balzac or Chateaubriand is to
ring a new change on the pathetic fallacy. The

fact remains that they were the chief forces of their period; European literature still feels the impact of their personalities. They made history and any one who can run and is not blind may read this history. No doubt when the corridor of time lengthens between them and newer generations the pathos of distance will again operate and fresh critical perspective form.

Let me confess that the thinkers united under the title of "Egoists" are a fortuitous grouping. No particular theory of life is adduced therefrom; if you believe in the salve of "altruism," then, as William James would say, it is your truth; or, if you follow Walter Pater's poetic injunction, and burn always with a clear, hard flame of some artistic enthusiasm, go ahead and burn, but watch yourself—that way neurasthenia lies. Nearly all the men in the book lived their lives "to the fullest"; and were generally unhappy. Those who returned to belief in religion seemed happy. At this juncture I sha'n't exclaim: *Ergo!* However, it is a holy and wholesome act to retire to the "seven solitudes" of your ivory tower and there come face to face with the one reality in this world of fluctuating images — your own soul (your "subliminal self," is the precise psychic slang-phrase).

John Henry Newman, in his Apologia, spoke of "the thought of two and two only absolute and luminously self-evident beings, myself and my Creator." That is a crystallisation of the Higher Egoism. For dolorous souls, disenchanted by the deceptions of life, these words of Cardinal Newman light the strait and difficult pathway to the veritable *Turris Eburnea*. But for those to whom the world is a place to collect bric-à-brac, stale "truths," reputations for respectability, other people's money, and earth-worms, the aphorism of Nietzsche must suffice as an epitaph: "Some souls will never be discovered unless they be first invented."

What Maeterlinck wrote:

Maurice Maeterlinck wrote thus of James Huneker: "Do you know that 'Iconoclasts' is the only book of high and universal critical worth that we have had for years—to be precise, since Georg Brandes. It is at once strong and fine, supple and firm, indulgent and sure."

The *Evening Post* of June 10, 1915, wrote of Mr. Huneker's "The New Cosmopolis":

"The region of Bohemia, Mr. James Huneker found long ago, is within us. At twenty, he says, he discovered that there is no such enchanted spot as the Latin Quarter, but that every generation sets back the mythical land into the golden age of the Commune, or of 1848, or the days of 'Hernani.' It is the same with New York's East Side, 'the fabulous East Side,' as Mr. Huneker calls it in his collection of international urban studies, 'The New Cosmopolis.' If one judged externals by grime, by poverty, by sanded back-rooms, with long-haired visionaries assailing the social order, then the East Side of the early eighties has gone down before the mad rush of settlement workers, impertinent reformers, sociological cranks, self-advertising politicians, billionaire socialists, and the reporters. To-day the sentimental traveller 'feels a heart-pang to see the order, the cleanliness, the wide streets, the playgrounds, the big boulevards, the absence of indigence that have spoiled the most interesting part of New York City.' But apparently this is only a first impression; for Mr. Huneker had no trouble in discovering in one café a patriarchal figure quite of the type beloved of the local-color hunters of twenty years ago, a prophet, though speaking a modern language and concerned with things of the day. So that we owe to Mr. Huneker the discovery of a notable truth, namely, that Bohemia is not only a creation of the sentimental memory, but, being psychological, may be located in clean and prosperous quarters. The tendency has always been to place it in a golden age, but a tattered and unswept age. Bohemia is now shown to exist amidst model tenements and sanitary drinking-cups."

ICONOCLASTS:
A Book of Dramatists

12mo. $1.50 net

CONTENTS: Henrik Ibsen—August Strindberg—Henry Becque—Gerhart Hauptmann—Paul Hervieu—The Quintessence of Shaw—Maxim Gorky's Nachtasyl—Hermann Sudermann—Princess Mathilde's Play—Duse and D'Annunzio—Villiers de l'Isle Adam—Maurice Maeterlinck.

"His style is a little jerky, but it is one of those rare styles in which we are led to expect some significance, if not wit, in every sentence."
—G. K. CHESTERTON, in *London Daily News.*

OVERTONES:
A Book of Temperaments

*WITH FRONTISPIECE PORTRAIT OF
RICHARD STRAUSS*

12mo. $1.50 net

"In some respects Mr. Huneker must be reckoned the most brilliant of all living writers on matters musical."
—*Academy, London.*

MEZZOTINTS IN MODERN MUSIC
BRAHMS, TSCHAÏKOWSKY, CHOPIN, RICHARD STRAUSS, LISZT, AND WAGNER

12mo. $1.50 net

"Mr. Huneker is, in the best sense, a critic; he listens to the music and gives you his impressions as rapidly and in as few words as possible; or he sketches the composers in fine, broad, sweeping strokes with a magnificent disregard for unimportant details. . . . A distinctly original and very valuable contribution to the world's tiny musical literature."
—J. F. RUNCIMAN, in *London Saturday Review.*